Praise for *China Now*

China Now offers the best negotiation advice now available for cross-border dealmakers hoping to forge value-creating agreements in the world's fastest growing major economy. In an easy, informal style, this book excels at efficiently conveying a sense of historical context, the dos and don'ts of effective negotiation, and an all-important recognition of critical regional variations.

> —James K. Sebenius, Gordon Donaldson Professor of Business Administration, Harvard Business School, and Vice Chair, Program on Negotiation, Harvard Law School

For many American executives, China is still inscrutable. Few people writing about doing business in China can provide the practioner-academic and Chinese-American balance that Mark Lam and John Graham provide in *China Now*. It is a must read for all American managers and executives working with and negotiating with Chinese partners. The book holds the keys for building successful, long-lasting business relationships in China.

> —Katherine Xin, editor-in-chief, *Harvard Business Review* (China), Professor of Management, Michelin Chair in Leadership and Human Resource Management, China Europe International Business School (Beijing), and Professor of Leadership and Organizational Behavior, IMD (Switzerland)

Few companies, especially those operating globally, can afford to ignore doing business in China or business with Chinese partners. This book permits a rapid assimilation of knowledge on how to understand the Chinese psyche, cultural background, and business mores, as well as others' business experiences of working in China. Vivid descriptions of various cultural traits, as well as rich examples of positive and negative experiences, provide a backdrop and a way to prepare for challenging, but potentially rewarding business ventures.

> —David Pyott, CEO and Chairman, Allergan, Inc.

A great primer for someone seeking an entry and additional insights to doing business in China. The book is very relevant and current, given the business environment is changing so quickly as China embraces commercial acumen, tools, and infrastructure . . . not only to compete, but to lead on the worldwide playing field going into the twenty-second century.

> —Greg Spierkel, CEO, IngramMicro, Inc.

A magnificent treatment of Chinese and American negotiation styles and what this means in face-to-face business interactions. Lam and Graham provide us with an original, integrative account of the cultural and psychological foundations of cross-cultural negotiations and weave these into a masterful specification of practical guidelines. This is a splendid book with much value for practitioners and academicians alike.

> —Richard P. Bagozzi, Professor of Marketing, University of Michigan

China has changed faster than the misconceptions held by most international business people. John Graham and Mark Lam provide a clear framework of Chinese history and culture to help readers prepare for, negotiate, and establish sustainable business relationships. Their advice and strategies are born of true insights, not stereotypes.

> —David Murphy, President, Saatchi & Saatchi

This is an exceptional analysis of a complex culture and a sophisticated business community. A must read for western business people.

—Edwin D. Fuller, President and Managing Director, Marriott

China Now is a must read for any foreigner wanting to succeed in the world's most challenging and fastest growing market. Mark Lam and John Graham provide a unique and very necessary perspective to the complex dynamics of negotiating with the Chinese. The multitude of lessons learned and prescriptions are provocative, insightful and, most of all, practical.

—Dean Yoost, former Managing Partner in both China and Japan, now Senior Advisor to the Group Companies of PricewaterhouseCoopers in Japan

CHINA NOW

DOING BUSINESS IN THE
WORLD'S MOST DYNAMIC MARKET

N. MARK LAM
JOHN L. GRAHAM

McGraw-Hill

New York Chicago San Francisco Lisbon London Madrid
Mexico City Milan New Delhi San Juan Seoul
Singapore Sydney Toronto

1 2 3 4 5 6 7 8 9 0   FGR/FGR   0 9 8 7 6

ISBN-13: 978-0-07-147254-8
ISBN-10: 0-07-147254-1

This publication is designed to provide accurate and authoritative information in regard to the subject matter covered. It is sold with the understanding that the publisher is not engaged in rendering legal, accounting, or other professional service. If legal advice or other expert assistance is required, the services of a competent professional person should be sought.

> —*From a declaration of principles jointly adopted by a committee of the American Bar Association and a committee of publishers.*

McGraw-Hill books are available at special quantity discounts to use as premiums and sales promotions, or for use in corporate training programs. For more information, please write to the Director of Special Sales, Professional Publishing, McGraw-Hill, Two Penn Plaza, New York, NY 10121-2298. Or contact your local bookstore.

This book is printed on acid-free paper.

To my family
　　　　　—Mark Lam

To my teachers—Thomas R. Wotruba, John G. Myers,
Richard P. Bagozzi, John G. Gumperz, Roy A. Herberger Jr.,
Edward T. Hall, and Philip R. Cateora
　　　　　　　　　　—John Graham

CONTENTS

ACKNOWLEDGMENTS

We have so many friends and colleagues to thank for their help with our book:

Jason Dedrick, Bronwyn Fryer, Joanna Ho, Vivian Kuo, Wen Wen Lam, T.Y. Lau, Mark Lemly, Andy Liang, James McCoun, C.T. Teng, James Tong, Katherine Xin, Larry Wong, Dean Yoost, and Zhong Xue Ping.

We would like to specifically thank Charles Liu and Monty Ma for their contributions to Chapters 10 and 11, respectively.

Jill Marsal and Sandra Dijkstra recognized the potential for our book early on. And Jeanne Glasser, Pattie Amoroso, Maureen Harper, and Lauren Lynch at McGraw-Hill helped us improve the book greatly.

Thanks to all!

CHAPTER 1

SHANGHAIED IN SHANGHAI?

Denver omelets, Vienna sausage, London broil, Boston baked beans, and Boston cream pie—we can think of many city names used as adjectives and as "improper" nouns—you may want to wash down your dessert with a Singapore sling or a Manhattan. And perhaps Sandy Dennis and Jack Lemmon were "New Yorked" in the movie *The Out-of-Towners.*[1] Indeed, perhaps you've been "New Yorked" yourself.

But, there is only one city honored in Webster's Dictionary as a verb—*Shanghai.* Here's what the dictionary says:

> **shang·hai** \shanj-'hi\ vt *shang·haied; shang·hai·ing* [Shanghai, China; from the formerly widespread use of this method to secure sailors for voyages to the Orient (1871)] (1) To put aboard a ship by force often with the help of liquor or a drug; (2) to put by force or threat of force into or as if into a place of detention; or (3) to put by trickery into an undesirable position.*[2]

You may recall Stan and Ollie being knocked unconscious with a frying pan, thrown down the hold of a tramp steamer, and shanghaied in the Laurel & Hardy classic *The Live Ghost.* Certainly many modern-day managers have felt shanghaied in their negotiations with their Chinese counterparts. We start the book with one such story in which an American executive was sure he had been "put by trickery into an undesirable position" during high-level business negotiations in Shanghai.

The Inside Track, Or So It Seemed

The pole position, the inside track, sitting in the driver's seat, all described Jim Paulsen's circumstances in January 1995. In March 1994 he had been appointed the first-ever president of Ford of China, and job one was negotiating a joint venture with Shanghai Automotive Industry Corporation. Unfortunately, Paulsen and his Ford Taurus didn't get the Chinese checkered flag. Why GM Buicks have hit Beijing boulevards first makes for a great story, filled with international relations machinations and corporate miscalculations. Cultural differences were key. Let us explain.

Ford Motor Company has always been one of the most global firms on earth. Everyone recognizes the blue oval logo. Indeed, Henry Ford was hawking his wares in urban China about the same time that Pearl Buck was writing about feet binding in rural China in her 1930s classic, *The Good Earth*. Henry Ford II was one of the first American executives to meet with Deng Xiaoping after China reopened its economic doors in 1978.

Moreover, Ford had moved into the local area faster than GM. At the start of the race Ford already had three parts-related joint ventures in China with a fourth in the works.

Although American Motors/Chrysler had been producing Jeeps in Beijing for some 10 years, the Shanghai Automotive deal was really the first major production venture open to American firms. Shanghai Auto was the largest and most profitable of all Chinese automakers, already producing Audis in a joint venture with Volkswagen. The Shanghai plant was targeted for production of about 100,000 sedans and 200,000 vans per year—a $2 billion capital investment.

Ford had been talking with the Shanghai folks in secret for sometime. But events in Washington, D.C. put the negotiations on the front pages in both countries. On February 6, 1995, the Clinton administration announced the imposition of trade sanctions on China for its continuous violations of intellectual property agreements, slapping 100 percent tariffs on $1.08 billion in cellular phones, sporting goods, and plastic articles coming from the Middle Kingdom.

The Beijing response was twofold. First, retaliatory tariffs were placed on CDs, video games, films, cigarettes, and alcoholic beverages coming from the United States to China. Second, the threat was made that all talks with American automakers about joint ventures would be suspended. Both Washington and Beijing put a February 26 deadline on discussions after which sanctions would go into effect.

On February 14 Lu Jian, president of Shanghai Auto, announced that both Ford and GM had been instructed to submit their final bids "by the end of the month." Previous to the 14th the identity of the Chinese company negotiating with Ford had been confidential. Moreover, Shanghai Auto had been talking with Japanese firms as well. In an interview with the *Wall Street Journal* Mr. Lu stated, "Toyota was just tooting its horn because of the threat of a trade war with the United States . . . I told them frankly that, while we hope at some point to have cooperation with them, we will continue now to negotiate with the Americans. Toyota is at the back of the line."[3]

It really didn't matter whether it was Toyota's demonstrated reluctance to share technology with the Chinese or the latter's obvious need to bolster the credibility of their counterthreats regarding the auto talks with the Americans. In fact, both circumstances probably worked together to push Ford and GM to the front of the line. But, please note Mr. Lu's further comments in the *Journal*: "Everything is on track except for the possibility of a trade war. If a trade war breaks out, then everything is delayed, maybe canceled. If there is no trade war, then I can tell you that we will choose Ford or GM." Finally, we doubt that Mr. Lu spoke of the two American firms with consideration to alphabetical order.

Jim Paulsen in the Driver's Seat

So, as of mid-February, Ford was in the lead. And, Jim Paulsen was at the wheel. After visits to the U.S. Trade Representative and the Commerce and State Departments in Washington, D.C.,

Paulsen and his wife stopped over in southern California for a couple of weeks of cross-cultural training at the University of California Merage School of Business. That's where we first met. Jim told us that he was appalled by the lack of knowledge about China displayed by all the Clinton appointees he had talked with.

We had been recommended to Jim by the folks at the Ford Executive Development Center in Detroit. We had provided advice and training to executives there for a number of years regarding their Japanese business associations. About 2,000 of their executives had been through a three-day program of our design[4] on negotiating with the Japanese. However, now the topic was China, a very different cup of tea! Jim and his wife spent most of the two weeks at the university working with our Katherine Xin, a Beijing native who is now the Michelin Chair in Leadership and Human Resource Management at the China Europe International Business School (CEIBS) in Shanghai. Better cross-cultural training for a leadership role in China was available nowhere else.

Jim Paulsen is a very bright and an affable Midwesterner. An engineer by training and a career-long Ford man, he had worked on plant-related issues in several foreign countries including Mexico, the Czech Republic, Poland, and France. However, much to our surprise, he had had no previous experience living overseas. Jim had spent the previous 18 months traveling back and forth to China working on the Shanghai Auto deal and others.

Ford "put the peddle to the metal" with the announcement by CEO Alex Trotman that the company was sponsoring a research program for developing environmentally friendly auto engines with the Chinese Academy of Science. On February 16 he handed Song Jian, the Science and Technology Minister of China, a set of keys to a shiny new Ford Taurus, fitted with an engine that ran on a mixture of gasoline and methanol.

Meanwhile the trade row fizzled. As one pundit put it, threatening trade sanctions made sense for both sides in the piracy dispute, but actually implementing them made no sense at all. That is, talking tough served to consolidate domestic political power in both China and the United States, but neither country could really afford the costs of a trade war. So the issue was settled by the end of February, of course only to arise again the following year.

However, the duel between the American carmakers was still on. GM followed Ford almost immediately with its own announcements about technology transfers to Chinese institutes. In March the firm contributed 1 million yuan (about $120,000 at the time) to establish the Delphi Automotive Systems Technology Institute at the prestigious Tsinghua University in Beijing. Oh, by the way, Tsinghua also happens to be the alma mater of many of China's senior leaders. In China, alma mater matters. It matters more than most westerners can imagine, and the arrangement at Tsinghua was just the first of several planned as components of the larger GM-China Technology Institute involving GM's technical centers and research labs.

Jim Paulsen was particularly good at managing the negotiations with the Ford home office. Jacques Nasser, then product development vice president in Detroit, had nixed a key product adaptation for the Chinese market. Because the Tauruses would mostly be driven by chauffeurs in China, leg room had to be maximized in the back seat—not a cheap change. Paulsen knew the Detroit organization well enough to risk going over Nasser's head directly to Alex Trotman. He won that battle, but the war waged on over the summer.

Enter Shirley Young

The key event in the race was GM's introduction of Shirley Young into its pit crew. Yes, women can and often do make a difference in international business negotiations. Ms. Young not only brought a marketing imagination to the GM team, but she also brought great *gaunxi* (connections). Let's look at the list.

Young had joined GM in 1988 as vice president of Consumer Market Development. She had been a consultant to GM since 1983 and had worked for a variety of communications and marketing strategy firms, including a stint as president of Grey Strategic Marketing. She served on the boards of the Promus Companies, Bell Atlantic, and the Bombay Company. She was a vice chair of the nominating committee of the New York Stock Exchange and was a member of the Business Advisory Council for the U.S. State Department Agency for International Development. Ms. Young was also chair of the Committee of 100, a national Chinese-American leadership group, and on the board of the Shanghai Symphony Orchestra (the last after a $125,000 donation made by GM). In the educational community Ms. Young was a trustee of Wellesley College, Philips Academy Andover, and the Interlochen Center for the Arts, and on the board of directors of the Associates of the Harvard Business School. Her numerous awards included Woman of the Year separately for the American Advertising Federation and the Chinese American Planning Council. Yes, very well connected in the United States.

And, get a load of her China credentials. Ms. Young was born in Shanghai, and she still has relatives there. She speaks Mandarin fluently. Her father, Clarence Kuangson Young, is a hero in both China and Taiwan, having been killed by the Japanese when he was China's consul general to the Philippines during World War II. As a Tsinghua alum, he is memorialized on the campus in Beijing. Also, her stepfather was at one time China's ambassador to the United States, the United Kingdom, and France. Yes, great *guanxi*.

GM appointed Young as an advisor to Rudolph Schlais, the GM vice president in charge of China operations. Schlais himself had negotiated three joint-venture agreements in China before. But, GM also had her maintain a reporting relationship to a marketing vice president in Detroit. Thus, her role was more than an underling to Schlais. Her job was to promote technology transfer and to impart marketing expertise in China.

Perhaps even more important than her professional brilliance, her connections, and her rèsumè was the way she managed the negotiations. From the spring into the late summer the negotiations involved great numbers of Chinese executives and dignitaries who descended on Detroit to study their potential partners. Young organized GM's 1,000 plus Chinese-American employees to meet and greet the visitors and formed a committee to advise the company on relations with China. She was likewise successful in delivering the top American executives to Shanghai. For example, GM CEO John Smith made three trips to Shanghai during the negotiations. Five of GM's top seven executives also did the Shanghai shuffle during September and October. Such a dedication of executive resources was unprecedented in the history of the firm's international alliance efforts. Shanghai Auto executives were also treated to a trip to Brazil to see up close GM's new high-tech operations there. Rio is nice during the summer!

Shirley Young well understood that there is no such thing as inter*national* business. Nations don't talk to one another. Nor do companies talk to one another. Only people do. There is only inter*personal* business. Particularly for the Chinese, face-to-face meetings and relationships between *people* at all levels are the essential elements of successful negotiations.

The Last Lap

On August 25 Vaughn Koshkarian replaced Jim Paulsen as president of Ford of China. Koshkarian's bio included a Northwestern MBA and 33 years at Ford, mostly in the finance chain of command. During the 1980s he worked in both Japan and Europe. Yes, he brought more international experience to the job than Jim Paulsen, but he still had no specific experience in China and no Chinese language skills. Jim Paulsen had served just 19 months in Beijing before retiring. According to him, it was actually more like seven months in Beijing, six months in Shanghai, and six months in airplanes flying between the two. Changing drivers was Ford's admission that it had fallen behind in the race.

The Post-Race Analysis

GM and Shanghai Auto inked their deal on October 31 in Detroit. Plans were to produce 100,000 midsized Buick Regals by 1997 in a new billion-dollar assembly plant in Shanghai. Eventually minivans would be produced as well.

Both Ford and GM had invested and/or committed millions of dollars in establishing technology institutes and component parts manufacturing facilities during the negotiations. At the time a Ford spokesperson in Beijing blamed the lost contract on the Taurus sedan—it was "too modern" despite the engineering changes Jim Paulsen had forced through the Dearborn bureaucracy. Alternatively, GM explained that beyond its car capabilities it offered up technology from both its Hughes Electronics Corp. and Electronic Data Systems units. Ford couldn't match those broad computer technologies.

Jim Paulsen later reminisced in *Time* magazine, "We tried to find out more about how they were arriving at their decisions, but we didn't have enough Chinese-speaking people to establish close contact with the officials in Shanghai. We were playing catch-up and with fewer resources."[5] In the same article Wayne Booker, president of Ford's Asia Pacific operations and Jim Paulsen's boss, added, "You can't understand a foreign market unless you have capable, experienced nationals on staff."

Where Was Lawrence Wong When We Needed Him?

We agree with the gist of Booker's post-race analysis, but we would add that "experienced nationals" need to be at or near the top of American foreign ventures, particularly in China. Jim Paulsen had been a very successful executive at Ford, but he simply did not have the rèsumè for success *in China*. Training can go only so far. Even two weeks of the best possible cross-cultural training cannot make up for a lack of foreign living experience in an international manager's credentials. In a very real sense Jim Paulsen was not shanghaied in Shanghai by either Shanghai Auto or GM. Jim Paulsen was actually shanghaied in Detroit by Ford itself.

The odd thing from our point of view is that Ford had the ideal person for the job already in the company. The key blunder made by those in charge in Dearborn was not choosing Larry Wong to be the first president of Ford of China. Let's look at Wong's credentials circa 1995.

Dr. Lawrence T. Wong was a 32-year man at Ford as a corporate executive and research engineer. He earned his Ph.D at Michigan State University in aerospace engineering while with the company. Recall that Shanghai Auto was interested in technology—Wong had technology in spades. But he also had the other right stuff for managing relationships in China. Raised in China, he was a native Mandarin and Cantonese speaker. For 11 years he was president of Ford of Taiwan. Through his leadership and the *guanxi* he cultivated, Ford became the dominant carmaker there. Larry Wong was elected "Taiwan Businessman of the Year" in 1994.

Perhaps the best measure of Wong's capabilities is his current position. In 1996 he was given the reins of what he calls another transportation company—the Hong Kong Jockey Club. He was appointed the first ethnic Chinese to head the most important horse racing operation in the world. The Hong Kong Jockey Club has an annual turnover of $12 billion. That's right, $12 billion. $1.5 billion is returned to the people of Hong Kong in taxes amounting to 11 percent of the island's tax base. The club also donates some $130 million per year to charities. For example, it funded the construction of the $300 million Hong Kong University of Science and Technology, one of Asia's most prestigious universities.

The question this case raises is, Why did Ford miss the opportunity to choose Larry Wong to head its negotiation team in the first place? How could Ford, one of America's best global companies, make such a blunder? We answer these questions and many others in the pages that follow.

Finally, as a postscript, we are happy to report that in January 1998 Ford finally did wise up and appoint an ethnic Chinese executive to a senior position in Beijing. Mei Wei Cheng has now replaced Vaughn Koshkarian as chairman and CEO of Ford of China (Koshkarian was bumped up to CEO, and later to president of Ford Asia Pacific). Cheng was a vice president and regional executive for General Electric's appliance businesses based in Hong Kong. And, at long last, in April 2001 Ford completed a 50–50 joint venture agreement with Chongquin Changan Automobile Company, China's third largest automaker, to produce 50,000 small cars in Sichuan province in the southwest. But Ford has still not recovered from being shamed in Shanghai. In 2005 GM took over market leadership from Volkswagen affiliated brands, and it still outsells Ford-produced cars in China by a three-to-one ratio (665,000 to 220,000 units).

Conclusion

We have included Shanghai in the introduction of our book for two additional reasons. Our use of the term implies two fundamental facts about twenty-first century China. First, Shanghai is where the action is—it is again the vortex of commercial activity in East Asia. Second, Shanghai is different from the other parts of China. In Chapters 11–15 we discuss in some detail how negotiation behaviors and business systems vary across regions of the Greater China. The remainder of the book is divided into five parts. Chapters 2–5 include the necessary historical, cultural, and regulatory/legal background that provide the context for American/Chinese commerce. Chapters 6–10 focus on differences in negotiation styles that often cause problems when Americans meet Chinese across the negotiating table. As mentioned above, in Chapters 11–15 regional differences are considered. Chapters 16 and 17 regard the growingly controversial topic of intellectual property rights in China. And in Chapter 18 we speculate about the future of U.S./China commercial relations. By the way, it's no accident that we included 18 chapters in the book. Eighteen (or any number ending in eight) is a very lucky number in Chinese culture. The number eight (八, *ba*) said in Chinese sounds like the word for "prosperity" (发, *fa*). Of course, your reading of these 18 chapters will help you achieve prosperity in your adventures and ventures in the Middle Kingdom.

Notes

1 Goldie Hawn and Steve Martin starred in the 1999 remake of the 1970 original with Dennis and Lemmon.
2 *Merriam-Webster's Collegiate Dictionary*, 11th edition (Springfield, MA: Merriam-Webster, 2002).
3 Joseph Kahn, "Chinese Car Maker Plans to Pick Ford or GM as Partner," *Wall Street Journal*, February 14, 1995, page A18.
4 Actually, the program involved negotiation simulations and videotaping, and the material was presented using the format described in John Graham's book with Philip Cateora, *International Marketing*, 13th ed. McGraw-Hill, 2007.
5 Frank Gibney, Jr., "Detroit Gets into Gear Eagerly, Awkwardly and Finally, America's Big Three Are Staking Their Future on the World's Most Potentially Lucrative Car Market. Can They Outrun the Japanese?" *Time International*, July 15, 1996, page 28+.

PART I

THE NECESSARY BACKGROUND FOR NEGOTIATIONS WITH CHINESE BUSINESSPEOPLE

CHAPTER 2

HISTORY AND CULTURE OF THE CHINESE PEOPLE

There are about 5,000 years of Chinese history to study if one cared to. Indeed, Jim Hodgson, former U.S. ambassador to Japan, recommends that anyone traveling to another country for commerce ought to read the encyclopedia section on that country at the very least. We don't disagree with the ambassador, but we do offer this chapter as a hors d'oeuvre for that larger meal. And the canapés we're serving here may just help you avoid appearing an ethnocentric fool to your Chinese business associates. Read the encyclopedia (*Britannica* includes 188 pages on Chinese history) or a good book on the topic, and you may even impress.

For luck (and for fun) we're listing the 18 things you most need to know about China's past. First we discuss the six key people in Chinese history. Then we list the six key events or turning points. We close the discussion with brief descriptions of six prominent themes tracking across the millennia in China.

Central Figures of the Middle Kingdom

Confucius (552–479 B.C.)

There was King Kong, the great ape that held Fay Wray, Jessica Lang, and Naomi Watts in the palm of his hand. Remember Kung Fu fighters? How about the old TV show *Kung Fu* with

David Carradine as the "Little Grasshopper"? And then there's the famous saying from Confucius: "A picture is worth a thousand words." All this pop culture and lore is derived from the name, life, and teachings of a Chinese philosopher who lived some 2,500 years ago. Born Kong Qui or Kong Zhongni, he was known to his disciples by the honorific term Kong Fuzi[1] (no, not meaning "big ape," but rather "Master Kong"). The Latinized version is Confucius, which is in common usage in the West today.

The best guess by historians is that Confucius was born in 551 or 552 B.C. to impoverished descendants of nobility in what is now the Shandong province about halfway between Shanghai and Beijing. The beginnings of a China had appeared, but the dozen or so different states still vied for power in the immediate region. This created a landscape of chaos and constant change.

Confucius may have considered himself a conservative, talking frequently about the "Ways of Former Kings." However, many of his ideas were revolutionary and in many ways predated and presaged those of European Enlightenment philosophers such as John Locke. Like Locke he argued against heredity in the determination of status and power, and he argued that government should serve the people rather than vice versa.

He offered a moral code based on benevolence roughly represented by the notion, "Do not impose on others what you yourself do not desire." Sound familiar? He maintained that a society organized under this moral code would be both prosperous and politically stable (that is, safe from attack). Reverence for scholarship and kinship were fundamental lessons as well.

Confucius was not a legend in his own time. He did travel and teach widely in the region, but he died in his seventies as a junior counselor in his native state of Lu. His disciples, some in high offices, spread his ideas first orally. After a couple of generations his teachings were set down in writing as sayings in the *Lun Yu* or *Analects* which survive to this day. And these writings served as the foundation for Chinese education for some 2,000 years until the 1911 Nationalist Revolution overthrow of the Qing dynasty. During those two millennia knowledge of the Confucian texts was the primary requisite for appointment to the offices of government.

Other Chinese philosophers have been important to the country as well—Mo Zi, Mencius, Yang Zhu, and so on. But Confucius was and is clearly one of the most influential thinkers of all time and all places. Even today, as communism fades from thinking on the mainland, a revival of Confucian ideas has gained popularity.

Qin Shi Huangdi, the First Emperor (260–210 B.C.)

The postcard pictures of the terracotta army on display in Xian in the middle of the Middle Kingdom don't do the subject justice. The great halls that now cover the bit of the army excavated so far are basketball-stadium-sized, and the thousands of gray soldiers and horses stand 6-feet erect and are seemingly ready for battle. This menacing array has stood that way for more than 2,000 years! This is but a minor part of the legacy of the first emperor of China.

In 246 B.C. when Zheng became the new king of Qin, the consolidation of the surrounding states had already begun. By 221 B.C. he had conquered all his neighbors and pronounced himself Shi Huangdi, the first emperor of China. However, his empire was about as organized and orderly as a Brazilian *futbol* crowd with weapons. But organize the place he did.

First, he divided all the conquered lands into provinces that were in turn divided into prefectures. The remnants of the old feudal administrations were eliminated, and a new hierarchy of officials was appointed to govern. Weights, measures, and money were made uniform to make tax collection more efficient. The language was also standardized so that appointed officials could be easily transferred among the provinces. Local styles of writing and characters were forbidden. Finally, to encourage trade among the different regions of the empire, it was ordered that all carts should have axles of the same length, thus allowing them to fit into the road ruts north and south. Finally, Qin Shi Huangdi commanded the Great Wall to be built (actually this meant connecting and extending a series of smaller ones) along the northern border of the empire.

The true legacy of this hardworking and ruthless first emperor is China itself. At the time Qin was known in India under the Sanskrit name Cinasthana, which yielded the name China. The organization of government Qin Shi Huangdi conceived is also reflected in modern China. And, perhaps most importantly the language he unified unites the Chinese psyche around the world now, more than two millennia after his death.

Wang An-shih, the Great Reformer (1021–1086)

After the almost immediate demise of the Qin dynasty, history records the rise and fall of four more—the Han, Xin, Sui, and Tang. The next, the Song dynasty, saw China become one of the leading nations of the world of the time. Much of that power and prosperity can be attributed to the ideas and aspirations of one man, Wang An-shih.

Wang had been a famous poet, but he was a low-level bureaucrat until 1069 when a new emperor, Shen Tsung, appointed him his second privy councilor. As a close advisor to the throne, Wang was able to begin implementation of reform proposals he had made 11 years earlier in his "Ten Thousand Word Memorial."

Wang An-shih was the John Maynard Keynes of his time. He believed in fiscal stimulus as the best way to strengthen the country. He devised a system to provide cheap government loans to both farmers and merchants, and he pumped currency into the economy. He also established a more efficient market-based system of government procurement. He strengthened the navy and merchant fleets, and he used the duties collected from the burgeoning international trade to further stimulate the economy.

The conundrum facing all previous emperors was how strong to make the military—too strong and it tended to take things over and drain the economy; too weak and the empire was susceptible to invasion. To improve the military, Wang set up arms development and horse-breeding agencies and organized a new national militia system. The smaller standing army with a large reserve militia devised by Wang proved to be the best balance.

The Song dynasty thrived under the new rules. Industry, technology, literature, and art all flourished. All the major innovations of the premodern world—paper, printing, gunpowder, and the compass—were known and used by the Chinese of the Song dynasty. The population of Kaifeng, the capital, grew to over 1 million (this was equal to the total population of contemporary England), and Kaifeng was by far the largest and richest city on earth.

Genghis Khan, the Mongol Invader (1162–1227)

Ultimately walls never work. The Great Wall could not withstand the Great Khan's ambition: "One sole sun in the sky, one sole sovereign on earth." He and his hordes of horsemen took Beijing in 1215 and razed it to the ground. Genghis (also Chenghiz) Khan then diverted his destruction to the west (Persia and Europe) until his death in 1227. His grandson, Khubilai Khan (1215–1294) finished the conquest of China, finally taking the remainder of the southern Song Empire in 1279.

During the Mongol dynasty, for the first and last time in history, the entire overland trade route between the Near and Far East was under one authority. Trade, released from the bureaucracy of the Chinese system, burgeoned, and merchants' influence grew. The Khan's armies put gunpowder to harsh use in controlling the rest of the empire. Religious pluralism was allowed including Christianity, Islam, Judaism, Daoism, Confucianism, and Buddhism. The Khan ordered the building of the Forbidden City and the completion of the Grand Canal south from Hangzhou to Beijing.

But, ultimately the Mongols grew to prefer the pampering of the palace to the temperance of the tent. The gradual sinicization made them soft. After the death of Khubilai the eastern empire declined until Chinese rule was reestablished in 1366. But the empire never ascended to the apex of nations again. The development of Chinese culture had been arrested by the Mongols' destructiveness and autocratic restrictions on individuality and innovation. Indeed, perhaps the greatest legacy of the Khans was a Chinese xenophobia that persists to this day.

Sun Yat-sen, Father of the Republic of China (1866–1925)

The Ming dynasty fended off Manchurian advances for the next 300 years. However, in 1644 China again fell under the thumb of foreigners—the Manchus' rule lasted into the twentieth century. The foreign yoke chafed on the Chinese, and a young Dr. Sun Yat-sen fomented a Chinese republican uprising in Guangzhou in 1895. It failed, and Sun fled to Japan and then England.

In London he was captured by Manchu agents and held at the Chinese embassy. A note delivered in secret to a British doctor who had been his teacher in Hong Kong and some fast diplomacy secured his release. The incident created instant world fame for the young doctor. He spent the next 15 years studying Western political and social trends and traveling to Japan, France, and the United States soliciting support for his cause.

Back home the Manchu regime was beginning to splinter from a growingly rebellious Chinese army and new popular uprisings. Finally, in 1911 the dam burst, and 15 provinces declared their independence. Dr. Sun was welcomed back to Shanghai as the provisional president of the Republic of China. He held the job for two months. His government in Nanjing then deferred to a newer republican government in Beijing, signifying the end of Manchu rule in all of China.

Dr. Sun had won—dynastic control of China was finished. It took another two decades for Sun's protégé, General Chiang Kai-shek, to wrest control of most of the country from a variety of warlords. But, Dr. Sun's seeds of western democracy were planted in the good earth of the ancient empire.

Zhou Enlai, Statesman (1898–1976)

If Chairman Mao[2] Zedong was the fist and the face of the Communist Revolution, Zhou Enlai was its brains and heart. Mao controlled; Zhou negotiated.

Zhou studied abroad first in Japan and then in France. He learned his communism in the latter, and represented the Communist Chinese Party (CCP) in Europe between 1921 and 1924. He then returned to Guangzhou to help Sun Yat-sen, Chiang Kai-shek, and the Nationalist Party (KMT) gain greater control of the nation. At that time Zhou was appointed deputy director of the political department of Whampoa Military Academy, and Chiang was its commandant. In 1927 the rightist Chiang purged the communists from the KMT, and Zhou barely escaped with his life.

It was then that Zhou joined Mao in the countryside where the latter was forming the Red Army. Mao knew the peasants and the revolution. Zhou knew everyone and everything else. They made a powerful team that ruled China until both their deaths in 1976. After the Long March in 1935 it was Zhou who negotiated the tactical alliance with the KMT to fight the Japanese invaders. Chiang Kai-shek resisted the alliance, and his own generals arrested him in Xian. Only Zhou's hasty trip there saved Chiang from execution.

After the war he again represented the CCP in an American-sponsored, but vain attempt to make peace with the KMT. After the communist takeover of China in 1949, he negotiated a "30-year" treaty of alliance with the Soviets. During the 1950s he traveled widely in Europe, Asia, and Africa proclaiming the last to be "ripe for revolution." He participated in the Geneva Convention that settled the partition of Vietnam. During the late-1960s Cultural Revolution Zhou was the primary voice of restraint amidst the Mao-created chaos. He met with Henry Kissinger in 1971 to set up President Nixon's meeting the next year with Chairman Mao in Beijing. Finally, in perhaps his most enduring act, he reinstated into the Communist leadership Deng Xiaoping, the great economic reformer of the 1980s and 1990s.

Turning Points and Key Events

Portuguese Ships Reach China (1514)

Toward the middle of the second millennium politics, conquests, and thieves made the Silk Road between Europe and China less efficient. The Chinese responded to the problem first with a series of seven voyages of discovery and expansion. In 1403 Cheng Ho commanded the first massive Ming merchant and military fleet sailing south toward India and Africa. Some records suggest it included 27,000 men in 200 ships, some of which were more than 400 feet long and weighed 1,500 tons. This compares with Columbus's crew of 87 in three ships, the largest of which was about 100 feet in length and 100 tons. This unusual[3] Chinese adventurism was big business, but apparently it didn't turn a profit. The seventh voyage in 1431–1433 was the last. After that China closed its doors to international trade, and many believe this marked the beginning of the Middle Kingdom's 400-year slide into mediocrity and worse.

The Venetians and Muslims who controlled the Mediterranean trade at the time made the Spaniards, Portuguese, and English pay dearly for spices and silk from east Asia. So Vasco da Gama and his Portuguese comrades headed south and east, finally reaching the coast of China in 1514. Chinese xenophobia led to closed harbors and dead Portuguese ambassadors. But in 1535 the persistent Portuguese were able to gain a foothold at Macau (one that they would only relinquish 464 years later).

The price for spices and silk in Lisbon dropped by 80 percent. Yes, 80 percent! The other European seafaring nations followed close behind and brought with them the influences of trade and Christianity. Often the sales pitch was made with cannon. Now in the third millennium China still resists these western "gifts."

First Opium War and the Treaty of Nanjing (1839–1842)

During the early 1800s the British taste for tea was creating a huge trade deficit with China. Silver bullion was flowing fast in an easterly direction. Of course, other goods were being traded, too. Exports from China also included sugar, silk, mother-of-pearl, paper, camphor, cassia, copper and alum, lacquerware, rhubarb, various oils, bamboo, and porcelain. The "barbarians" returned cotton and woolen textiles, iron, tin, lead, carnelian, diamonds, pepper, betel nuts, pearls, watches and clocks, coral and amber beads, birds' nests and sharks' fins, and foodstuffs such as fish and rice. But, the tea-for-silver swap dominated the equation.

Then came the English East India Company epiphany. Opium. Easy to ship, high value to volume and weight, addicting to customers; what a great product! At the time the best opium came from British India, and once the full flow began, the tea-caused trade deficit disappeared fast. The emperor complained and issued edicts, but the opium trade burgeoned. One of the taller skyscrapers in Hong Kong today is the Jardine-Matheson Trading House.[4] Its circular windows are reminiscent of the portholes of its clipper-ship beginnings in the opium trade.

In 1836 some high-ranking Chinese officials advocated legalizing opium. The foreign supplies boosted production and shipments in anticipation of exploding sales. Then the emperor went in the opposite direction and ordered the destruction of the inventories in Guangzhou. By 1839 the trade was dead. The British responded by sinking junks in the Pearl River and blockading all Chinese ports.

The "magically accurate" British cannon pointed at Nanjing yielded negotiations there in 1842. The Chinese ceded Hong Kong and $21 million pounds to the British. Ports at Xiamen, Fuzhou, Ningbo, and Shanghai were opened to trade and settlement by foreigners. Hong Kong thus became the gateway to a xenophobic China, particularly for the last 50 years. Perhaps most importantly, China recognized for the first time its loss of great power status. The Celestial Kingdom came down to earth.

Ultimately the Opium War was over foreign access to Chinese trade, and the treaty of Nanjing really didn't settle the issue. A second opium war was fought between 1857 and 1860. In that imbroglio the British and French forces combined to destroy the summer palace in Beijing. Such new humiliations yielded more freedoms for foreign traders, and notably the treaty specifically included provisions allowing Christian evangelism throughout the realm.

Taiping Rebellion (1851–1864)

One consequence of the humiliation at the hands of foreigners was a loss of confidence in the Chinese government. The resulting disorder came to a head in Guangxi, the southernmost province of the Empire. The leader of the uprising was a peasant who grew up near Guangzhou, Hong Xiuquan. He aspired to be a civil servant but failed the required Confucian-teachings-based exam. When in Guangzhou for his second try at the exam he came into contact with Western Protestant missionaries and later began to have visions of God.

After flunking the exam for a fourth time in 1843, he began to evangelize, presenting himself as Christ's brother. In the next seven years he attracted 10,000 followers. In 1851 he was crowned by his followers as the "heavenly king" of the "Heavenly Kingdom of Peace." Despite their adopted label, they revolted, cut off their pigtails in defiance of the ruling Manchus, and began to march north. With the fervor of the religious zealots they were, they fought their way through the capital at Nanjing and almost to Tianjin by 1855.

Then things started to unravel. Chinese opposition forces organized. Because foreigners did not appreciate Hong's interpretation of the scriptures, his 88 concubines, or his attacks on Shanghai, they formed another army against him. Hong took his own life just before the final defeat and the recapture of Nanjing.

Estimates of the death toll from the Taiping Rebellion are between 20 and 40 million! We repeat: 20–40 million Chinese lives were lost. By contrast, "only" 2 million were killed in the Communist Revolution. The Taiping Rebellion is the single most horrific civil war in the history of the world. Surely Hong Xiuquan was insane. Furthermore, other rebellions occurred in China during this time—the Muslim one in the northwest is most notable (1862–1878). However, based on these events in the mid-1800s, it is easy to see why the Chinese leadership is wary of religious movements even today.

Sino-Japanese War and Treaty of Shimonoseki (1894–1895)

In 1281 a Chinese/Mongol invasion fleet on its way to Japan was destroyed by a typhoon or what the Japanese called a *kamikaze*. The Chinese fleet was also destroyed in 1894, this time not by a divine wind, but by Japanese cannon. The battle was about Korea. The Chinese saw it as a domain.

Once again China was humiliated by foreigners, this time by a despised neighbor that they had long considered a tributary nation of pirates. The Treaty of Shimonoseki was draconian and included independence for Korea, cession of Taiwan, the Pescadores Island, the Liaodong Peninsula (just west of Korea), and millions of dollars in indemnity.

Within a week Germany, France, and Russia forced Japan to return the peninsula, but the Chinese had to dole out more cash for that. That diplomacy gave the Russians an entrée to Manchuria via an ensuing secret alliance with China. The other Western countries (not the United States) saw the weakened China as open for dismemberment. Only their infighting arrested the activity. And, of course, Taiwan was ruled by Japan for the next 50 years until Japan's defeat in World War II.

Establishment of the People's Republic of China (1949)

Recall that Zhou Enlai's 1936 mercy mission to Xian saved Chiang Kai-shek's life and ensured that a united China would stand against the onslaught of the Japanese. The red army fought the Japanese in the north, and, with the aid of the Soviets, at war's end it controlled much of the territory formerly claimed by the Japanese. General George Marshall was unable to broker a peace, and in 1946 the civil war began again.

Even though China was supported by the United States, Chiang had not been ready for the quick demise of the Japanese brought on by the atomic bomb. Early on the Nationalist armies were successful, but they suffered a critical defeat in Manchuria in 1948. Chiang's autocratic, some say repressive, style won him few converts. Meanwhile the Communist forces continued to attract followers, and their hugely superior numbers began to hold sway. Beijing and Tianjin fell to them in January 1949. In April the Communists crossed the Yangtze and the Nationalists fled to Taiwan. The war was over.

The People's Republic of China (PRC) was formally established by Mao Zedong's decree at Tiananmen Square in Beijing on October 1, 1949. Tibet was reoccupied in 1951. The great majority of the Chinese people welcomed the "liberation" and its concomitant strong central government and land reforms. They were tired of the chaos. Collectivization of the countryside proceeded until the first peasant resistance in 1957. About this time the first large-scale purges of Mao's critics also occurred. In the early 1960s Mao was dealing with criticism from the Soviets and his own leadership. He broke with the former and began to purge the latter.

The Great Leap Forward of the late 1950s and the Cultural Revolution of the 1960s proved to be both economic and social disasters for the PRC. The 1970s saw continued economic stagnation. All these events have lead to the more recent economic reforms promoted by Deng Xiaoping, moving the country toward free enterprise since the 1980s. However, the Communist Revolution can be seen to have accomplished positive social reforms as well. Of particular note are the elevated position of women in society and substantial successes in arresting the population explosion.

The Cultural Revolution (1966–1976)

The low point for China during the last 50 years began in 1966. Chairman Mao was again tired of his high-level critics, and he was losing his grip on the leadership of the party. To help regain control, he formed the Red Guards, which were groups of militant, aggressive college and high school students, into paramilitary units throughout the country. The Red Guards attacked everything traditional. Ridicule of the intellectuals forced the educational system to collapse. Historical sites and relics were destroyed. "Capitalist roaders" such as Deng Xiaoping were banished to the countryside and threatened with death. The ensuing chaos almost led to civil war. Finally, in August 1968 Mao ordered the Red Guards disbanded, and the army restored order.

But great damage had been done. Some of the brightest people of a generation spent years on farms rather than in classrooms. Without the benefit of a formal education, many of these people who were displaced by the Cultural Revolution, now in their fifties and sixties, continue to work in menial jobs today. The Chinese often refer to the decade between 1966 and Mao's death in 1976 as the "ten wasted years."

Fortunately Deng Xiaoping survived the countryside and reemerged as de facto leader of the nation after just a few short years. He repudiated the Cultural Revolution and began the important process of reform toward his vision of a "socialist market economy." The measured opening of China to international trade begun by Deng in 1978 continues to this day.

Central Themes of the Middle Kingdom

The Language

The association between national borders and linguistic boundaries is close and clearly more powerful than politics. Witness the demise of the Soviet Union or Yugoslavia. Other aspects of culture also come into play, such as religion and cuisine. But, language generally defines nations.

Thus, we have the politically incorrect notion of a "greater China." Its citizens reside in the PRC (including Hong Kong), Taiwan, and indeed the rest of the world. It isn't just Communist or Catholic, Republican or Democratic. Sons and daughters of Chinese immigrants in Vancouver, Los Angeles, Kuala Lumpur, Manila, and Sydney are all learning to think of themselves as Chinese in their Saturday morning language classes and in hearing their folks talk at home. Indeed, the kids are not just studying characters; they are also studying character. Learning the language, any language, inculcates values and ways of thinking *very deeply*. First generation immigrants to the United States often complain about how America has corrupted such values as working hard in the second generation. But, the language acquisition keeps the values intact, if below the surface. Of course, Hebrew lessons have served to keep Jewish culture intact in the same way around the world and over the centuries.

Learning written Chinese is a matter of memory. Rather than learning an alphabet and how to combine letters to form sounds and words, the student of Chinese must memorize about 5,000 commonly used individual characters. Most characters originally included pictorial information and hints at pronunciation. However, over the centuries most of that information has disappeared, and memory must be depended upon. This hard work unites Chinese speakers in a special, cultural way. It also discourages creativity. It should also be noted that on the mainland simplified characters have been officially adopted, while in Hong Kong, Taiwan, and to a certain extent Japan the traditional characters are still in use.

In China today hundreds of dialects and languages are still spoken. However, the vast majority of the people can communicate in writing using Chinese characters. Despite the common written language, those in the northern provinces cannot talk to southerners. In the north Mandarin is the dialect, in the Yangtze River delta it's Shanghainese, and in the south it's Cantonese. There are eight major dialects, but since 1949 the government has encouraged everyone to learn to speak Mandarin. Today in Hong Kong you can catch the evening news in either Cantonese or Mandarin. The last is also the official language of Taiwan.

Ideas Flow from the South

A favorite saying in south China is, "They make the rules in Beijing, we interpret them in Guangzhou." The saying reflects the historical fact that new ideas have flowed from south to north in China. Part of this has to do with the fact that the northern invaders have tended to bring with them violence, but little innovation. The sinicization of the Mongols and the Manchus is well documented. Alternatively, Guangzhou (old Canton) and the Pearl River delta were the first places the Europeans landed, and they brought technology and religion with them.

Even before the Europeans arrived, new ideas flowed north. Water transportation was used in the wet south, and the technology moved north with the digging of major canals. The half-cylindric shape of roofing tiles used widely in the north was most likely derived from split bamboo shelters in the south. Rice and tea were first cultivated in the south as well.

Because of the aforementioned European influences, it is no surprise that the Taiping Rebellion madness started in the south. Sun Yat-sen was first exposed to Western thinking during his medical school days in British-held Hong Kong. Even today manufacturing and business systems and the associated wealth are spreading from the entrepreneurial south to the state-owned enterprises in the north. It was for good reason that following the death of Chairman Mao, that the first free farmers' market opened in China was in Guangzhou.

The Silk Road

The Silk Road connected the two world powers at the time of Jesus. The "three kings of the Orient" bearing gifts most likely traversed part of the well-worn 4,000 miles between Xian and Rome. The road passed through modern Afghanistan and delivered goods to Mediterranean ports in Syria. Virtually no one traveled the entire route. Depending on politics and the like, goods were bought and sold by a series of intermediaries along the way.

Silk went west while gold, silver, and woolens went east. Not only did goods make the trip, but ideas did as well. Buddhism and Christianity came east. So did Marco Polo between 1271 and 1297. Technology went west—paper, the foot-stirrup, the crossbow, the wheelbarrow, magnetism, and gunpowder among other innovations.

Integration and Disintegration

Reading across the millennia of Chinese history, a clear cyclicity is apparent—strong leaders unite the country, but the dynasties decay eventually and collapse. Perhaps China is no different from other parts of the world in this regard, but it's still a history unfamiliar to most Americans.

After the fall of the Han dynasty in 220 A.D., it was more than two centuries before the country was reunited. The collapse of the Tang Dynasty in 906 yielded 70 years of chaos. The Jin and Song Dynasties split the empire (1126). Genghis Khan divided the empire, but his grandson Kublai united it again under Mongol rule in 1279. The British took Hong Kong (1842). In just 13 years (1851–1864) the Taiping Rebellion killed tens of millions of Chinese. The Japanese took Taiwan (1895). The Russians took Manchuria (1898). The Boxer Rebellion (1898–1900) divided the country. The Japanese took Manchuria (1905). The Nationalists divided the country in 1911, and the fight began for control among the last emperor, the Japanese, and the Communists. The PRC took back Tibet (1951), Hong Kong (1997), and Macau (1999) and is now "negotiating" for Taiwan.

Some people in the West today make book that China will go the same direction as the Soviet Union. But, the stronger lesson of history is the resiliency of China as a united state. Perhaps the better bet is the peaceful reunification of Taiwan with the mainland.

Invasions

Between the Muslim invasion of Guangzhou in 758 and the Japanese aggression in 1931–1937, we count a dozen other foerign military incursions—Tibetans (763), Jurcheds (1126), Mongols (1234 and 1449), Portuguese (1535), Japan (1592 and 1894), Manchus (1629), British (1839 and 1860), French (1860), and Germany (1897).

Note that the United States is not on the list. At this point in time it's quite difficult to imagine anyone invading China ever again. In

1964 China set off its first atomic bomb. It has good rocket technology and more than 2 million men in uniform. Indeed, state-to-state warfare makes little sense for anyone anymore.

Given the history, it is easy to see why the Chinese people are xenophobic. However, with both United Nations and World Trade Organization membership, we can now see China getting over the bad experiences of the last two millennia. Perhaps an unfamiliar feeling of security is beginning to set in. If this is the case, that's good news for everyone.

The Weight of Population

The xenophobes here in the United States would have us believe that China will return to its international adventurism of the Ming Dynasty some day. Recall the vast Chinese fleets prowling the Indian Ocean area in 1403–1433. In 1407 they invaded and vanquished Vietnam. China kept that conquest for all of 21 years. Its modern disputes with the Vietnamese and Filipinos over the Spratley Islands in the South China Sea are often offered as evidence of its potential expansionism.

However, all this silliness ignores the Chinese government's primary problem, one that it has always had and will always have—keeping peace among its huge population. The famine problem has been solved by the green revolution. The population growth has been at least temporarily arrested through the one-child policy of the PRC.

The current problem is that almost 70 percent of the 1.3 billion Chinese live in rural areas and mostly inland. However, the two most important migration trends in the world today are urbanization and movement to the coasts. The Chinese authorities have to manage not only the steady economic growth needed to provide increasing numbers of free enterprise jobs for the millions leaving the inefficient state-owned enterprises, but also an unprecedented migration from country center to city coast. They will need all the help they can get!

Timeline of Chinese History

BC

c. 1.5–0.5 million	Homo erectus living in China near Beijing, Lantian, Yuanmou and other sites
c. 80,000	Appearance of modern man, Homo sapiens, in China
c. 7,000	Beginnings of agriculture and of the Neolithic period
c .2550	Reign of the Yellow Emperor (legendary)
c. 2300	Reign of Yao (legendary)
c. 2200	Reign of Shun (legendary)
c. 2140	Yu the Great controls the great flood (legendary)
c. 2100	Beginning of the Xia dynasty (historicity uncertain)
c. 2100	Beginning of the Chinese Bronze Age
c. 1600	Tang the Accomplished overthrows the last Xia king and establishes the Shang dynasty
c. 1300	Earliest Shang inscriptions on oracle bones
c. 1100	Reign of King Wen of Zhou
c. 1050	The forces of King Wu of Zhou defeat those of the last Shang king in the Battle of Muye: end of the Shang dynasty
c. 900	Emergence of horse nomadism in the steppes north of China
841	Earliest certain date in Chinese history
c. 820	Zhou china attacked by the Xianyun (probably mounted warriors from the north)
771	King You of Zhou killed in attack on the royal capital by rebellious vassals and barbarians
770	First year of the reign of King Ping of Zhou, enthroned in the eastern Zhou capital near modern Luoyang; beginning of Spring and Autumn period
c. 650	Chinese begin to cast iron
552 or 551	Birth of Confucius
479	Death of Confucius

463	Beginning of Warring States period
c. 450	Long defensive wall built on the borders of the state of Qi
256	Zhou kingdom finally annihilated by the state of Qin
221	King Zheng of Qin completes the conquest of all the Chinese states and declares himself First Emperor of the Qin dynasty
214	Completion of the first Great Wall of China
210	Death of the First Emperor of Qin
209	Outbreak of uprisings against the Qin dynasty
206	Han dynasty established
c. 140	Confucianism becomes the dominant state philosophy
138–126	Zhang Qian travels from China to Bactria and Sogdiana
c. 90	Sima Qian finished the first complete history of China

AD

9–23	Reign of Wang Mang, only emperor of the Xin dynasty; all land declared state property
c. 65	Buddhism reaches China
105	Cai Lun brings paper to the attention of the emperor
184	Rebellion of the Yellow Turbans begins
220	Final collapse of the Han dynasty; China splits into three states
c. 250	Tea drinking begins to spread through China
c. 399–414	Fa Xian travels from China to India
589	Sui dynasty reunites China
605	Completion of the first Grand Canal, linking the Yangtze with the Yellow River
610	Grand Canal extended south to the Qiantang River

c. 629–45	Xuan Zhuang's journey from China to India
641	A Chinese princess marries the King of Tibet
668	Chinese subjugate Korea
690–701	Reign of the Empress Wu
694	Buddhism ceases to be treated as a foreign religion
751	Battle of the Talas River; Chinese power in Central Asia destroyed by the armies of Islam
755–7	Rebellion of An Lushan
758	Muslims from Arabia and the Persian Gulf burn and loot Guangzhou
763	Tibetans invade China and briefly occupy Chang'an
843	Large quantities of Buddhist church property seized by the government
868	Earliest surviving dated printed book produced in China
875	Outbreak of rebellion of Huang Chao
906	Tang dynasty collapses; China again divided
c. 901	Paper money first used in China
919	Gunpowder begins to be used in China
932–53	Printing of the complete texts of the Confucian Classics
975	China reunited during the reign of the first emperor of the Song dynasty
1044	Description of the magnetic compass in a Chinese text
1069	Reforms of Wang Anshi
1126	The Song capital, Kaifeng, falls to Jurched invaders, who establish the Jin dynasty in north China
1161–5	Song armed forces repulse Jin attacks
1194	Major flood and change of course of the Yellow River
1234	The Mongols complete the conquest of north China and destroy the Jin Dynasty

1271–97	Marco Polo in China
1279	Khubilai Khan completes the conquest of south China
c. 1290	The Grand Canal is rebuilt and extended
1294	John of Montecorvino establishes a permanent Christian mission in Beijing
1368	The Ming dynasty is founded with its capital at Nanjing
1403–33	Voyages by large Chinese junks to India and East Africa
c. 1412	Rebuilding of the Great Wall
1421	The Ming court moves to Beijing, and perhaps a Chinese fleet explores the coast of America
1449	The Mongols invade China and seize the sixth Ming emperor
1514	Portuguese ships reach the China coast
1535	The Portuguese first begin to use Macao
1581	Tax reform: the land tax and poll tax are combined under the "single whip system"
1592	The Japanese invade Korea
1598	Chinese forces push the Japanese out of Korea
1601	Matteo Ricci, Jesuit missionary, establishes himself in Beijing
1629	Manchus loot Beijing
1629–45	Rebellion of Li Zicheng
c. 1640	The first tea is brought to Europe
1644	Li Zicheng seizes Beijing and overthrows the Ming dynasty; Wu Sangui invites the Manchus through the Great Wall to help drive Li Zicheng out of Beijing; the Manchus establish themselves in China, moving their capital to Beijing
1683	The Manchus take Taiwan, completing their conquest of China
1689	The Treaty of Nerchinsk partially settles the border between Russia and Manchuria

1720	The Manchus incorporate Tibet into the Qing empire
1729	An imperial edict forbids the selling and use of opium
1790–1	Qing forces subjugate Nepal
1793–4	First British embassy to China, led by Lord Macartney
1793–1804	White Lotus rebellion
1816	Second British embassy to China, led by Lord Amherst
1834	The British East India Company's monopoly of the China trade is abolished
1836–9	The opium trade at Guangzhou is suppressed by the Chinese
1839–42	First Opium War
1842	Treaty of Nanjing: Hong Kong Island ceded to Britain, Shanghai opened as a "treaty port"
1851–64	Taiping rebellion kills 20 to 40 million Chinese
1853	Taiping rebels take Nanjing
1853–68	Nian rebellion
1855	The Yellow River floods and changes its course; the northern section of the Grand Canal loses its water and falls into disuse
1855–73	Muslim rebellion in Yunnan
1857–60	*Arrow* War or Second Opium War
1860	British and French forces enter Beijing and destroy the Yuan Ming Yuan summer palace
c. 1862	The Empress Dowager Ci Xi becomes the dominant force at the Qing court
1862–78	Muslim rebellion in northwest China
1863	Robert Hart becomes inspector-general of the Chinese Customs service
1879	Japan annexes the Ryukyu Islands
1894–5	Sino-Japanese War
1895	Treaty of Shimonoseki: Taiwan is ceded to Japan
1897	The Germans seize Jiaozhou Bay and Qingdao and force the Chinese to grant a lease

1898	Russia obtains a lease on Port Arthur and Dalian
1898	Britain obtains leases on Weihaiwei and the New Territories of Hong Kong
1898	The "Hundred Days of Reform"
1898–1900	The Boxer uprising
1900	Siege of the Foreign Legations; Western troops occupy Beijing
1904–5	Russo-Japanese War; Japan takes over Russian interests in Manchuria
1908	Death of the Empress Dowager Ci Xi; accession of the last emperor, Pu Yi
1911	The Nationalist Revolution overthrows the Qing dynasty
1912	Yuan Shikai becomes first president of the Chinese Republic
1914	Outbreak of First World War; Japan attacks German concessions in the Far East and takes Qingdao
1915	Yuan Shikai accepts Japan's "Twenty-one Demands"
1916	Yuan Shikai abandons plans to become emperor and dies soon afterwards
1917	Brief restoration of the last Qing emperor; China enters the First World War against Germany
1919	The May Fourth Movement: Chinese students demonstrate against the Versailles settlement
1921	First general meeting of the Chinese Communist Party
1922	Japan returns Qingdao to Chinese control
1925	Sun Yat-sen dies; Chiang Kai-shek becomes leader of the Chinese Nationalists
1926–8	The Northern Expedition succeeds in establishing Nationalist control over much of China
1930	Britain return Weihaiwei to China
1931	Japan seizes much of Manchuria
1933	The League of Nations condemns Japanese aggression in China: Japan walks out of the League

1934	Pu Yi becomes emperor of the Japanese puppet state of Manchukuo
1934–5	The Long March
1936	The Xian Incident; the Chinese Nationalists and Communists form a united front against Japan
1937	Outbreak of war between China and Japan
1941	U.S. volunteer fliers form the "Flying Tigers" in Kunming
1945	The USSR attacks the Japanese in Manchuria; Japan surrenders
1946	Resumption of civil war between Nationalists and Communists
1949	Founding of the People's Republic of China
1950	U.S. Seventh Fleet sent to the Taiwan Straits to prevent a Communist invasion of the island; China sends troops into Korea
1951	The People's Liberation Army takes control of Tibet
1953	End of the Korean War
1957	"Hundred Flowers" campaign
1957–9	Anti-rightist campaign
1958	The Great Leap Forward; People's Communes established
1960	Split between China and the Soviet Union
1962	China defeats India in a war over the border of Tibet
1964	China explodes its first atomic bomb
1966	Outbreak of the Great Proletarian Cultural Revolution
1971	Death of Lin Biao; the People's Republic of China replaces Taiwan at the United Nations
1972	President Nixon visits China
1975	Zhou Enlai announces the "Four Modernizations"
1976	Death of Zhou Enlai; death of Mao Zedong
1977	The "Gang of Four" are arrested
1979	The U.S. recognizes the People's Republic of China
1981	First Special Economic Zones established

1989	Suppression of the democracy movement in Beijing
1993	Exchange rate of the Chinese yuan allowed to float
1995	Chen Yun, last of Den Xiaoping's major Maoist opponents, dies
1996	U.S. President Clinton, after his election for a second term, agrees to exchange state visits with Jiang Zemin
1997	Deng Xiaoping dies on 19 February at age 92; Hong Kong is handed back to the People's Republic of China by Britain; Jiang Zemin pays an official visit to the USA, during which he obliquely admits that the use of military force to suppress demonstrations in 1989 was an error
1998	Li Peng retires as Premier at the end of his term of office and is replaced by Zhu Rongji; U.S. President Clinton visits China
1999	Almost 2,500 people are killed by an earthquake in Taiwan; Jiang Zemin visits the UK and other Western countries; Portugal returns Macau to China
2000	Chen Shuibian is elected the first non-Guomindang President of Taiwan; elections to the Legislative Council in Hong Kong attract only a 43.6% turnout, with the Democratic Party receiving only 34.7% of the vote; Cheng Kejie, a vice-chairman of the Standing Committee of the National People's Congress, is executed for corruption; the U.S. grants China permanent normal trade relations (PNTR), opening the way for China to become a full member of the World Trade Organization (WTO)
2001	WTO membership achieved
2008	Beijing Olympic Games
2010	Shanghai World Expo

Notes

1 Also often spelled K'ung-fu-tzu.
2 Certainly a good argument can be made that we should list Chairman Mao as the key person of this period. However, we do correctly credit Mao with fomenting the Communist Revolution in a later section of the chapter. But, as in the case of Wang An-shih during the Song Dynasty, advisors can play decisive roles in history. So, while the Chairman lies in state in Tiananmen Square, we list his loyal advisor in this section of the book as being the more influential, even if debatably so.
3 These voyages are among the few instances in the history of Chinese attempts at expansion beyond their traditional borders.
4 This old firm is the model for the excellent James Clavell novels about Hong Kong, *Taipan* and *Noble House*.

CHAPTER 3

ECONOMIC DEVELOPMENT AND THE TRAJECTORY OF THE GREATER CHINA

Nobody predicts that China's economic performance will flatten out. So far William Overholt has been right. He predicted in his 1993 tome, *The Rise of China*,[1] almost exactly the unprecedented dynamic development we're seeing there more than a decade later. We haven't even gotten to the Beijing Olympics (2008) or the Shanghai World Expo (2010) yet. On the other end of the seer scale are folks like Gordon Chang and his 2003 complaint, *The Coming Collapse of China*.[2] Minxin Pei supports this view in his essay in *Foreign Policy* magazine:

> *China's economic boom has dazzled investors and captivated the world. But beyond the new high-rises and churning factories lie rampant corruption, vast waste, and an elite with little interest in making things work better. Forget political reform. China's future will be decay, not democracy.*[3]

So who's right? Up or down?

Indeed, China's 5,000 years of history as reported in Chapter 2 supports either view. Cyclicality is a central theme. In this chapter we consider the question from five perspectives. First, we consider the broader context of economic growth in China's neighborhood, East Asia. Next we present a broad overview of China's recent growth and the associated difficulties. Third, we compare economic development in China with that of its peers—India and Russia. Fourth, we take a quick look at similar instances of dramatic growth, albeit in the smaller countries of Japan, Korea, and Taiwan. Finally, we focus on a series of issues that should influence growth rates in China for years to come.

The Rise of East Asia

Asia has been the fastest-growing area in the world for the past three decades, and the prospects for continued economic growth over the long run are excellent.[4] Beginning in 1996, the leading economies of Asia (Japan, Hong Kong, South Korea, Singapore, and Taiwan) experienced a serious financial crisis, which culminated in the meltdown of the Asian stock market. A tight monetary policy, an appreciating U.S. dollar, and a deceleration of exports all contributed to the downturn. Despite this economic adjustment, the 1993 estimates by the International Monetary Fund (IMF) that Asian economies would have 29 percent of the global output by the year 2000 have been on target. As sources of new products and technology and as vast consumer markets, the countries of Asia—particularly those along the Pacific Rim—are just beginning to hit their stride.

The most rapidly growing economies in this region are in the group sometimes referred to as the Four Tigers (or Four Dragons): Hong Kong, South Korea, Singapore, and Taiwan. Often described as the "East Asian miracle," they were the first countries in Asia, besides Japan, to move from a status of developing countries to newly industrialized countries. They have grown from suppliers of component parts and assemblers of Western products to major global competitors in electronics, shipbuilding, heavy machinery, and a multitude of other products. In addition, each has become a major influence in trade and development in the economies of the other countries within its spheres of influence. The rapid economic growth and regional influence of the member countries of the Association of Southeast Nations (ASEAN) over the last decade has prompted the U.S. Trade Representative to discuss free-trade agreements—Singapore has already signed up. These countries are vast markets for industrial goods and, as is discussed later, important emerging consumer markets.

The Four Tigers are rapidly industrializing and extending their trading activity to other parts of Asia. Japan was once the dominant investment leader in the area and was a key player in the economic development of China, Taiwan, Hong Kong, South Korea, and other countries of the region. But, as the economies of other Asian countries have strengthened and industrialized, these countries are becoming more important as economic leaders. For example, South Korea is the center of trade links with north China and the Asian republics of the former Soviet Union. South Korea's sphere of influence and trade extends to Guangdong and Fujian, two of the most productive Chinese special economic zones, and it is becoming more important in interregional investment as well.

China Itself

Aside from the United States, there is no more important single market than China.[5] The economic and social changes occurring in China since it began actively seeking economic ties with the industrialized world have been dramatic. China's dual economic system, embracing socialism along with many tenets of capitalism, has produced an economic boom with expanded opportunity for foreign investment that has resulted in annual gross national product (GNP) growth averaging nearly 10 percent since 1970. Most analysts predict that an 8 to 10 percent average for the next 10 to 15 years is possible. At that rate China's GNP should equal that of the United States by 2015. All this growth is dependent on China's abilities to deregulate industry, import modern technology, privatize overstaffed, inefficient state-owned enterprises (SOEs), and continue to attract foreign investment.

Two major events that occurred in 2000 are having a profound effect on China's economy: admission to the World Trade Organization and the United States' granting China normal trade relations (NTR) on a permanent basis (PNTR). China's entry to the WTO cut import barriers currently imposed on American products and services. The United States is obligated to maintain the market access policies that it already applies to China, and has for over 20 years, and to make its normal trade relation status permanent. After years of procrastination, China has begun to comply with WTO provisions and has made a wholehearted and irrevocable commitment to creating a market economy that is tied to the world at large.

An issue that concerns many is whether China will follow WTO rules when it has to lower its formidable barriers to imported goods.[6] Enforcement of the agreement will not just happen. Experience with many past agreements has shown that it is often next to impossible to get compliance on some issues. Some of China's concessions are repeats of unfulfilled agreements extending back to 1979. The United States has learned from its experience with Japan that the toughest work is yet to come. A promise to open markets to U.S. exports can be just the beginning of a long effort at ensuring compliance.

Because of China's size, diversity, and political organization, it is better to think of it as a group of five regions rather than a single country—a grouping of regional markets rather than a single market. (The regions are discussed in more detail in Chapter 11.) There is no one-growth strategy for China. Each region is at a different stage economically and has its own link to other regions as well as links to other parts of the world. Each has its own investment patterns, is taxed differently, and has substantial autonomy in how it is governed. But while each region is separate enough to be considered individually, each is linked at the top to the central government in Beijing.

China has two other important steps to take if the road to economic growth is to be smooth: improving human rights and reforming the legal system. The human rights issue has been a sticking point with the United States because of China's lack of religious freedom, the Tiananmen Square massacre in 1989, the jailing of dissidents, and its treatment of Tibet. The U.S. government's decision to award PNTR reflected, in part, the growing importance of China in the global marketplace and the perception that trade with China was too valuable to be jeopardized over a single issue. However, the issue remains delicate both within the United States and between the United States and China.

Meanwhile, China continues to reinvent itself. At the 2002 Communist Party's National Congress, Hu Jintao was selected as general secretary. But, perhaps more important than his selection was the admission of private entrepreneurs into the Party. This signifies a huge transformation of the Chinese Communist Party from a class party representing workers and peasants into one representing the people as a whole.

Despite these positive changes, the American embassy in China has seen a big jump in complaints from disgruntled U.S. companies that are fed up with their lack of protection under China's legal system. Outside the major urban areas of Beijing, Shanghai, and Guangzhou, companies are discovering that local protectionism and cronyism make business tough even when they have local partners. Many are finding that a Chinese partner with local political clout can rip off its foreign partner and, when complaints are taken to court, influence courts to rule in its favor.

Actually there are two Chinas—one a maddening, bureaucratic, bottomless money pit; the other an enormous emerging market. There is the old China, where holdovers of the Communist Party's planning apparatus heap demands on multinational corporations, especially in politically important sectors such as autos,[7] chemicals, and telecom equipment. Companies are shaken down by local officials, whipsawed by policy swings, railroaded into bad partnerships, and squeezed for technology. But there is also a new, market-driven China that is fast emerging. Consumer areas, from fast food to shampoo, are now wide open. Even in tightly guarded sectors the barriers to entry are eroding as provincial authorities, rival ministries, and even the military challenge the power of Beijing's technocrats.

No industry better illustrates the changing rules than information technology. Chinese planners once limited imports of PCs and software to promote homegrown industries, but the Chinese preferred smuggled imports to the local manufacturers. Beijing eventually loosened the restraints, and Microsoft is now the dominant PC operating system. A market whose modernization plan calls for imports of equipment and technology of over $100 billion per year, with infrastructure expenditures amounting to $250 billion through the remainder of the decade, is worth the effort. Indeed, China is now the second biggest market for personal computers, following only the United States.

The Race among China, Russia, and India

During the 1980s the Japanese changed the game of international competition from one involving military spending to one based on overall economic performance. At the end of the decade the Japanese were winning the new game, and among their trophies they counted the likes of Pebble Beach Golf Course and Rockefeller Center. Russia smartly dropped out of the military game in 1989 and thus engaged China in one of the greatest economic and political experiments in history. Great debates have swirled around the question of which road to prosperity was the more direct—the "big bang" democratic liberalization of the Russian political economy or the more controlled incrementalism of Chinese reforms. In Exhibits 3.1 and 3.2 we've included the New India. With the Internet, we Americans can finally "see" the other side of the planet and the competitive and market potentials of the other billion-person country.

The metric we're using for economic development—gross domestic product (GDP) per capita adjusted for purchase price parity(PPP)—is the best measure of quality of life the economy is delivering to the average person. But, a word of caution is in

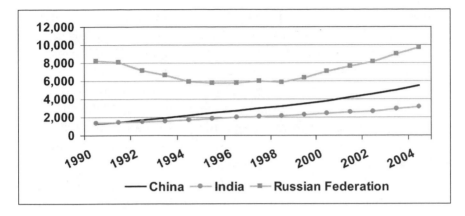

Exhibit 3.1   GDP per Capita PPP (Current International $)
(*Source: World Development Indicators*)

order—all statistics coming from developing nations have to be taken with a grain of salt. Indeed, you can find good arguments that the Chinese overestimate their economic growth rates, and you can also find good arguments that they underestimate. The main point is that Chinese statistics are generally unreliable and

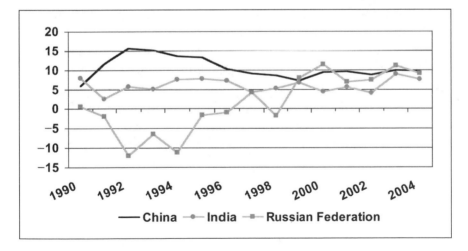

**Exhibit 3.2   GDP per Capita PPP—Percent Change
(Current International $)** (*Source: World Development Indicators*)

subject to political manipulations. We're getting all these data from the World Development Indicator database, which is managed by the World Bank. But even these data should not be considered accurate—they are just the best measures available.

Looking at Exhibits 3.1 and 3.2 you can see that Russia started out ahead, but stumbled badly during the early 1990s and, of course, in 1998. Its dismal economic performance in 1998 was the source of the only finance joke we've ever heard: "Do you know the difference between a dollar and ruble? In 1998 it was a dollar." Indian growth has hovered at around 5 percent, and Chinese growth at about 10 percent during the period. But, overall the Russians still lead the game, and their trajectory so far in the twenty-first century is the same as China's. So, in 2005 the average Russian had an annual income of $9,863; the average Chinese, $5,495; and the average Indian, $3,115. By the way, the average American had an income of $39,618 that year.

The biggest difference in the three economies can be seen in Exhibit 3.3. The growth in net inflows of foreign direct investments (FDI) in China is astonishing. Indeed, for 2003, the last year in which all countries reported, China's FDI (at $54 billion) even eclipsed that of the United States (at $40 billion).[8] The best FDI estimates for China during 2005 were over $60 billion. As you can see in Exhibit 3.3, the Russian and Indian economies are not attracting nearly the same level of investment. So, as FDI is a leading indicator of economic development, it will be hard for the Russians and Indians to keep up.

Of course, China has a huge advantage in garnering FDI—overseas Chinese have served to funnel investment dollars to the Middle Kingdom. Hong Kong has always served that purpose, but Taiwan and the diaspora in all the other places where Chinese people have immigrated throughout Southeast Asia and the rest of the world have helped mightily as well. It is an axiom of the international political economy that immigration creates an easy path for trade and capital flows.

Information infrastructure is also an important leading indicator of economic development. Exhibits 3.4 and 3.5 include the

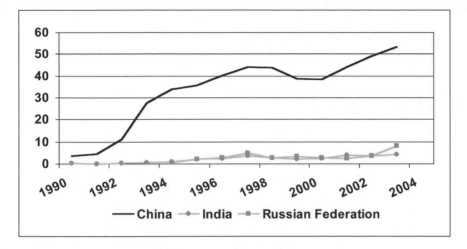

**Exhibit 3.3   Foreign Direct Investment, Net Inflows
(BoP, Current U.S. $) BoP = balance of payments**
(*Source: World Development Indicators*)

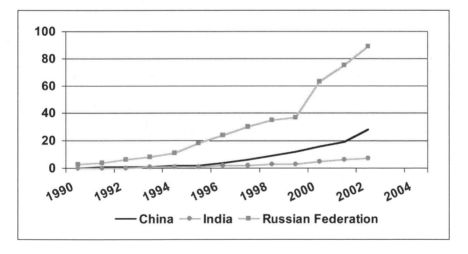

Exhibit 3.4   Personal Computers (per 1,000 People)
(*Source: World Development Indicators*)

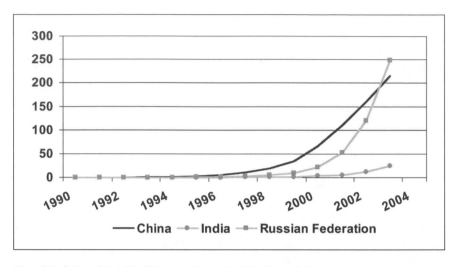

Exhibit 3.5   Mobile Phones (per 1,000 People)
(*Source: World Development Indicators*)

penetration of personal computers and cell phones for all three countries. Clearly the Russians are winning this aspect of the race. Although the Chinese purchase of IBM's PC business will certainly help them in the technology infrastructure race, the government's heavy-handed censorship will be a hindrance to future economic development.

Finally, the quality of the educations systems will have the biggest impact on the economic trajectory of these three nations. By most accounts India is in the lead when it comes to higher education. Diana Farrell, director of the McKinsey Global Institute, reports that India is producing a substantially larger number of young professionals than is China.[9] However, China's universities are catching up. In particular, the growth of China's business schools is currently exploding. But, of the three, India has had the longest tradition of excellent business education.

Japan and South Korea as Models of Growth

How hard is it to sustain 10 percent growth rates? A look at China's closest neighbors provides some insight into this difficult question. (See Exhibits 3.6 and 3.7.) The economies of all three countries have grown steadily over the last three decades. Indeed, you cannot even see the so-called "Japanese malaise" during the 1990s, because our metric controls for population growth rates and deflation. Both South Korea and Japan experienced slowdowns associated with the 1997 Asian economic crisis. But, because Japan has a national fetish for economic stability, the average Japanese person continued to be better off from the mid-1970s to the present, with only one instance of decline, that is, −.033 percent in 1999. Of course, the South Korean decline during that period was steeper, but the recovery was also fast. And, apparently China weathered that storm even better. So these data give hope that China can sustain steady growth, even if it is not at a double-digit level.

One caveat is in order though. As compared to the steady growth of its two smaller neighbors, China's trajectory is a bit

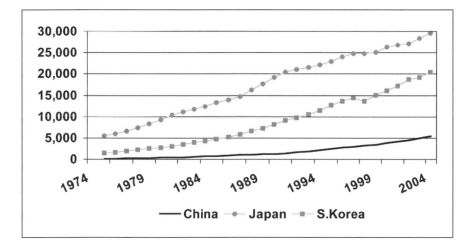

Exhibit 3.6   GDP per Capita PPP (Current International $)
(*Source: World Development Indicators*)

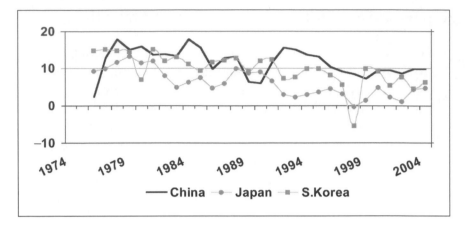

Exhibit 3.7   GDP per Capita PPP—Percent Change (Current International $) (*Source: World Development Indicators*)

more volatile than it appears. This is because most of the growth in China is along the coast and around the big cities. Much of the nation still does not participate. So, what is estimated as a 10 percent growth rate for the entire country really translates to perhaps a 15–20 percent growth rate for parts of the country and significantly less for other parts of the country. Furthermore, that level of growth is clearly unsustainable.

Indeed, an initial ominous sign of this problem was the 2006 bust in the Shanghai housing market. There the Shanghai housing market was the hottest on the planet. At least temporarily things have turned bitterly cold. Prices in some apartment complexes there fell by a third. For the first time folks in Shanghai experienced "upside down" mortgages. Moreover, about 1 million new housing units are under construction in Shanghai alone. At this writing the immediate hope is that this new Chinese overbuilding disease will not spread to the other big cities.

Then There's Spain in 1993

A popular T-shirt on the streets of Barcelona in 1992 pictured a Spaniard with his empty pants pockets turned out and the caption,

"Spain 1993." You may recall that both the Olympic Games and a Worlds Fair were staged in Barcelona and Seville, respectively, in 1992. The world celebrated these wonderful events, and the Spaniards spent lavishly putting on the show. Quite a fiesta! In fact, the Spanish spent so lavishly that the economy and the people suffered shortly thereafter. Its traditional 6 percent growth rate slowed to zero in 1993. The T-shirt makers were right.

Now fast-forward to the 2008 Olympics in Beijing and the 2010 Worlds Fair in Shanghai. Any ideas for T-shirts circa 2011? Indeed, China is sucking up half the world's cement and steel rebar to ready itself for the big parties at the end of the decade. It's certain that there will be a 2011 slowdown caused by the immense party preparations. The question is how slow will the slowdown be?

A U.S. Slowdown Will Hurt China

Speaking of Shanghai and its cooling housing market, what about the United States? The only thing that's kept our debt-ridden economy afloat has been the unprecedented appreciation in housing prices here. We've borrowed on our houses to fill our garages and closets. And our spending has fueled mediocre domestic growth and a wonderful growth in imports from China. Indeed, on the West Coast we expect another fall traffic jam at our ports, the ships coming from China filled with goodies for Wal-Mart shelves.

The only thing keeping Congress from rattling the "trade saber" over the huge trade deficit with China is the ongoing conundrum of the Middle East. But, if the economy suffers a substantial downturn in housing prices, then an immediate victim will be trade with China. That's a safe bet. And, curtailed exports from China will precipitate a slowing of growth there.

There's an even a bigger gorilla on the horizon—the American Baby Boomers are or will be retiring. Our health-care and pensions systems no longer make sense after 2010, that is, if they do now? The end of the national parties in Beijing (2008 Olympics) and Shanghai (World Expo 2010) will coincide with the beginning of the economic turmoil associated with the American retirement bust. Yikes!

The Green Opportunity

With respect to the 2008 Olympics, you have to wonder whether the marathoners will be able to go the distance given the summer dust storms and exhaust fumes. If the wind blows away the automobile generated pollution, will it bring the dust from Gobi Desert with it? Quite a conundrum? The burgeoning Chinese demand for energy is pushing oil prices to new highs. They've got coal to burn, but the pollution associated with that practice is unfortunately easy to see, if not hard to breathe. Certainly a lack of energy can slow economic growth—that's a worry.

However, as we learned from the energy-less Japanese following the OPEC oil crisis of the mid-1970s, shortages can also breed creativity in fuel savings. You don't need oil under your feet to live a good life. In fact, there's plenty of evidence around that having oil under your feet often leads to a bad life—think Nigeria or Iraq. William McDonough[10] is quite eloquent in making the case that China will actually lead a new green revolution:

> *Indeed, the very urgency of China's environmental problems is forcing a flowering of innovation. And its search for solutions will have global impact, opening up vast markets for forward-looking energy and technology companies while simultaneously creating a rich seedbed for new types of ecologically intelligent products, services, and technologies.*

Scott Samuelsen, director of the National Center for Fuel Cell Research at the University of California, Irvine, not only agrees, but he adds to the argument. Samuelsen would be the first to tell you that innovations, no matter how apparently advantageous, are fundamentally disruptive. And so it is with green technologies such as electric cars. When Toyota first introduced its model in

California, the car was quite popular with consumers. But neither the car dealers nor the oil companies appreciated the advance. The electric cars require less maintenance, thus reducing the most profitable aspect of auto dealers' offerings. And, the oil companies saw revenue losses because consumers could just charge up at home. So both industry groups lobbied hard against the subsidies given the new technology, and ultimately they defeated it. Toyota withdrew its product from the marketplace. China is different. There is no infrastructure yet to be disrupted. It makes the perfect "seedbed" for experiments with electric vehicles and such.

Political Reform and Economic Development

It is our belief that economic development leads to political reform. The best evidence for this assertion comes from East Asia itself. Look at Japan, South Korea, Taiwan, and the PRC. As the economies in these countries have grown, oligarchy and cronyism have declined. Of course, declines of cronyism haven't occurred fast enough for most. But, the causal relationship is undeniable. It may be that the Russian approach to reform and then development may also work. But, violence rates in Russia remain among the highest in the world, and President Vladimir Putin appears to continue his backsliding toward autocracy.

The question the critics such as Minxim Pei and Gordon Chang have to answer is not whether corruption, oligarchy, and inefficiency exist in China. They do. Rather, the important question is, What is the trajectory of these maladies? At this writing they are in decline in China. And continued economic growth will accelerate their decline. Please consider the impact of WTO membership as an indicator of the trajectory of China. We ask you, the reader, to sit back in your chair for a moment and consider the situation. (If you're near a window or perhaps at 35,000 feet somewhere over the Pacific, put the book down and take a look out at the big picture.) Then answer the question for yourself. Are things improving in China or not?

Finally, Taiwan helps in all this. Not just economically, but as an inspiration for good behavior on the part of leaders on the mainland. Recall that historically China has gone through waves of integration and then disintegration. The only path to complete integration, bringing Taiwan back into the fold, is through trade and economic prosperity. That's a 50-year project. So maybe the time to worry about "the coming collapse" is sometime in the latter half of this century.

Conclusion

In the long run the economic strength of China will not be as an exporting machine but as a vast market. The economic strength of the United States comes from its resources and productivity and the vast internal market that drives its economy. China's future potential might better be compared with America's economy, which is driven by domestic demand, than with Japan's, driven by exports. China is neither an economic paradise nor an economic wasteland. It is a relatively poor nation going through a painfully awkward transformation from a socialist market system to a hybrid socialist/free market system, not yet complete and with the rules of the game still being written.

Despite the obstacles we describe in this chapter, there are also many reasons for long-term steady growth of Greater China. Indeed, nobody on the planet can afford to see a collapse of China. And trade is leading not only to economic prosperity in the region, but also to peace. We remain bullish on China. We vote UP!

Notes

1   William J. Overholt, *The Rise of China* (New York: Norton, 1993).
2   Gordon C. Chang, *The Coming Collapse of China* (New York: Random House, 2001).

3 Minxin Pei, "The Dark Side of China's Rise," *Foreign Policy*, March–April 2006, pp. 32–40.

4 Visit *Asia Week* for current information on Asian countries: www.asiaweek.com.

5 *The Economist*, "How China Runs the World Economy," July 30, 2005, pp. 11, 61–63.

6 Don Lee, "No Easy Answers on China Trade," *Los Angeles Times*, June 4, 2005, pp. C1, C2.

7 Brian Bremner and Kathleen Kerwin, "Here Come Chinese Cars," *BusinessWeek*, June 6, 2005, pp. 34–36.

8 We should note that America's FDI jumps all over the place—in 2000 it was $321 billion, and in 2004, $116 billion.

9 Diana Farrell, "India Outsmarts China," *Foreign Policy*, January–February 2006, pp. 30–31.

10 William McDonough, "China as a Green Lab," *Harvard Business Review*, February 2006, pp. 38–39.

U.S. IMPEDIMENTS TO TRADE WITH CHINA: THE GOOD, THE BAD, AND THE UGLY

We believe that the most important sort of international relations is that between managers and companies, not that between politicians. The best empirical evidence for the veracity of our assertion is the current state of affairs across the Taiwan Straits. The newspapers cover the saber rattling in Beijing, Taipei, and Washington. What the journalists miss is the more salient trade-created interdependence among the three "nations" that makes military action impractical. Thus, we consider trade to be the main ingredient of international relations and politics to be simply the background music. But, of course, sometimes the background music can get very loud.

It was in 1807 when Thomas Jefferson came up with trade sanctions as an innovation in diplomacy. The donkeys he endeavored to persuade then were quite big and quite stubborn, England and France. The goal was to get these warring nations to leave American ships (including those headed to and from Canton) alone on the high seas. Lacking a competitive navy, our third president dreamed up the trade embargo—rather than using trade as a carrot, he planned to withhold trade and use it as a stick. However, instead of changing French or English policies and behaviors, Jefferson's policy actually endangered New England traders. They complained:

Our ships all in motion, once whiten'd the ocean;
They sail'd and return'd with a Cargo;
Now doom'd to decay, they are fallen a prey,
To Jefferson, worms, and EMBARGO.[1]

Jefferson's embargo fell apart in just 15 months. It was the War of 1812 that settled the problems with English aggression at sea.

We should have learned from Jefferson's folly that government trade sanctions rarely have their intended consequences. But we didn't. Consider the track record of trade sanctions in the last century. In 1940 the United States told the Japanese to get out of China—the ensuing embargo of gasoline and scrap metal lead directly to the Pearl Harbor attack. Since 1948 Arab countries have boycotted Israel. Given that countries trade most with their close neighbors, you have to wonder how much this lack of trade has promoted the continuing conflicts in the area. Israel is still there. In 1959 Castro took over Cuba; for more than 50 years the United States has boycotted sugar and cigars, and Castro is still there. OPEC's 1973 oil flow slowdown was intended to get America to stop supporting Israel. However, the dollars still flow fast to Israel and now Egypt as well.

In 1979 the United States told the Soviets to get out of Afghanistan. They refused. America boycotted the Moscow Olympics and stopped selling them grain and technology. The Soviet response— they continued to kill Afghans (and, by the way, Soviet soldiers) for another 10 years. Moreover, in 1984 they and their allies' athletes stayed away from the L. A. Olympics. And the high-tech embargo didn't work anyway. A San Diego division of Caterpillar John had worked for in the mid-1970s lost millions of dollars in service contracts for Soviet natural gas pipelines. These revenues were lost permanently, because the Soviets taught themselves how to do the maintenance and overhauls. In 1989 John walked through a Moscow weapons research facility—it had every brand of computer then available in the West, IBMs, Apples, and the best from Taiwan and Japan, as well.

Perhaps the 1980s multilateral trade sanctions imposed on South Africa hastened Apartheid's demise. But, look how well the world's 10-year embargo of Iraq changed policy there. Using trade as a weapon killed kids while Saddam celebrated at $12 million birthday parties. Indeed, the best prescription for Middle East peace (and American taxpayers' wallets, by the way) is all sides dropping all embargoes.

After 1949 we treated Communist China in a similar way with a complete trade embargo until 1972, and more recently requiring annual approval of normal tariff rates for trade. But, as China became less communist during the 1990s, these restrictions faded away, ultimately resulting in congressional and presidential approvals of both permanently normalized trade relations (PNTR) and World Trade Organization (WTO) ascension for China. Despite this dramatic progress, three aspects of American trade regulation continue to make it more difficult for our firms to do business in China: (1) the Foreign Corrupt Practices Act (FCPA); (2) national security-based export controls on high-technology exports; and (3) immigration and travel restrictions. These government policies are frequently complained about with respect to trade with China, and they are the subjects of this chapter.

The Good—The Foreign Corrupt Practices Act (FCPA)

Our story starts with a foreign donation to a political campaign in Japan. In international relations 1972 was a watershed year. In February Richard Nixon traveled to China, and his meetings with Zhou Enlai resulted in the opening of mutual trade offices, thus beginning the détente that continues to this day. In September of that same year the newly elected prime minister of Japan, Kakuei Tanaka, made a similar trip and opened diplomatic relations with China. These were good things.

Just two years later both Nixon and Tanaka were forced to resign from office amid scandals involving political misbehavior. We all know about Watergate, so we won't go into that here. In Japan in 1972 Tanaka had accepted campaign donations of at least $2 million from Lockheed Corp. In 1974 the scandal erupted there, Tanaka was forced to resign, and in 1983 he was finally convicted of corruption. Congress was so disgusted with Lockheed's behavior (Nixon's, too), and the foreign bribery of some 450 other American multinationals disclosed in a Securities and Exchange Commission (SEC) investigation, that the 1977 Foreign Corrupt Practices Act (FCPA) was passed and signed into law by President Carter. American executives working in China are now dealing with its 30-year-old incarnation.

Background—A Question of Culture

The moral question of what is right or appropriate poses many dilemmas for American executives at home. Even within a country, ethical standards are frequently not defined or always clear. The problem of business ethics is infinitely more complex in the international marketplace because value judgments differ widely among culturally diverse groups. That which is commonly accepted as right in one country may be completely unacceptable in another. Giving business gifts of high value, for example, is generally condemned in the United States, but in many countries of the world gifts are not only accepted but also expected.[2]

The Western Focus on Bribery

Before the Enron and WorldCom crises, to most Americans the word *corruption* meant bribery. Now in the domestic context fraud has moved to the more prominent spot in the headlines. However, during the 1970s for U.S. companies engaged in international markets, bribery became a national issue as mentioned. At the time, there were no U.S. laws against paying bribes in foreign countries. But, for publicly held corporations, the SEC rules required accurate public reporting of all expenditures. Because the payoffs were not properly disclosed, many executives were faced with charges of violating SEC regulations.

The issue took on proportions greater than that of nondisclosure because it focused national attention on the basic question of ethics. The business community's defense was that payoffs were a way of life throughout the world: If you didn't pay bribes, you didn't do business. But the decision to pay a bribe creates a major conflict between what is ethical and proper and what is perceived as profitable and sometimes necessary for business. Many global competitors perceive payoffs as a necessary means of accomplishing business goals. A major complaint of U.S. businesses was that other countries did not have legislation as restrictive as that of the United States.

Despite such objections from American executives, the FCPA was approved in 1977 and was substantially revised (some say emasculated) in 1988. The U.S. Commerce Department provides a brief explanation of the law (see box).

Penalties are substantial. Firms are subject to fines of $2 million, and executives can be sentenced to up to five years in prison and a $100,000 fine. Under federal criminal laws other than the FCPA, individuals may be fined up to $250,000 or up to twice the amount of the gross gain or gross loss if the defendant derives pecuniary gain from the offense or causes a pecuniary loss to another person. Violations of the Books and Records Provisions can result in fines of $5 million for executives and 20 years in prison, and $25 million for firms. Defendants are also subject to serious civil actions as well. The federal government may also revoke export licenses and bar involved persons from the securities business.

Compliance and training programs for employees and joint-venture partners will help avoid problems and can even act as an insurance policy against prosecution; that is, the "Federal Sentencing Guidelines for Organizations," issued by the U.S. Sentencing Commission and applicable to criminal violations of all federal statutes such as the FCPA, require federal courts

BASIC PROVISIONS PROHIBITING
FOREIGN CORRUPT PAYMENTS[3]

Antibribery Provisions. The FCPA's basic antibribery prohibition makes it unlawful for a firm (as well as any officer, director, employee, or agent of a firm or any stockholder acting on behalf of the firm) to offer, pay, promise to pay (or even to authorize the payment of money, or anything of value, or to authorize any such promise) to any foreign official for the purpose of obtaining or retaining business for or with, or directing business to, any person. A similar prohibition applies with respect to payments to a foreign political party or official thereof or candidate for foreign political office.

Payments by Intermediaries. It is also unlawful to make a payment to any person, while knowing that all or a portion of the payment will be offered, given, or promised, directly or indirectly, to any foreign official (or foreign political party, candidate, or official) for the purposes of assisting the firm in obtaining or retaining business. "Knowing" includes the concepts of "conscious disregard" or "willful blindness."

handing down criminal sanctions to take into account the existence or absence of effective corporate compliance programs. The presence of an effective compliance program can significantly reduce a corporation's sentence, in some cases by as much as 95 percent, while the absence of such a program can increase the sentence.[4]

As one might guess, Lockheed has perhaps the single best training program regarding the FCPA. It issues to its employees a list of "red flags" to focus vigilance. Its list is included at Exhibit 4.1. You will notice that first on the list is: "The payment is being made in a country with a widespread history of corruption." That leads us directly to China and the larger international context of bribery.

"Red flags" appear most commonly as proposed contracts or billing requests are reviewed. Any of the following requests are widely accepted as indications that a representative or distributor may be taking action that could expose a company to potential FCPA liability.

- The payment is being made in a country with a widespread history of corruption
- A representative or distributor refuses to confirm that he or she will abide by the provisions of the FCPA
- A representative or distributor has family or business ties with government officials
- A representative or distributor has a bad reputation in the business community
- A representative or distributor requires that his or her identity not be disclosed
- A potential government customer of authorizing agency recommends a representative or distributor
- A representative's or distributor's business seems to lack sufficient staff to perform the services offered
- A representative or distributor is new to the business, or cannot provide references to document claimed experience
- A representative or distributor makes unusual requests, such as requests to backdate or alter invoices
- A representative or distributor asks for commissions that are substantially higher than the "going rate" in that country
- A representative or distributor asks for payment by unorthodox or convoluted means, such as through bank accounts outside the country where the services are being offered
- A representative or distributor requests over-invoicing
- A representative or distributor requests checks be made out to "bearer" or "cash" or requests payments to be made in cash or by some other anonymous form
- A representative or distributor asks for an unusually large credit line for a new customer
- A representative or distributor requests unusually large bonuses or similar payments

    or

- A representative or distributor requests substantial and unorthodox up-front payments

Exhibit 4.1   "Red Flags" Indicating Potential Violations of the Foreign Corrupt Practices Act

International Cooperation

The U.S. advocacy of global antibribery laws has led to an accord by the member nations of the Organization for Economic Cooperation and Development (OECD) to force their companies to follow rules similar to those that bind U.S. firms. To date 33 of the world's largest trading nations, including the United States, have signed the OECD Convention on combating the bribery of foreign public officials in international business transactions. In Latin America, the Organization of American States (OAS) has taken a global lead in ratifying an agreement against corruption. Long considered almost a way of business life, bribery and other forms of corruption now have been criminalized.

Leaders of the region realize that democracy depends on the confidence the people have in the integrity of their government and that corruption undermines economic liberalization. The actions of the OAS coupled with those of the OECD will obligate a majority of the world's trading nations to maintain a higher standard of ethical behavior than has existed before. Unfortunately, India, China,[5] and other Asian and African countries are not members of either organization. The actions of the OECD and OAS reflect the growing concern among most trading countries regarding the need to bring corruption under control. International businesspeople often justify their actions in paying bribes and corrupting officials as necessary because "corruption is part of their culture," failing to appreciate that it takes two to tango—a bribe giver and a bribe taker.

An international organization called Transparency International[6] (TI) is dedicated to "curbing corruption through international and national coalitions encouraging governments to establish and implement effective laws, policies and anticorruption programs." Among its various activities, TI conducts an international survey of businesspeople, political analysts, and the general public to determine their perceptions of corruption in 159 countries. In the Corruption Perception Index (CPI), shown in part in Exhibit 4.2, Iceland, with a score of 9.7 out of a maximum of 10, was perceived to be the least corrupt of the countries ranked. TI is very

TRANSPARENCY INTERNATIONAL'S CORRUPTION PERCEPTION INDEX (CPI) 2005
(LOWER SCORES = GREATER PREVALENCE OF BRIBERY)

TOP 20 PERTINENT OTHERS			PERTINENT OTHERS		
RANKING	COUNTRY	SCORE	RANKING	COUNTRY	SCORE
1	Iceland	9.7	*32*	*Taiwan*	*5.9*
2	Finland	9.6	39	Malaysia	5.1
3	New Zealand	9.6	40	S. Korea	5.0
4	Denmark	9.5	47	Czech Rep.	4.3
5	*Singapore*	9.4	59	Thailand	3.8
6	Sweden	9.2	62	Brazil	3.7
7	Switzerland	9.1	65	Mexico	3.5
8	Norway	8.9	65	Turkey	3.5
9	Australia	8.8	70	Saudi Arabia	3.4
10	Austria	8.7	*78*	*China*	*3.2*
11	Netherlands	8.6	88	India	2.9
12	United Kingdom	8.6	107	Vietnam	2.6
13	Luxembourg	8.5	117	Philippines	2.5
14	Canada	8.4	126	Russia	2.4
15	*Hong Kong*	8.3	130	Cambodia	2.3
16	Germany	8.2	130	Venezuela	2.3
17	*U.S.*	7.6	137	Indonesia	2.2
18	France	7.5	152	Nigeria	1.9
19	Belgium	7.4	158	Bangladesh	1.7
20	Ireland	7.4	158	Chad	1.7

Exhibit 4.2   Transparency International's Corruption Perception Index (CPI) 2005 (lower scores = greater prevalence of bribery) (*Source: www.transparency.de*)

emphatic that its intent is not to expose villains and cast blame, but to raise public awareness that will lead to constructive action. As one would expect, those countries receiving low scores are not pleased; however, the effect has been to raise public ire and debates in parliaments around the world—exactly the goal of TI.

So how prevalent is bribery in the areas covered in this book? According to TI, managers in Singapore and Hong Kong are less likely to accept bribes, and managers in Taiwan and particularly the PRC are more likely to take bribes than comparable Americans. Singapore was ranked 5 (at 9.4), Hong Kong 15 (8.3), United States 17 (at 7.6), Taiwan 32 (5.9), and China 78 (3.2).

Impact of the FCPA

The answer to the question of bribery is not an unqualified one. It is easy to generalize about the ethics of political payoffs and other types of payments; it is much more difficult to make the decision to withhold payment of money when the consequences of not making the payment may affect the company's ability to do business profitably or at all. With the variety of ethical standards and levels of morality that exist in different cultures, the dilemma of ethics and pragmatism that international businesses face cannot be resolved until the anticorruption accords among the OECD and OAS members are fully implemented and multinational businesses refuse to pay extortion or offer bribes.

Even though convictions under the FCPA are few and far between (just four during the years 1990–2004[7]), the law has had a positive effect. According to the latest Department of Commerce figures, since 1994 American businesses have bowed out of 294 major overseas commercial contracts valued at $145 billion rather than pay a bribe. This information corroborates the academic evidence cited above. Even though there are numerous reports indicating a definite reduction in U.S. firms paying bribes, the lure of contracts is too strong for some companies. Lockheed Corporation made $22 million in questionable foreign payments during the 1970s. More recently the company pled guilty to paying $1.8 million in bribes to a member of the Egyptian national parliament in exchange for lobbying for three air cargo planes worth $79 million to be sold to the military. Lockheed was caught and fined $25 million, and cargo plane exports by the company were banned for three years. Lockheed's actions during the 1970s were a major influence on the passage of the FCPA. The company now maintains one of the most comprehensive ethics and legal training programs of any major corporation in the United States as mentioned.

Recent cases of potential FCPA violations involving American firms in China include Lucent Technologies, InVision Technologies, Alltel Information Services, and Diagnostic Products Corp. (DPC). Lucent fired the president, COO, a marketing executive, and a finance executive in its Chinese operations after discovering internal control deficiencies. "The company added that it had reported the potential violations of the FCPA to the U.S. Department of Justice and the Securities and Exchange Commission, and said it is cooperating with both agencies. The move was disclosed in a regulatory filing with the SEC. The company said the problems in China were discovered as part of a review of operations in 23 countries."[8] A $1 million Alltel bribe to the chairman of China Construction Bank (CCB) has resulted in the house arrest of that executive and investigations in both China and Monterey, California. Why Monterey? That's where the bribe was offered, on the Pebble Beach Golf Course. Finally, in Exhibit 4.3 we have included the Department of Justice press release announcing the indictment of DPC in China. This is not the kind of thing you want to read about your company.

It would be naïve to assume that laws and the resulting penalties alone will put an end to corruption. Change will come only from more ethically and socially responsible decisions made by both buyers and sellers, and by governments willing to take a stand. The FCPA indubitably makes transactions in China more work for Americans. Literally, more due *diligence* is required. Employee training and vigilance will be particularly important. Some still argue that this impedes American efforts to sell there. However, OECD and OAS nations are starting to enforce their own anti-bribery statutes, thus reducing Americans' competitive disadvantage. Indeed, many American firms use the FCPA as an "excuse" for not paying bribes. Also, by most accounts the Chinese themselves are getting better at managing the problem. In fact, as their

United States of America
Department of Justice

FOR IMMEDIATE RELEASE   CRM
FRIDAY, MAY 20, 2005   (202) 514-2008
WWW.USDOJ.GOV   TDD (202) 514-1888

DPC (TIANJIN) LTD. CHARGED WITH VIOLATING
THE FOREIGN CORRUPT PRACTICES ACT

WASHINGTON, D.C.—Acting Assistant Attorney General John C. Richter of the Criminal Division today announced the filing of a one-count criminal information charging DPC (Tianjin) Co. Ltd.—the Chinese subsidiary of Los Angeles-based Diagnostic Products Corporation (DPC)—with violating the Foreign Corrupt Practices Act of 1977 (FCPA) in connection with the payment of approximately $1.6 million in bribes in the form of illegal "commissions" to physicians and laboratory personnel employed by government-owned hospitals in the People's Republic of China.

The company, a producer and seller of diagnostic medical equipment, has agreed to plead guilty to the charge, adopt internal compliance measures, and cooperate with ongoing criminal and SEC civil investigations. An independent compliance expert will be chosen to audit the company's compliance program and monitor its implementation of new internal policies and procedures. DPC Tianjin has also agreed to pay a criminal penalty of $2 million.

(continued)

Exhibit 4.3   FCPA Filing

The bribes were allegedly paid from late 1991 through December 2002 for the purpose and effect of obtaining and retaining business with these hospitals. According to the criminal information and a statement of facts filed in court, DPC Tianjin made cash payments to laboratory personnel and physicians employed in certain hospitals in the People's Republic of China in exchange for agreements that the hospitals would obtain DPC Tianjin's products and services. This practice, authorized by DPC Tianjin's general manager, involved personnel who were employed by hospitals owned by the legal authorities in the People's Republic of China and, thus, "foreign officials" as defined by the FCPA.

In most cases, the bribes were paid in cash and hand-delivered by DPC Tianjin salespeople to the person who controlled purchasing decisions for the particular hospital department. DPC Tianjin recorded the payments on its books and records as "selling expenses." DPC Tianjin's general manager regularly prepared and submitted to Diagnostic Products Corporation its financial statements, which contained its sales expenses. The general manager also caused approval of the budgets for sales expenses of DPC Tianjin, including the amounts DPC Tianjin intended to pay to the officials of the hospitals in the following quarter or year.

The "commissions," typically between 3 percent and 10 percent of sales, totaled approximately $1,623,326 from late 1991 through December 2002, and allowed Depu to earn approximately $2 million in profits from the sales.

DPC Tianjin's parent company, Diagnostic Products Corporation, is the subject of an FCPA enforcement proceeding filed earlier today by the U.S. Securities and Exchange Commission. The SEC ordered the company to cease and desist from violating the FCPA and to disgorge approximately $2.8 million in ill-gotten gains, representing its net profit in the People's Republic of China for the period of its misconduct plus prejudgment interest.

The Department of Justice acknowledges the cooperation and assistance provided by the Pacific Regional Office of the Securities and Exchange Commission.

The criminal case was prosecuted by Deputy Chief Mark F. Mendelsohn and Trial Attorney Adrian D. Mebane of the Fraud Section, Criminal Division, at the U.S. Department of Justice, with assistance from the U.S. Attorney's Office in the Central District of California.

Exhibit 4.3   FCPA Filing (*Continued*)

financial operations become more global, we are able to help them directly in curtailing bribery—whether they like it or not.

How? Most interestingly the FCPA applies to 50 of China's largest firms including CNOOC, ASAT Holdings, China Telecom, China Life Insurance, Lenova, and Shanda Interactive, because those firms are listed on American stock exchanges. That puts them and their employees under the jurisdiction of the U.S. Securities and Exchange Commission. Indeed, it is most ironic that the person most responsible for enforcing the FCPA with respect to these Chinese companies is SEC Chairman Christopher Cox.

The Bad—National Security Laws Damage American Competitiveness

This story also starts with a foreign donation to a political campaign, this time in the United States. In April 1996 Al Gore attended a "political fund-raiser" at the Hsi Lai Buddhist Temple in Hacienda Heights, California. Pictures were taken. Later it was also revealed that the Clinton–Gore campaign had accepted donations from a variety of dubious sources with Chinese surnames including John Haung and Johnny Chung. The latter allegedly laundered a $35,000 donation[9] from one Liu Chaoying, a Chinese (PRC) aerospace executive. Circa 1998 this little mess was congealing into a nice big wedge issue to be used by the Bush campaign against Gore in the 2000 election. The pictures were there for the negative TV ads—almost perfect. All the Republicans needed to add to the mix was a little spy scandal, and in 1999 Christopher Cox was there to help out.

In May 1998, after accusing President Clinton of "trading U.S. security for Beijing funds,"[10] Newt Gingrich appointed his House colleague Chris Cox to head a committee to investigate allegations that Loral Space and Communications and Hughes Electronics Corp. gave Chinese customers protected technology. On January 3, 1999, what became known as the "Cox Committee" began to report its findings. Later in the year the declassified findings were reported directly in the form of the book, *The Cox Report* (Washington, D.C.: Regnery, 1999). The work of the Cox Committee and its findings were roundly criticized as politically biased: "An exercise in amateur-hour paranoia," said Tom Plate in the *Los Angeles Times*. "Hill report on Chinese Spying faulted, five experts cite errors, 'unwarranted' conclusions by Cox panel," Walter Pincus in the *Washington Post*; ". . . misleading, inaccurate, and damaging to U.S.-China relations, according to a team of policy analysts at Stanford University," *Associated Press*. Beyond its dubious contents, the back cover of the book well demonstrates the blatant use of xenophobia not only to sell the book, but also to sell the political message. There the headline in bold half-inch letters blares "China's Target: America." Its intention was to fuel the fears of the American people.

We have reprinted below John's own criticism from the *Orange County Register*, July 11, 1999:

U.S. Xenophobia Is Only Directed at the East

I'm not sure how big the Chinese are on irony, but the latest salvo from Capitol Hill is a humdinger. Apparently, they're stealing our rocket technology. The irony? Think back for a moment to who invented rockets in the first place!

Conservative Congressman Christopher Cox's congressional committee charges the Chinese with a criminal curiosity that challenges our national security. According to the allegations the boys in Beijing have been sniffing around our missiles and satellites for at least twenty years, and most recently with the help of American aerospace firms Hughes and Loral.

I don't doubt the Chinese have broken some rules and remedial steps should be taken. Indeed, I trust the objectivity of Congressman Bereuter's (R-Nebraska) vote on Cox's Committee—he's a long-term expert on trade with Asia and a genuine advocate of increased trade.

What I don't like is the xenophobic and racial overtones of picking on China. It's very hard for me to believe that the Russians aren't getting from us even more aerospace technology out of their currently cozy relationship with NASA and the associated American firms. Can we be really comfortable in assuming that China is a greater threat to American national security than is Russia? And what about the earlier cases of both French and Israeli military/industrial espionage? Indeed, all four countries are big sellers on the global weapons market, and all four have good reason to be curious about, even aggressive about American technology. Why does Cox's Committee focus on China only?

Fear of foreigners is a natural thing; and the more foreign, the greater the fear. Indeed, our best pals these days are the British. Same language, same religion, a shared Anglo culture, we love their brands and call their TV "educational," and they own more of America than any other foreign nation. British accents make people sound smarter. This is so even though we've fought two wars against them and they very certainly have their own separate national interests.

As Americans go East from England, the fear of foreignness begins to grow. Just pass through the Chunnel and they're already speaking unintelligibly, rejecting American TV, and eating horses and frogs and snails, oh my! Go all the way to East Asia and they're using characters instead of an alphabet, beliefs are based on Confucius and Buddha, and the diet includes raw fish in Japan or dogs, cats, rats, lizards, snakes, grubs, bugs, and quite literally anything with digestible protein in China.

Burlington Coat Factory recently committed a major faux pas *by importing parkas from China with accurately labeled dog hair collars. In America it's OK to have a collar on your dog, but not a dog hair collar around your neck. From the Chinese perspective why would you waste the fur of something you eat. Don't Americans sit on leather wallets?*

This strange Chinese culture can only be understood with respect to famine. Starvation (true starvation, not the typical American January calorie cutting) changes values and behaviors. Recall how your fellow Americans behaved during the gas crunches of the 1970s. If you doubt you'd eat your own pet dog or cat in a crisis, I suggest you rent the movie Alive *or read again about the Donner Party. The current one-child policy in China, with all its ugly social consequences, is comprehensible in the context of a history of mass starvation. Chinese views about human rights and individual freedoms must also be understood in the context of the civil chaos associated with famine.*

So, because the language, religion, values, and culture of East Asians are more different (than Europeans) we tend to understand them less and fear them more. And these fears have had and still have effects on our foreign policies. Harken back to Christopher Cox's own congressional district of the 1920s. Then the Orange County Farm Bureau took the lead in promoting the racially motivated anti-Asian immigration policies of the time.

Recall the shrill outcry of the 1980s when Japan bought so much American real estate and so many American companies. One of Newsweek's *1987 cover stories was, "Your Next Boss May Be Japanese." Even then the British owned more of America. And now why don't we hear the same alarm about European investments in America? Japan's 1980s appetite for American assets pales in comparison to Germany's 1990s gorging on the likes of Bankers Trust, Random House, and Chrysler. Indeed, history tells us we should fear Germany more than Japan. But, instead we fear the more unfamiliar. Our xenophobia dominates our remembrance.*

Many Japanese even complain that dropping the bomb on Hiroshima and not Berlin was racially motivated. Thank God, history belies that particular accusation. But, generally the behavior of many Americans feeds such Asian perceptions of American racism. After President Bush's visit to Japan (you may recall he barfed on the Prime Minister) with the CEOs of Ford, GM, Chrysler in tow, sales of Japanese imported cars plummeted. German sales did not. In the mid-eighties two companies, Toshiba of Japan and Kongsberg of Norway, illegally sold technology to the Soviet Union for making submarine propellers quieter. The consequences for Toshiba were far greater than those for the Nor-

wegian firm. And China still has to bargain for Most Favored Nation status every year.

*I urge Congress to broaden the scope of the Cox Committee. Aerospace technology transfers to all foreign countries should be considered—Russia, France, Israel, and Japan included. A focus on the Peoples Republic of China smacks of racism and the wedge politics of fear. A focus on China smacks of Clinton baiting. A focus on China does great damage to our political, commercial, and personal relations with potentially powerful friends. Our leaders in Washington must be very careful to avoid letting xenophobia cloud their vision of the evolving global political economy. And finally we should remember that the Chinese may yet have some technology to give us in return, **given a context of cooperation and creativity**. Indeed, isn't it Chinese technology that makes our 4th of July celebrations so spectacular?*[11]

There were at least four consequences of *The Cox Report*. First, the Wen Ho Lee crucifixion commenced at the Los Alamos National Laboratory. How ironic that an immigrant from Taiwan would be accused by the FBI of spying on behalf of the Peoples Republic of China. But, he did have the requisite Chinese surname to serve the political purposes of those involved. We suppose if Robert E. Lee had been working there, he would have been persecuted as well. The climax of the case as described in the *Wall Street Journal* was revealing: "In excoriating officials for their treatment of Wen Ho Lee, Federal District Judge James A. Parker said one question remained unanswered: 'What was the government's motive?' There is an answer to that question, a chilling one. It is: politics."[12] Most recently, the U.S. government and five news organizations agreed to pay Wen Ho Lee $1.65 million to settle his lawsuit against them for violating his privacy.[13]

Second, the companies involved in the original Gingrich allegations, Loral, Hughes, and Boeing (the new owner of Hughes' satellite operations) were forced to pay the federal government $52 million in fines for allegedly "transferring rocket technology" to the Chinese.

Third, the China wedge issue did work against Al Gore in the 2000 presidential campaign. Indeed, because the race was so close, all strategies employed by the Bush campaign proved to be important.

Fourth, the House passed legislation to tighten restrictions on the export of high-technology products and services worldwide. These restrictions continue to hamper the sales of America's most important export, our technology. Indeed, the top categories of U.S. exports to China remain high-technology goods—integrated circuits, powered aircraft, computers/components, soybeans (perhaps not so high tech), and telecommunications equipment. While it is true that U.S. exports to China have been increasing quickly during recent years, we lost shares of both satellite sales worldwide and total exports to China. Our share of satellite sales worldwide fell from 45 percent in 1999 to 42 percent in 2000, while our share of total exports to China declined from 12 percent to 10 percent. These billions in business were lost primarily to European competitors. Indeed, the Europeans are pressing their advantage. AIRBUS is building a new assembly plant in Tianjin as American companies continue to be stymied by political machinations at home. We cannot blame solely Mr. Cox for this national loss of commercial competitiveness in China. Our mistaken bombing of the Chinese embassy in Belgrade in May 1999 certainly exacerbated tensions. The more general identification of China as the "next big threat to American national security" made things worse as well. But, what makes *The Cox Report* stench so great is its obvious political motivations.

High-Tech Export Restrictions circa 2007

U.S. firms, their foreign subsidiaries, or foreign firms that are licensees of U.S. technology cannot sell a product to a country in which the sale is considered by the U.S. government to affect national security. Further, responsibility extends to the final destination of the product regardless of the number of intermediaries that may be involved in the transfer of goods.

During the latter half of the twentieth century, an extensive export control system was created to slow the spread of sensitive technologies to the former Soviet Union, China, and other communist countries that were viewed as major threats to U.S. security. The control of the sale of goods considered to have a strategic and military value was extremely strict. But with the end of the Cold War, export controls were systematically dismantled, that is, until 1999 when the Cox Committee reported Chinese espionage activities and American aerospace companies transferring sensitive technology irresponsibly. As mentioned, following the report, legislation was passed again restricting the export of products or technologies that might be used by other countries for defense applications.

The events of September 11, 2001, added another set of restrictions related to weapons of mass destruction (WMD). Unfortunately, many of the products used in WMD are difficult to control since they have dual purposes; that is, they have legitimate uses as well as being important in manufacturing WMD. For example, Iraq, which was allowed to import medical equipment despite a U.N. embargo, purchased, under the pretext of medical benefits, six machines that destroy kidney stones. The manufacturer accepted the claim that Saddam Hussein was concerned about kidney stones in the Iraqi population and began shipping the machines. However, integral components of these machines are high-precision electronic switches that are also used to set off the chain reaction in thermonuclear weapons. When 120 additional switches as "spare parts" were ordered, a red flag went up, and the shipments were stopped.

There are countless numbers of dual-purpose technologies that are exported from the United States. A sticking point with dual-purpose exports is the intent of the buyer. Silicon Graphics Inc. (SGI) sold computer equipment to a Russian nuclear laboratory that contended it was for non-military use, which would have been legal. However, the Department of Justice ruled that since the equipment was purchased by a government-operated facility involved in both civil and noncivil activities, SGI should have applied for the correct export license. SGI paid a fine of $1 million plus a $500,000 fine for each of the export violations. National security laws prohibit a U.S. company, its subsidiaries, joint ventures, or licensees to sell controlled products without special permission from the U.S. government. The consequences of violation of the Trading with the Enemy Act can be severe: fines, prison sentences, and, in the case of foreign companies, economic sanctions. And, the larger consequence of these largely politically based laws is a general loss of competitiveness for American firms in international commerce.

And the Ugly—America's Immigration Policies Hamper Trade with China

The complaints come from everywhere it seems. The complaints are about the ugly face America presents visitors and immigrants via our visa and work permit policies. America's scientists suggest that the nation is losing its lead in technology creation at the universities because our immigration policies are limiting our search for the smartest graduate students to half the world. The World Trade Organization (WTO) may take up criticism of U.S. immigration policies regarding visa programs for temporary workers. Company after company reports lost sales because foreign executives, particularly those from China, cannot easily visit the U.S. for commercial reasons. For example, David Cunningham, Jr., president of FedEx's Asia Pacific Division, groused to a *New York Times* reporter, "We are in essence restricting trade by restricting visas. Businesspeople take their business elsewhere."[14] Two years in a row the Merage Business School at the University of California Irvine delivered executive training programs in Orange County for managers from China's largest motor vehicle company, First Auto Works. The ranks of both visiting groups (and the associated dollars associated with the exportation of our education services) were halved by visa problems. And, of course, as we argue in Chapter 8, American negotiators are always at a disadvantage when they cannot negotiate at home. American immigration and travel restrictions deliver that disadvantage regularly to American companies.

We particularly appreciate the concise comprehensiveness of an article on the topic from a neutral third-country[15] press, the *Agence France-Presse*, and have reprinted it here:

Strict US Visa Policy Scares away Students, Investors

A teenage Asian girl with a valid student visa was handcuffed and deported for entering the United States five days earlier than stipulated, highlighting strict American immigration policy.

A 79-year-old British historian, who came to work at the US Library of Congress on the life of US former chief diplomat Henry Kissinger, was herded on arrival in a wheelchair at Washington's Dulles airport to a small room facing a superintendent with a revolver in his hip for no apparent mistake.

Although all his travel papers were in order, "I was stopped and treated rather disgracefully," lamented Sir Alistair Horne at a conference in Washington Tuesday.

Stringent enforcement of US visa policy and seemingly overzealous immigration officers following the September 11, 2001 terror attacks are not only scaring away foreign students and tourists but dampening the investment climate of the world's richest nation and taking a toll on its economy, experts told the conference organized by the Center for Strategic and International Studies.

Among the other cases cited to highlight the economic, security, scientific and diplomatic implications of changes in US visa policy were:

* *An international business conference in Hawaii had to be shifted to Hong Kong at the last minute because the organizers could not obtain travel papers for most of its participants, who were from China.*
* *Some of US aviation giant Lockheed Martin Corporation's testing of its civil space activities have been delayed because visas could not be obtained on time for Russian scientists.*

- *A company in northern Illinois waited in vain for seven months for its prospective buyers from China to get a visa to inspect its products and close a multimillion dollar sale. Eventually the company became bankrupt and was auctioned off.*

According to one private sector study, US businesses lost nearly 31 billion dollars in sales between 2002 and 2004 because foreign executives could not get into the United States to purchase American goods and services or attend trade shows.

From 2003 to 2004, there was a roughly 30 percent decline in the number of applicants for US graduate programs and correspondingly 20 percent decline in admissions, university figures showed.

The situation is critical and requires the personal intervention of President George W. Bush, former defense secretary Frank Carlucci told the conference.

He said Bush should act to stop further erosion of US popularity overseas.

"It is part and parcel of the anti-Americanism around the world and if the President is serious about addressing that, in that context, he has to address visa policy," Carlucci said.

"President Bush can demonstrate leadership and demonstrate that the country is not anti-foreigner and that we are not closing the gates and he can encourage the bureaucracy to make sense out of a patchwork quilt—it is slowly coming together but needs to come together much faster."

Lockheed Martin's corporate international business development vice-president Richard Kirkland said "what is important is predictability and process" of getting approval for visas.

Nearly 100 percent of aerospace programs in the United States involve some form of foreign participation or content, he said.

"America's post-9/11 visa policy is threatening our country's economic security, and reforms are needed to boost US exports, maintain our technological leadership and create jobs," said Don Manzalo, head of the small business committee at the House of Representatives.

"Multinationals are setting up shop overseas to avoid our arbitrary visa process," said Monzalo, who is campaigning for a fast track visa program for companies.

He had brokered a deal between the United States and China earlier this year allowing executives to travel between the two countries under a single visa for 12 months instead of seeking new visas for each trip.

The Migration Policy Institute, an independent think tank which studies movement of people worldwide, said Tuesday it was convening a bipartisan panel of US lawmakers, business leaders and public policy and immigration experts to consider immigration reforms.

"Neither national security nor individual liberties can be properly safeguarded in the United States without sensible and effective immigration laws," said Lee Hamilton, among those who led a special commission that investigated the 2001 terror attacks.

William Webster, former CIA and FBI head, said by scaring away foreign students, "we are losing an opportunity for public diplomacy because the best ambassadors we can possibly have are these students."

Jordan's ambassador to Washington Karim Tawfiq Kawar said there had been a drop of more than 30 percent of students from the Arab world coming to the United States to study.

A survey showed 65 percent of students from six Middle East countries still wanted to study in the United States but "only one quarter of those who came here had a positive experience."

Conclusion

We can remember back in the 1980s when America's trade deficit with Japan catalyzed tensions between our countries. Now that China has taken over the role of "number 1 trade problem" the déjà vu is powerful.

In 2003 J. W. Marriott, representing the president's own Export Council, sent President Bush a letter exhorting that political pressure be applied to China to reduce its trade barriers. Mr. Marriott specifically represented the complaints of the council as:

- The undervalued Chinese currency
- Nontariff barriers
- Subsidies to local Chinese companies
- Impediments to foreign investments
- An underdeveloped capital market

The president has since gone to work on all issues and has made some progress—the Chinese have begun to gently increase the value of the yuan, for example.

Then, in August 2004, in recognition that policies of the U.S. government were causing part of the trade deficit with China, Mr. Marriott wrote: "As members of the President's Export Council, we respectfully ask that you reinstitute and bring to rapid completion the thorough review of U.S. policy of unilateral sanctions at the beginning of your Administration." Mr. Marriott followed in September 2004 with, "We therefore recommend that U.S. technology export controls should rely on strengthened corporate compliance processes, rather than regulating individual transactions."

We certainly agree. Actually, even Chris Cox agreed in 1999 that some high-tech restrictions made little sense then: "The brute fact of life is the availability of this technology."[16] But, relaxing high-tech export restrictions is moving far too slowly in the current xenophobic environment promoted by the current administration. *The Cox Report* is completely representative of the dangerous political use of xenophobia. Indeed, it is the antithesis of the book you are reading now. It is the antithesis of *China Now*.

In order to get to a rational trade policy that encompasses easing restrictions both on high-tech exports and on visas related to commerce, we must first shift our thinking in the country back to reality and away from fear. Yes, terrorism is a big problem. But, framing it as a "war" is not only counterproductive, but dangerous. The Europeans treat terrorism as a criminal problem. Certainly it's more than that, but terrorism is nothing like the former Soviet threat, World War II, Vietnam, or even the current carnage in Iraq. Other nations, including China, are not now and never will be a military threat to the United States. Let us say it again. Other nations are not a *threat*. Other nations are an *opportunity* for American firms. Until we accept this fundamental truth, even the good advice of Mr. Marriott and his council will have little impact on improving America's international commercial competitiveness.

Notes

1   From Leland D. Baldwin, "Shipbuilding on the Western Waters," *Mississippi Valley Historical Review*, 1933, pages 29–44.
2   See www.ethics.org and www.business-ethics.org for more pertinent information.
3   *USIA Electronic Journal*, 3 (5), November 1998.
4   This paragraph is quoted from www.haynesboone.com.
5   Bribery is attracting greater attention in all countries. Please see Kam-hon Lee, Gong-ming Qian, Julie Yu, and Ying Ho, "Trading Favors for Marketing Advantage: Evidence from Hong Kong, China, and the Unites States," *Journal of International Marketing*, 13(1), 2005, pp. 1–35.
6   www.transparency.org.
7   John R. Wilke and Stephen Power, "U.S. Escalates Daimler Probe," *The Globe and Mail*, August, 2005, p. B1.
8   Paul Taylor, "Lucent Fires Four Staff in China," *Financial Times*, April 7, 2004, p. 24.
9   The reader might note the difference in the dimensions of the Lockheed donation to Tanaka ($2 million in 1972 dollars) versus the Chaoying/Chung donation to Clinton/Gore ($35,000 in 1996 dollars).
10 Tom Rhodes, "Clinton 'Traded US Security for Beijing Funds,'" *The Times* (London), May 21, 1998, p. 17.

11 Some may just assume that this diatribe against Mr. Cox is simply sour grapes from John's three losses against him in the Orange County congressional elections of 2000, 2002, and 2004. Actually, the reason John entered the races against the deeply entrenched incumbent was to protest Cox's politically motivated mischaracterizations of China.

12 Anthony Lewis, "It Did Happen Here," *Wall Street Journal*, September 16, 2000, p. 15.

13 David G. Savage, "Government, News Media Settle Suit by Wen Ho Lee," *Los Angeles Times*, June 3, 2006, p. A1.

14 Keith Bradher, "For Chinese, U.S. Products Don't Measure Up," *New York Times*, November 18, 2005, p. 3.

15 But of course, are the French ever really neutral when in comes to the United States? "Strict US Visa Policy Scares Away Students, Investors," *Agence France-Press*, May 4, 2005.

16 Peter G. Gosselin, "Cox Backs Easing Rules on Computer Sales to China Exports," *Los Angeles Times*, June 11, 1999, p. C1.

CHAPTER 5

THE CHINESE LEGAL AND BUSINESS ENVIRONMENT

In 1882 Judge Roy Bean (played by Paul Newman in the 1972 western) was the law in Texas west of the Pecos River. He didn't need a gavel or a bailiff to keep order in his court. He had his own large caliber pistol for that purpose. One of Bean's most outrageous rulings occurred when an Irishman was accused of killing a Chinese worker. Rapping his pistol on the bar, he's reported to have proclaimed, "Gentlemen, I find the law very explicit on murdering your fellow man, but there's nothing here about killing a Chinaman. Case dismissed." We're more civilized now, more than 100 years later, although we suppose Wen Ho Lee, the persecuted Los Alamos National Laboratory scientist, might disagree.

In 1982 the Chinese legal system was about as organized Judge Bean's. Indeed, up until 1978 there were no lawyers in the country at all. Back then, Communist Party bureaucrats in Beijing made the rules. Local magistrates and feudal lords interpreted them, and the army and police enforced them. As in Judge Bean's court, nobody argued and nobody protested; in fact, protesting was against the law. Now, in the first decade of the twenty-first century, the Chinese legal system is getting organized fast. However, in many respects the wild west metaphor still pertains.

Indeed, we love James McGregor's comparison of changes in China to the previous American experience:[1]

> *China is [simultaneously] undergoing the raw capitalism of the Robber Baron era of the late 1800s; the speculative financial mania of the 1920s; the rural-to-urban migration of the 1930s; the emergence of the first-car, first-home, first-fashionable clothes, first-college education, first-family vacation, middle-class consumer of the 1950s; and even aspects of social upheaval similar to the 1960s.*

Before you delve deeper into this chapter, you might want to get yourself a cup of coffee. In order to be complete, our discussion borders on tedium. If you are an attorney, this material will be an interesting flavor of cake. If you're not an attorney, it may be a bit less fun to consume. History is always a good place to start.

Historical Underpinnings

A nation's legal system always evolves from a particular political, social, and economic environment and thus carries with it particular legal values and social heritage. In order to understand the contemporary Chinese legal system and business environment, we have to look back and study the pertinent aspects of the nation's culture, tradition, and history and understand how these factors influence today's fast-evolving legal system.

Traditional Legal Culture

Development of Chinese legal ideologies can be traced back some four millennia. About that time the society transformed from slavery to feudalism, and conflict between different interest groups induced the first major ideological dispute between two main schools of thought—Confucianism and Legalism. Confucianists asserted "*li*" (a ritual concept related to human manners) as the fundamental concept of government and advocated that the achievement of social order should rely on cultivation of ethical norms and individual morality. The Legalists, on the other hand, asserted "*fa*" (a penal concept related to legal punishment) as the primary measure of government and advocated that social order be achieved by implementing regulations and punishment.

Throughout the feudal dynasties, Confucianism dominated the ideologies of government, while still allowing the concept of *fa* to exist. Under traditional social hierarchy, both ethical formulas and regulatory measures were used by government to maintain social control. However, *fa* was often included only as a supplemental means of last resort for maintaining social control. Under such legal and social culture, there was a general ignorance of legal rights in society. Judicial function was subsidiary to executive administration, and the legal codes were used primarily to enforce corporal punishment. In Chinese society, the concepts of personal laws and rights were not adopted until the early twentieth century.

Earlier Legalization Efforts

The traditional legal norm was challenged in late 1800s. However, at the turn of the twentieth century, domestic socioeconomic unrest and foreign pressure awakened the need for change in the nation's societal structure. The Chinese began to recognize the need for a formal legal system, and thus, legal scholars and intellectuals began to pursue reform.

In 1902, the Qing government began to create a national court system and revise old legal codes. In efforts to establish constitutional reform, a constitutional committee was established in 1907. In 1911, the Criminal Procedure Codes and Civil Procedure Codes were drafted, adopting the jury and lawyer system from European and Japanese models. However, they collapsed with the Qing dynasty in 1911.

That same year the Republican Revolution, led by Sun Yat-sen, overthrew the feudal dynasty and founded the Republic of China

(ROC). The interim Nanjing government partially adopted the Qing law and formalized the ROC provisional constitution, as well as various other revolutionary laws and decrees. However, the efforts of introducing western law to China based on the European continental system were retarded in 1912, when the Northern Government reinstated old Qing codes and set forth a series of codes and decrees pursuing a warlord autocracy. As a result, the Nationalists' efforts for legal reform suffered setbacks.

In 1927 the government reevaluated the Qing codes. The Nanjing government created a "Six Codes" system, including constitutional law, civil law, civil procedure law, criminal law, criminal procedure law, and administrative law. The Nationalists' legal system was developed with reference to the European Continental model, but it incorporated Nationalist principles. The Republic's legalization efforts established the Chinese legal system, to some extent, in the direction of modernization. However, the development was rather slow because of social and political unrest.

After the Communist takeover in 1949 the Nationalists' legal system was abolished, including all laws and the Six Codes. In the early 1950s, legal enforcement was formulated by a mixture of statutes, rules, decrees, and regulations. The laws were discharged by regional "people's courts."

In 1954, a new constitution was established, calling for the independence of judicial power. The government's realization of the urgency to establish a formal legal system resulted in efforts to implement comprehensive codes based largely on the Soviet model.

However, the efforts to build a Socialist legal system in the mid-1950s were brought to an abrupt halt by the Anti-Rightist Campaign in 1957–1958. The concepts of judicial independence and equal protection under the law were attacked as "bourgeois" legal doctrines. In early 1959, the nation's lawyer system was abolished.

Even though there were meager efforts to reinstate a legal system in the early 1960s, China experienced a period of 20 years, from the Anti-Rightist campaign of the late 1950s through the end of the Cultural Revolution (1966–1976), without laws.

Recent Legal Reform

In late 1976, the Cultural Revolution came to an end. In 1977, Deng Xiaoping resumed power and launched a campaign of economic development. The government was determined to reinstate its legal system to ensure social and political reform and economic development throughout China. The 1978 Communiqué of the Third Plenum of the 11th Central Committee of the Chinese Communist Party contemplated the establishment of a "socialist legal system," for the first time signifying a shift from a course of destructive sociopolitical campaigns to constructive socioeconomic development.

In early 1978, the National People's Congress (NPC) enacted a constitution, thus reinstating a formal judicial system. In 1979, the Ministry of Justice was reinstated, and the procuratorate (this organization is similar in function to the U.S. Department of Justice) also regained power to exercise legal supervision. Subsequently, the NPC set forth a series of codes, such as PRC criminal law, criminal procedure law, and people's courts organic law in 1979. The enactment of the 1978 Constitution and implementation of related laws laid a foundation for restoration and reform of a legal system that was virtually destroyed during the political turmoil of the previous 20 years.

The pressing demands of social and economic reform required fundamental revisions of the nation's constitutional law. In 1982, the Constitution was adopted with comprehensive revisions of the previous Constitutions of 1954, 1975, and 1978. Under the 1982 Constitution, the principle of the independent judicial power was reestablished. In the 1980s, China began to heavily implement legal codes based on Western models. As we discuss later in this chapter, the 1982 Constitution has been amended three times since, in 1988, 1993, and 1999. To catch up with the trend of economic globalization, the Chinese government has undertaken the urgent task of assimilating the domestic legal system with international norms.

On December 11, 2001, China, one of the founding nations of General Agreement on Tariffs and Trade (GATT), joined the WTO. Prior to entry in the global trade body, the Chinese government had introduced extensive legal amendments and implementations, particularly those related to international trade and foreign investment. As a member of the WTO, China recently committed itself to further harmonize its economic market and legal system with that of the global environment. Nearly 3,000 national laws and 200,000 local ones have been either revised or abolished. Rules and policies previously regarded as inside information were made public. It is projected that many more legal amendments and adjustments will be made in years to come.

With China's recent rapid economic expansion, however, corruption and bureaucracy are still serious problems, threatening the nation's development and growth. Since early 2003, in order to tackle corruption and reduce the size of the existing bureaucracy, China's new president Hu Jintao has worked to strengthen the authority of the Constitution.

Legal and Administrative Infrastructure

Legislative—The People's Congresses

The National People's Congress (NPC) is constitutionally the highest organ of state power, with the Standing Committee as its permanent body. The NPC and its Standing Committee are charged with legislative power of the state. Under China's Constitution, the NPC has: (1) the state legislative power to enact, amend, and supervise the enforcement of the Constitution and other basic laws concerning criminal offenses and civil affairs; (2) the decisive power to examine and approve national economic and social plans and the state budget; and (3) the supervisory power to create and supervise the State Council, the Supreme People's Court, and the Supreme People's Procuratorate. It also has the power to appoint and remove high government officials.

The Standing Committee of the NPC exercises the highest state and legislative power during adjournments of the NPC. It interprets the Constitution and supervises its implementation, enacts and amends laws (with the exception of those which should be enacted by the NPC), partially supplements and amends laws enacted by the NPC when it is not in session, and interprets laws.

Certain special committees, both permanent and provisional, exist under the NPC to study, examine, and draw up related motions for the NPC and the NPC Standing Committee. Currently, there are eight permanent special committees: the Nationalities Committee; the Law Committee; the Financial and Economic Committee; the Educational, Science, Culture, and Public Health Committee; the Foreign Affairs Committee; the Overseas Chinese Committee; the Committee for Internal and Judicial Affairs; and the Committee on Protection of Environment and Resources.

Under the current Constitution and related laws, the NPC holds a session on the first quarter of each year convened by its Standing Committee. The NPC is elected for a term of five years.

Local People's Congresses and their Standing Committees are established at all levels of local government, from provincial to villages. Local People's Congresses at the provincial level are empowered to enact local laws and rules that do not conflict with the Constitution, national laws, or administrative regulations. In the nation's Special Economic Zones, the local People's Congresses are authorized preferentially to implement laws and regulations for foreign investment.

Judicial—the People's Courts

The people's courts, under the Constitution, are judicial organs of the state. In contrast to the U.S. dual (federal and state) court system, there is a uniform court system in China. The state establishes the *Supreme People's Court* (SPC), the local people's courts, and all other special courts. The SPC is constitutionally the highest judicial organ of the state.

Local people's courts are divided into three levels: higher people's court at the provincial level, intermediate people's court at the municipal level, and basic people's court at the county level. A basic people's court, when necessary, may establish a few people's tribunals. Each people's court generally consists of criminal, civil, economic, and administrative divisions. Courts above the county level may also establish other special divisions.

Special courts include the Military Court, the Maritime Court, and Railroad Transport Courts. Moreover, some special tribunals are established within higher or intermediate people's courts, such as the Intellectual Property Tribunal established in the Beijing intermediate People's Court since 1983. The Intellectual Property Tribunal hears cases concerning patent, trademark, and copyright (including computer software) infringement, and other cases concerning licensing agreements and unfair competition. Other analogous intellectual property tribunals have also been established in other jurisdictions. In addition, the Beijing Municipal Higher People's Court has established an Intellectual Property Appellate Division, which has exclusive jurisdiction for the whole nation analogous to the United State Court of Appeals for the Federal Circuit.

Legal Supervisory Organ— the People's Procuratorates

Under the Constitution, the people's procuratorates are state organs that exercise legal supervision, similar in concept to the U.S. Justice Department. The state established the *Supreme People's Procuratorates* (SPP, this is similar in function to the U.S. Justice Department), the local people's procuratorates, military procuratorates, and other special procuratorates. The SPP is constitutionally the highest procuratoral organ of the state. The procuratorates exercise procuratoral power independently, in accordance with the provisions of the law, and are not subject to interference by any administrative organ, public organization, or individual.

Local people's procuratorates are divided into provincial, municipal, and county levels. A procuratorate at the provincial or county level, when necessary, may establish its agency in special industrial or economic districts. Each people's procuratorate generally consists of criminal, civil, economic, and administrative divisions. A local procuratorate is subordinate to its superior procuratorate, and at the same time it is accountable to the local People's Congress and its Standing Committee.

The procuratorates have the right to investigate activities involving national security, to pursue public prosecution, to exercise legal supervision over the trial activities of the people's courts, and to exercise legal supervision over the investigations of the public security organs. The procuratorates investigate and prosecute unlawful conduct committed by governmental officials and law enforcement officers, such as white-collar crimes, wrongful prosecutions, and corruption.

Executive—the State Council

The State Council, the central people's government, is the *executive* body of the highest organ of state power, and thus the highest *administrative* organ of the state. The State Council is responsible to the NPC, or during adjournments of the NPC, to its Standing Committee. The personnel of the State Council include premier, vice premiers, state councilors, and ministers of various ministries or commissions.

The State Council exercises its executive power to adopt administrative measures; enact administrative rules and regulations and issue resolutions and decrees in accordance with the Constitution and the law; to exercise its leadership over its ministries or commissions and local governments at various levels; to implement the plan for national economic and social development of the state budget; to administer the civil affairs, public security, and judicial administration; to handle foreign affairs, and deal with treaties and agreements with foreign states.

The ministries and commissions may issue orders, directives, and regulations within their jurisdiction and may implement administrative decisions, orders, regulations, and specific measures empowered by the State Council. Among the 28 ministries and commissions, those that are most relevant to foreign trade and investment include the following: the Ministry of Science and Technology, Ministry of Land and Natural Resources, Ministry of Labor and Social Security, State Economic and Trade Commission, State Development Planning Commission, State Drug Administration, and State Environmental Protection Administration.

Among various ministries and commissions of the State Council, the Ministry of Justice is the judicial administrative organ of the state. The Ministry of Justice has power to supervise and guide lawyers, law firms, and legal associations. It is authorized to administer the licensing and discipline of attorneys. Since 1986, it is also responsible for the administration of national bar examinations. According to a new measure adopted in 2001, the Ministry of Justice, along with the Supreme People's Court and the Supreme People's Procuratorate, is responsible for administration of Uniform Judicial Examinations (effective 2002)—national uniform qualification examinations for those who want to enter the legal profession as judges, procurators, or attorneys.

Other administration organs under the State Council that have significant impact on the legal enforcement of intellectual property rights include: the State Copyright Bureau, the China Patent Bureau, and the Trademark Office of the State Administration of Industry and Commerce.

The significant impacts of the State Council on China's legal system can be demonstrated through the distribution of power. First, the executive branch has law-making power, delegated by the NPC and its Standing Committee, to enact provisional ad hoc administrative measures, resolutions, and decrees concerning specific national issues. The dynamic nature of the recent economic reform in China often makes the State Council de facto the most powerful law-making body.

Second, the executive branch has the administrative power to issue national administrative regulations and rules in accordance with the existing Constitution and laws. These administrative rules and regulations are as powerful as those enacted by the Standing Committee of the NPC and are often supplemented by commissions and ministries of the State Council.

Third, as mentioned earlier, the executive body has the administrative power of legal enforcement and management. The Ministry of Justice is responsible for administering judicial execution, managing laws and regulations, and the administrative enforcement of intellectual property rights for three separate administrative branches: the State Copyright Bureau, the State Patent Bureau, and the Trademark Office of the State Administration of Industry and Commerce.

Local Governments

Local governments are state administrative organs at the local level. All are subordinate to the leadership of the State Council. Under the central government, people's governments are established for provincial regions, autonomous regions, and municipalities directly under the central government; at the municipal level of municipalities and autonomous prefectures; at the county level of counties, autonomous counties, and municipal districts; and at the township level of townships and villages.

At and above the county level, the local governments are responsible for local economic and social development, local civil affairs, public security, and judicial administration. The provincial governments may implement administrative rules and regulations within their jurisdiction. Local governments of provinces and large cities approved by the State Council may also enact local administrative regulations and specifications granted that they do not conflict with the Constitution, national laws, and basic administrative rules and regulations. Furthermore, local governments of Special Economic Zones are responsible for making certain local administrative specifications for their special economic demands. In the area of intellectual property, administrative organs for enforcement and management of patent, trademark, and copyright have been established in provinces, capitals of provinces, Special Economic Zones, and some major cities across the country.

The Legal Profession and Its Administration

As mentioned earlier, China's legal system did not emerge until the turn of the twentieth century. And, it wasn't until the late 1970s, when China launched its massive economic reform program, that reliance on lawyers became a generally accepted concept. Today, China has about 115,000 lawyers. Compared to other countries, particularly the United States, this is a tiny number (see Exhibit 5.1).

Administration of and Regulations for Lawyers

After 1949, China's lawyers were administered solely under the Ministry of Justice. The administration has been shifted to a system with both judicial supervision under the Ministry of Justice and professional administration under the All-China Lawyers Association. Under the new system, China's lawyers associations are no longer run by judicial administration organs, although lawyers associations and law firms are still subject to guidance and supervision by judicial administration organs.

In 1980, the legislature formalized the Interim Regulations on Lawyers (effective January 1, 1982), signifying China's effort to reconstruct its legal system. More recently, the passage of the PRC Law on Lawyers in 1996 (effective January 1, 1997) reinforced China's commitment to legal reform.

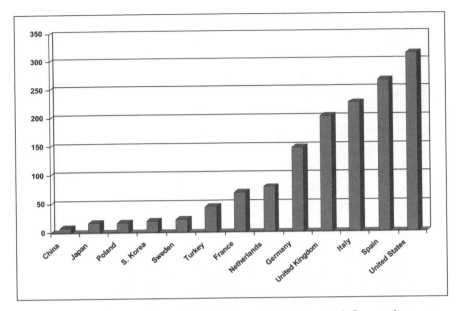

Exhibit 5.1   Lawyers per 100,000 People in Selected Countries
(*Sources: Council of Bars and Law Societies of Europe (www.ccbe.org) 2005; Ichiko Fuyuno, "Japan Grooms New Lawyers," Wall Street Journal, March 13, 2004, pp. A18–A19; and Qin Jize, "Lawyers Playing a Bigger Role," China Daily, June 17, 2005.)*

The 1996 Law on Lawyers is the most comprehensive and authoritative law regulating lawyers since 1949. It is the first law to recognize the concept of an independent legal profession and emphasize the need for lawyers to represent clients. Unlike the 1980 Interim Regulations, the 1996 Law on Lawyers no longer defines lawyers as "state legal workers" but rather as "personnel who have obtained a business license for lawyers' practice under the law and are providing legal services to the public." Lawyers shall "pursue independently the practice" under the law and exercise a high degree of professional and personal ethics. However, China's lawyers are not fully separate from the government since, under the law, lawyers, law firms, and bar associations are still subject to supervision and guidance of the judicial administration organs of the State Council.

In addition to provisions concerning lawyers' business organizations, bar associations, and legal aid programs, the 1996 Law on Lawyers has provisions on lawyers' rights, obligations, and professional responsibilities, and thus, through legislative power, ratifies some general rules on professional ethics and disciplines. In 1997, the All-China Lawyers Association formalized the Professional Ethics and Disciplinary Rules on Lawyers. With the demands from China's recent social, economic, and political development, it is expected that the Law on Lawyers will be revised and that some new administrative rules and regulations will be adopted in the near future.

Qualifications for the Legal Profession

Since China reinstated its legal system in late 1970s, the nation experienced rapid growth in the number of lawyers. As mentioned, in the last 20 years, the number of lawyers grew from virtually nothing to 115,000. Legal personnel increased by more than 10 percent annually in recent years. However, qualification is always a critical issue for the development of the profession. From the late 1970s through the mid-1980s, most lawyers were recruited from judicial personnel or other professions, many with little or no formal legal education and in some cases even without formal college education.

In order to enhance the qualifications of the legal profession, a national bar examination was established in 1986. The examinations were at first held once every two years starting 1986 and now once a year since 1993. Today the applicants must have at least three years of college law education (the three-year programs are referred to as *"zhuanke,"* while regular law education at the college level is designed for four years and is referred to as *"benke"*) or four years of college education in another discipline. Up until 2000, the national bar examinations were held 11 times, and the pass rate was around 10 percent. The uniform bar examination has helped to shape and standardize the legal profession.

Based on the national bar examination system, the judiciary established a Uniform Judicial Examination system to further improve the quality of the legal profession. The Ministry of Justice of the State Council, jointly with the Supreme Court and the Supreme Procuratorate, implemented the new measures. The separate examinations for the national bar, judges, and procurators, originally scheduled in 2001, merged into the first Uniform Judicial Examination, which was held in early 2002.

Business Organizations of Lawyers

In the past, Chinese lawyers were required to work in state-founded "legal advisory offices," which were defined as "public institutions under the organizational leadership and professional supervision of the judicial administration organs of the state." In 1988, the first "cooperative law firm," free of direct state supervision and financially independent of the government, was founded in Shanghai. In 1993, the Ministry formally authorized the establishment of cooperative law firms. The 1996 Law on Lawyers established more open and objective criteria for law firms. Since then, lawyers' business organizations take forms such as state-founded legal advisory offices, cooperative law firms, law firms in partnerships, state-funded law firms, and some special legal advisory offices. Currently, China has about 10,000 law firms across the country.

Regulations on Foreign Legal Representatives

In June 1992, the government granted foreign law firms formal rights to open branch offices in China. Since then, the government has enforced regulations on legal practices of foreign law firms. Right after China's entry into the WTO, new Regulations for the Administration of Representative Offices in China of Foreign Law Firms were adopted on January 1, 2002, setting new rules applying to the establishment of representative offices in China. Foreign law offices and their representatives may engage in activities that abide by the regulations, but they may not handle Chinese legal matters. They may, however, provide information to clients concerning the impact of China's legal environment.

Foreign law offices are permitted to provide legal services, such as legal consultation, to foreign clients for related international treaties and business laws and regulations; they may also offer legal services to foreign clients or Chinese law firms in legal matters related to foreign countries; and referral services through Chinese law firms to foreign clients regarding legal matters in China. Foreign attorneys thus primarily serve as advisors on business transactions.

The government restricts foreign law firms from engaging in practices in "China law matters," specifically issuing opinions about the law. Also, other foreign organizations and individuals are prohibited from engaging in legal service activities in China through the use of consulting companies or in other forms. Such restricted "China law matters" include: (1) taking part in litigation activities in China as a lawyer; (2) providing opinions or certification with regard to specific issues governed by Chinese law in contracts, agreements, articles of association, or other written documents; (3) providing opinions or certification with regard to acts or events governed by Chinese law; (4) giving an agent's opinion or comments concerning the application of Chinese law or concerning facts that involve Chinese law in one's capacity as an agent in the course of arbitration activities; and (5) carrying out registration, amendment, application, recordation, or other procedures with a Chinese government institution or other organization with governmental administration functions authorized by laws and regulations on behalf of a principal.

The regulations and implementing measures also provide rules on the application process, business commencement registration, annual inspections, rules and procedures for appointment of chief representatives and other representatives, the establishment of additional representative offices, employment of Chinese and foreign assistants, and other matters. Foreign representatives must have practiced for at least two years outside of China. The chief representative must have practiced for at least three years outside of China. Representatives must reside in China at least six months in each year, otherwise, registration may be denied in the following year.

The regulations on foreign law firms do not apply to the establishment of representative offices by law firms from Hong Kong, Macao, or Taiwan. Separate measures are formulated for representative offices of law firms from those areas.

Body of Laws and Regulations

Constitutional Law

China's Constitution, adopted in 1982 and most recently amended in 1999, is "the fundamental law of the state and has supreme legal authority." The frequent changes in the Constitution reflect Chinese leadership's constantly shifting vision of future society. Chinese constitutional law is mostly concerned with the state organizational structure rather than the balance of governmental power and the protection of fundamental rights of citizens. Nevertheless, the 1982 Constitution and its later amendments enhance protection of fundamental rights while reflecting the course of recent economic and legal reform.

In 1988, the first amendments to the 1982 Constitution affirmed the nation's earlier practice in economic reform and provided that the state allow "private economy" as a "complement to the socialist public economy."

In an effort to transform the socialist planned economy to a socialist market economy, the notion of "socialist market economy" was officially adopted by the 14th Congress of the CPC in 1992. The 1993 amendments to the Constitution ratified the notion of socialist "market economy," distinguishing it from the "planned economy" adopted in the previous versions. The 1993 amendments also indicate that the state is responsible for "economic legislation."

The 1999 amendments further stated that "individual economy, private economy and other nonpublic economy" are "important components" of the socialist market economy, and they ratified the notions of "ruling the country according to law." The legal system was envisioned as indispensable for the development of a market economy. To catch up with increasing economic globalization, the Chinese government realized the urgent task of adapting the domestic legal system to international norms.

Civil and Criminal Codes

In ancient China, as influenced by the traditional conception of "*xing*," legal codes emphasized criminal penalties. Thus, in imperial China civil matters were subsumed under the criminal codes. The situation did not change until the turn of the twentieth century. However, in the last century, civil and criminal codes experienced significant changes over time. Particularly since the late 1970s, the Chinese government has amended and reformed its civil and criminal codes.

For foreign nationals or business entities, civil and criminal codes may seem irrelevant; the most relevant of China's laws and regulations with respect to Americans are those relating to business, foreign investment, resources, or intellectual property. However, the relevant provisions of civil or criminal codes are actually very important in relation to other laws and regulations with respect to business issues.

Laws and Regulations on Commerce in General

Introducing competitive market mechanisms has been shown to be the key to driving China's economic reform initiated in the late 1970s. Over the past 20 years, China's economy has experienced a transition from a central planned system to a market-oriented system. The business environment has changed from one dominated by government-run enterprises to the one that coexists with government-run and privately owned enterprises.

In response to the demands of the emerging market, the government implemented a series of laws and regulations related to business and finance, which include contract law, corporation law, law on public bidding, and arbitration law. See our Web site, www.ChinaNowBook.com, for more details.

Laws and Regulations on Customs, Foreign Trade, and Investment

China's recent high economic growth rate has significantly benefited from foreign involvement. Foreign trade and investment are expected to play an increasingly important role in energizing China's opening market. Important laws and regulations affecting foreign trade and investment include regulations on foreign investment, equity joint ventures, and tariffs, to name only a few. For a complete list, see our Web site.

Laws and Regulations on Intellectual Property

For foreign traders and investors, protection of intellectual property rights is a major concern. Since the launch of its economic campaign to attract foreign investment, the Chinese government has made aggressive efforts to implement and enforce laws to protect intellectual property rights. However, the effectiveness of such protection is still far from satisfactory. Chinese intellectual property laws cover three major areas: patent law, copyright law, and trademark law. One must pay attention to the substantial differences between Chinese laws and their U.S. counterparts.

Laws and Regulations on Land and Resources

In the PRC, ownership of land and natural resources is retained by the state. Private entities may obtain only limited use or exploitation rights on land and natural resources. The Chinese government enacted laws and regulations to allow foreign parties to develop commercial land and explore or exploit certain natural resources, such as oil and gas. In addition, China has laws and regulations regarding the protection of the environment and conservation of nature and cultural resources. For a complete listing of the important laws and regulations on the environment and natural and cultural resources, see www.ChinaNowBook.com.

Administrative Rules and Policies

As mentioned above, the State Council has the power to adopt administrative measures, enact administrative rules and regulations, and issue resolutions and decrees in accordance with the Constitution and the law. The commissions and ministries of the State Council are charged with the power to implement administrative decisions, orders, regulations, and specific measures. Local governments of provinces and major municipalities may also implement specific local rules and regulations.

In view of the dynamic nature of China's economic development, the administrative regulations and the implementation of rules or policy decisions, though often provisional or local in their nature, should be scrutinized and may be considered as de facto. This is often the case in issues relating to foreign trade and investments, especially in Special Economic Zones.

Judicial Proceedings

In Chapter 10 we discuss dispute resolution options for those involved in business in China. As suggested by the discussion in this chapter, we hope you can avoid trying to settle your commercial disputes in the courtroom. All lawsuits are not lost by foreign firms—recently France's Hennessy cognac won a trademark lawsuit, and America's General Motors forced a settlement with China's Chery in another piracy dispute that made it to court. But the road is tough with ever-changing conditions. As a last resort, litigation is an uneasy option.

Under the PRC Civil Procedural Codes, the local people's court generally has jurisdiction over a civil dispute in the locality where the contract was signed or to be performed, the object of the litigation is located, the property of a foreign defendant exists, the representative or business organization of a foreign defendant is located, or where any torts occurred. Foreign national or entities may stipulate in a contract their right to choose a forum that is substantially related to the dispute. Otherwise, the general jurisdiction applies.

In general, local people's courts at all levels may have jurisdiction over a dispute involving foreign interests. The people's court has jurisdiction over contractual disputes involving Sino-foreign equity joint ventures, Sino-foreign cooperative joint ventures, or Sino-foreign cooperative exploration of natural resources. For patent disputes, an intermediate people's court may have jurisdiction if instructed by the Supreme People's Court. For maritime affairs or disputes, the Maritime Court has jurisdiction.

Under the PRC Civil Procedural Codes, a foreign national enterprise or organization, when initiating or responding to legal actions in the people's court, has the same litigation rights and obligations as Chinese citizens or entities. If foreign courts impose any restriction upon the civil litigation rights of a Chinese national or of Chinese entities, the people's courts will impose similar restrictions correspondingly to the national or entities of that foreign country. Foreign parties must retain Chinese lawyers to participate in the litigation. However, foreign parties may have an agent *ad litem* of their own nationality to represent their interests. If foreign parties are involved in civil disputes but do not reside in China, they may ask their embassy personnel to represent them to retain Chinese lawyers as legal counsel or Chinese citizens as agents *ad litem*.

Conclusion

We close the chapter with two scary little cases that demonstrate the legal pitfalls of doing business in China. Some people suggest that these cases are examples of "legal protectionism," where the Chinese government and judicial system are biased against foreign enterprises. We can't argue with this view. The only solace for foreign firms is the hope that legal conditions in China continue to improve. But, for Trayton Furniture and *Rolling Stone* magazine, things are not improving fast enough. The first was successfully sued by a vendor, and the second has been stymied by the Chinese bureaucracy. Read 'em and weep.

Trayton Furniture of Denmark[2]

The first time Simon Lichtenberg realized he was in trouble was a March afternoon when Liu Xiaoming, chief judge of a court from Leshan in Sichuan province, arrived at his door, having travelled the 2,300 miles to Shanghai with two police officers to deliver a court order freezing part of Mr. Lichtenberg's company's bank account and a section of its factory.

Five months later, Mr. Lichtenberg's company, Trayton Furniture, was on the losing end of a lawsuit from a Sichuan leather supplier. Lichtenberg's lawyer calls the situation a classic case of "legal protectionism," and Lichtenberg says it's a warning about doing business in the less developed parts of China.

The case is a rare glimpse of how such legal disputes can function.

Born in Denmark, Lichtenberg had been doing business in China for more than 10 years, starting as a timber trader. In 1997, he began manufacturing leather sofas for export to retailers such as Bo Concept and Ikea.

The business required little up-front investment or marketing, and the production costs were one-third of those in Scandinavia. The company now has 1,200 employees and profits of about Rmb20m ($2.4 million).

One big challenge facing Lichtenberg was getting hold of the leather. Until recently there were few suppliers, and the quality was often indifferent. That is how Trayton came in contact with Zhenjing Leather, a company based in Leshan, a small city 100 miles from the Sichuan provincial capital, Chengdu.

Lichtenberg says he was a little wary of Zhenjing—part of a group of businesses, including chemicals and coal, owned by He Zhenggang. It was in a far city and had a powerful position in the local economy. However, Zhenjing was then one of the largest leather companies in China and had been awarded a loan by the International Finance Corporation, an arm of the World Bank.

Over the course of 2004, Trayton bought Rmb37m ($4.6 million) worth of leather from Zhenjing. However, it complained about the quality of Rmb3m of the goods, where the top coating had started to peel off. After an independent testing company confirmed quality problems, Trayton says it decided to withhold payment and return the leather.

Lichtenberg did not hear back from Zhenjing until Mr. Liu, chief judge of the Wutongqiao district court in Leshan, arrived at his factory with a court order for nonpayment of goods. The ruling called for Rmb3m ($375,000) of cash in Trayton's bank account and Rmb4.2m ($525,000) of assets at the factory to be frozen.

According to Edward Epstein, one of Trayton's lawyers at Salans in Shanghai, the court order should have been invalid for a number of reasons. For a start, the original contract said disputes over quality would be handled in Shanghai. Moreover, there was no need to freeze any assets because Trayton could comfortably pay the Rmb3m ($375,000) if it lost the case.

However, the lawsuit was not issued on behalf of Zhenjing, but by one of its branch companies, Xinhua. To sustain this argument, the Sichuan company produced faxes of four sales invoices for leather goods issued by Xinhua, which it claimed overrode the original contract signed by Trayton and Zhenjing.

The court agreed. Mr. Liu's judgment ruled that the faxes counted as a contract, and it ignored the quality report about the leather.

By starting legal proceedings in the Wutongqiao district court, he had ensured that the entire legal case would stay close to home. Defendants in China get just one appeal, and that can be heard

only at the next level of the judicial system, in this case the intermediate court in Leshan.

Wang Liping, lawyer for the Sichuan company, says Trayton's
arguments missed the point. The faxes showed that Trayton did
have a business relationship with Xinhua. Moreover, she adds: "If
they deem the product to be of poor quality, they may sue Zhenjing Leather in Shanghai. But here we are talking about an issue
of payment default."

The appeal is scheduled to be heard in the Leshan court in the
near future, but Lichtenberg holds little hope of success.

Rolling Stone[2]

After a sell-out first issue, the Chinese edition of the iconic music
magazine *Rolling Stone* hit an obstacle. On March 29, 2006, Chinese officials said that the government had not approved the
cooperation between *Rolling Stone* and its local publisher, *Audiovisual World* magazine, which launched the U.S. periodical in
China in March 2006. "This kind of cooperation must be registered according to regulatory rules. . . . There are legal problems,
so this cooperation has been halted," said an official of the Shanghai bureau of China's press and publications administration.

The setback for *Rolling Stone*, which sold out a 125,000-copy
initial print run, highlights the legal and regulatory complexities
surrounding foreign involvement in China's magazine sector.

It could also signal official disapproval of the magazine's association with rock and roll lifestyles, in spite of the magazine's
decision to tone down its content for the Chinese market.

Beijing demands that ownership—and therefore final editorial
control—remain in Chinese hands even for the blandest period-
icals, forcing foreign publishers to work through joint ventures
and contractual link-ups with local license holders.

In spite of all-new content, the launch issue of *Rolling Stone*
was technically just another edition of *Audiovisual World*, which
retained its name on the cover, although this fact was overshad-
owed by *Rolling Stone*'s famous English-language masthead.

Such arrangements are routine in the Chinese magazine sector, which in recent years has seen the launch of foreign titles ranging from female fashion showcase *Vogue* to "lads' mag" *FHM*.

One Media Group, *Rolling Stone*'s regional licensee, declined to comment and Hao Fang, editor-in-chief of *Rolling Stone*'s Chinese edition, said he was unaware of a problem. However, a manager at *Audiovisual World* said that the Chinese publication was still trying to complete approval procedures for the link-up. "We will change our April magazine and the *Rolling Stone* name will be taken down. . . . The content will be our own," the person said.

Our advice? Invest in some good legal advice! However, even more important, do not be deceived by the appearance of the legal "system" just described. The only systematic thing about business law in China circa 2007 is that both the letter and rule of law are less important than the supervision and interpretation of the ubiquitous Communist party officials and the qualities and extent of your *guanxi* (your personal connections). The latter concept is detailed in Chapter 7.

Notes

1 James McGregor, *One Billion Customers* (New York: Wall Street Journal Press, 2005), p. 3.
2 Geoff Dyer, "How to Twist Long Arm of Law in China," *Financial Times*, March 30, 2006, p. 3.
3 Mure Dickie, "Rolling Stone Hits China Wall," *Financial Times*, March 30, 2006, p. 3.

Charles Liu's contribution to this chapter was immense and very much appreciated.

PART II

WHAT HAPPENS WHEN AMERICANS MEET CHINESE ACROSS THE NEGOTIATION TABLE?

CHAPTER 6

FREE ENTERPRISE COWBOYS

ADAM SMITH, JOHN WAYNE, AND THE AMERICAN NEGOTIATION STYLE[1]

"**S**aving face" is an important concept to understand. In Chinese business culture, a person's reputation and social standing rest on this concept. Causing embarrassment or loss of composure, even unintentionally, can be disastrous for business negotiations.

Thus runs the conventional wisdom about China as well represented in the popular media such as www.executiveplanet.com. Actually, useful anecdotes and rules about cultural differences can be found at that Web site regarding some 40 different business cultures around the world. We recommend you take a look. But really—"Face is important in China?"—duh! The problem with such anecdotes and rules is that they often don't help. They are too easily misunderstood or misinterpreted, and applying them badly may get you into worse trouble than not applying them at all. For example, consider the plight of one John Shipwright:

"Again? Not Again. They really want to talk about delivery *again*? I'm going insane!" John Shipwright's nodding head and calm demeanor belied the thoughts thus running through his head. He'd been in Shanghai now four days and three almost sleepless nights. He was tired and sick. His head still pounded from the endless rounds of toasts at the banquet the first night, and his stomach went queasy at the thought of the pig's skin and chicken's feet he managed to get down then. And now they wanted to talk about delivery again.

This was Shipwright's second trip to China. He had volunteered to "get things straightened out" with the new customer. In oilfield equipment sales the issues are many—price, quantity, design, delivery, warranty, service contract, technology transfer, and so on. Shipwright had carefully explained all the details about delivery dates and growing backlogs on Tuesday. They had settled on a six-month order-to-installation cycle and had moved on to the other issues. On Wednesday they asked about delivery again, and he had repeated much of the information about triple shifts, capital investment, and early delivery premiums. Again they had agreed on a six-month order-to-installation cycle. Now, first thing on Friday, they're asking about delivery again. That's when he snapped.[2]

How many hotshot American managers have been broken by this apparent Chinese relentlessness? Too many to count, we suppose. But is that the Chinese intent, to *break* the Americans? Perhaps? But, most of the time it is not. The serious problems we describe above are very likely attributable to cultural differences in negotiation processes in the two countries. Even though both potential business partners may be well intentioned, such differences can cause the breakdown, or even the blowup, of mutually beneficial commercial relationships.

The travail Mr. Shipwright suffered regarded cross-cultural differences in how concessions are made. He had thought the Chinese had agreed to a six-month delivery. They hadn't. They had just finished talking about it for the moment. To them, no issue is closed until all issues are. To Shipwright it had been decided twice before. When he "snapped" during their third broaching of the subject, the Chinese really didn't understand his "barbaric meltdown." What we might call venting in this culture made no sense to them and was a complete and extremely uncomfortable surprise.

Had Mr. Shipwright understood the differences in and logic behind the Chinese negotiation style, he might have handled things much differently. Instead of getting upset with the perceived lack of progress, the general disorganization of the discussions, and the Chinese's [apparently] bad ethics of reneging on previous agreements, he might have interpreted their repeated questions in another way. Actually, their focus on the delivery issue could have been seen as a sign of good progress and a signal of importance about their preferences.

The whys of Chinese behavior are important and sometimes hard for American executives to grasp. In this second section of the book we offer a master class, if you will, on the cultural differences that most often interfere in trans-Pacific negotiations. The differences in the Chinese style of negotiation run deep. Some of the explanations have to do with historical crowding, family farming, and a pictorial writing system. The 2,500 year-old teachings of Confucius have also had an important impact on how Chinese people interact with one another. The key points of difference are well summarized by the notions of face, social hierarchy, interpersonal harmony, connections, holistic thinking, and so on. But, before we get to those important topics in the next chapter, a quick review of American culture is in order. Indeed, "Know thyself" is Socrates's 2,500-year-old exhortation.

The John Wayne Style

Picture if you will the closing scenes of John Wayne's Academy Award-winning performance in *True Grit*. Sheriff Rooster Cogburn sitting astride his chestnut mare, a Colt .45 in one hand, a Winchester .73 in the other, whiskey on his breath, reins in his teeth, stampeding across the Arkansas prairie straight into the sights and range of villains' guns. A face-to-face shootout with four bad guys, and sure enough, the John Wayne character comes through in the end.

Great entertainment, yes! We know it's all fantasy. We know that in real life Sheriff Rooster Cogburn would have ended up face down in the blood and dust, alongside his dead horse. But it's more fun to see the fantasy nonetheless.

Such scenes from movies (think Clint Eastwood in *Unforgiven*, Daniel Day-Lewis in *Last of the Mohicans*, or even Uma Thurman in *Kill Bill*), TV, and books influence our everyday behavior in subtle but powerful ways. We tend to model our behavior after such John Wayne figures. And when everyone else plays the same game, the bluff and bravado often work. But such behavior becomes a problem when we sit face to face across a negotiating table with business executives who haven't grown up on a steady diet of American action heroes. Our minds play out the familiar scenes. But instead of six-guns, flintlocks, or samurai swords, our weapons are words, questions, threats and promises, laughter, and confrontation. We anticipate victory, despite the odds—four against one is no problem. But we are often disappointed to find it's not the movies. It's a real-life business negotiation. At stake are the profits of our companies, not to mention our own compensation and reputation. And like a real-life sheriff, we lose.

This scenario repeats itself with increasing frequency as American enterprise becomes more global. The cowboy bargaining style, which has served us well in conference rooms across the United States, does us great disservice in conference rooms across the sea.

Probably no single statement better summarizes the American negotiation style than "Shoot first, ask questions later," a phrase straight out of an old Saturday afternoon western. But the roots of the American negotiating style run much deeper than movies and television reruns. To understand the American approach to bargaining, we must consider more basic aspects of our cultural background—in particular, the seeds of Western thought, our immigrant heritage, our frontier history, the fundamental competitiveness of our social and business systems, and finally, much of the training in our present-day business and law schools.

The Roots of American Culture

Culture starts with geography.[3] Our ancestors adapted social systems and thinking processes to the problems and opportunities their environments presented. The cradle of ancient Western civilization is Greece 500 B.C. Look at a map and you'll see thousands of islands. That's the prominent geographical feature of Greece. Islands allow for individualism. Indeed, the word *isolation* comes from the French *isola*, or island. If you get mad at your neighbor, you can always move to another island, particularly when the seas are Aegean calm. You don't need his or her help to cast your net. In fact, you can't fit many folks into your boat anyway. And, of course, boats did get bigger and trade brought a flood of new ideas from all over the Mediterranean. Personal freedom, individuality, objective thought, and even democracy all come to us from this ancient island realm.

Now fast-forward two millennia. Throughout its history, the United States has been a nation influenced by its immigrants. Certainly the continuous mixing of ideas and perspectives brought from across the seas has enriched all our experiences. Every newcomer has had to work hard to succeed; thus the powerful work ethic of America. Another quality of our immigrant predecessors was a fierce individualism and independence—characteristics necessary for survival in the wide open spaces. But this quality does us disservice at the negotiating table. Negotiation is by definition a situation of *inter*dependence—a situation that Americans have never handled well.

We inherit more of this island/individualistic mentality from our frontier history. "Move out West where there's elbow room," ran the conventional wisdom of the first 150 years of our nation's existence. Americans as a group haven't had much practice in negotiating because they have always been able to go elsewhere if conflicts arose.

The long distances between people allowed a social system to develop with not only fewer negotiations but also shorter ones. A day-long horseback ride to the general store or stockyard didn't favor long, drawn out negotiations. It was important to settle things quickly and leave no loose ends to the bargain. "Tell me yes, or tell me no—but give me a straight answer." Candor, laying your cards on the table, was highly valued and expected in the Old West. And it still is today in our boardrooms and classrooms.

We must also recognize the uniqueness of the fundamental driving forces behind our social and business systems. Adam Smith in his *Wealth of Nations* published in 1776 well justified their emphasis in perhaps the most important sentence ever written in English: "By pursuing his own interest he frequently[4] promotes that of the society more effectually than when he really intends to promote it." In a stroke of his pen Smith solved the age-old conundrum of group versus individual interests. And, through his coauthor, one Benjamin Franklin, he inseminated the philosophy and structure of the most dynamic social system ever devised by humans.

Thus, in no country in the world are individualism and competitiveness more highly valued than in the United States. Indeed, see the empirical evidence for this assertion reported in Exhibit 6.1. Compare the 91 for the United States with the 17–25 for the much more collectivistic Chinese cultures.

We're at the top of the list, the end of the scale. Americans place higher value on individualism than folks from any other country. These numbers are based on the research of a Dutch international management scholar, Geert Hofstede. In 1970 he surveyed IBM employees around the world about their work-related values. From those data he developed four dimensions of

United States	**91**	Slovakia	52	**Hong Kong**	**25**
Australia	90	Spain	51	Serbia	25
Great Britain	89	India	48	Chile	23
Hungary	80	Surinam	47	Bangladesh	20
Netherlands	80	Argentina	46	**China**	**20**
New Zealand	79	Japan	46	**Singapore**	**20**
Italy	76	Morocco	46	Thailand	20
Belgium	75	Iran	41	Vietnam	20
Denmark	74	Jamaica	39	West Africa	20
France	71	Russia	39	Salvador	19
Sweden	71	Brazil	38	Korea (South)	18
Ireland	70	Arab countries	38	**Taiwan**	**17**
Norway	69	Turkey	37	Peru	16
Germany	67	Uruguay	36	Trinidad	16
South Africa	65	Greece	35	Costa Rica	15
Finland	63	Philippines	32	Indonesia	14
Estonia	60	Bulgaria	30	Pakistan	14
Luxembourg	60	Mexico	30	Columbia	13
Poland	60	Romania	30	Venezuela	12
Malta	59	Portugal	27	Panama	11
Czech Republic	58	Slovenia	27	Ecuador	8
Switzerland	58	East Africa	27	Guatemala	6
Austria	55	Malaysia	26		
Israel	54				

**Exhibit 6.1   Individualism/Collectivism Index (higher numbers =
more individualistic cultural values)** (Source: *Hofstede 2001.*)

cultural differences, the most salient of which is his "individualism/
collectivism scale."

The individualism/collectivism index (IDV) refers to the preference for behavior that promotes one's self-interest. Cultures
that score high in IDV reflect an "I" mentality and tend to reward

and accept individual initiative, whereas those low in individualism reflect a "we" mentality and generally subjugate the individual to the group. This does not mean that individuals fail to identify with groups when a culture scores high on IDV, but rather that personal initiative and independence are accepted and endorsed. Individualism pertains to societies in which the ties between individuals are loose; everyone is expected to look after himself or herself and his or her immediate family. Collectivism, as its opposite, pertains to societies in which people from birth onward are integrated into strong, cohesive groups, which throughout people's lifetimes, continue to protect them in exchange for unquestioning loyalty.

Of course our educational system also reflects Adam Smith's profundity. And, what goes on in the classrooms in our business and law schools in turn has a strong influence on our negotiating style. Throughout the American educational system we are taught to compete, both academically and on the sporting field. Adversarial relationships and winning are essential themes of the American socialization process. But nowhere in the American educational system is competition and winning more important than in case discussions in our law and business school classrooms. They who make the best arguments, marshal the best evidence, or demolish the opponents' arguments win both the respect of classmates and high marks. Such skills will be important at the negotiating table, but the most important negotiation skills aren't taught or, at best, are shamefully underemphasized in both business and legal training.[5] We don't teach our students how to ask questions, how to get information, how to listen, or how to use questioning as a powerful persuasive strategy. In fact, few of us realize that in most places in the world, the one who asks the questions controls the process of negotiation and thereby accomplishes more in bargaining situations.

A combination of attitudes, expectations, and habitual behaviors constitutes the John Wayne negotiation style. Each characteristic is discussed separately below, but it should be understood that each factor is connected to the others to form the complex foundation for a series of negotiation strategies and tactics that is typically American. We hope it is obvious that what we are talking about is the typical or dominant behavior of American negotiators. Obviously not every American executive is impatient, a poor listener, or argumentative. Nor does every American manager encounter difficulties during international negotiations. But many do, particularly when compared with businesspeople from other countries.

I Can Go It Alone

Most American executives feel that they should be able to handle any negotiation situation by themselves. "Four Chinese versus one American is no problem. I don't need any help. I can think and talk fast enough to get what I want, what the company needs." So goes the John Wayne rationalization. And there's an economic justification: "Why take more people than I need?" Another more subtle reason might be, "Why not take full credit for success? Why split the commission?" Often, then, the American side is outnumbered when it shows up for business discussions.

Being outnumbered or, worse yet, being alone is a severe disadvantage in a negotiation situation. Several things are going on at once—talking, listening, preparing arguments and explanations, formulating questions, and seeking approval. Numbers help in obvious ways with most of these. Indeed, on a Chinese negotiation team one member may be assigned the task of carefully listening with no speaking responsibilities at all. Consider for a moment how carefully you might listen to a speaker if you didn't have to think up a response to his or her next question. But perhaps the most important reason for having greater, or at least equal, numbers on your side is the powerful, subtle influence of nodding heads and positive facial expressions. Negotiation is very much a social activity, and the approval and agreement of others (friend and foe) can have critical effects on negotiation outcomes. Numbers can also be a subtle indicator of the seriousness and commitment of both parties to a negotiation.

Just Call Me Mary

Americans more than most other cultural groups value informality and equality in human relations. The emphasis on first names is only the tip of the iceberg. We go out of our way to make our clients feel comfortable by playing down status distinctions such as titles and by eliminating unnecessary formalities such as lengthy introductions. But all too often we succeed in making only ourselves feel comfortable, while our international clients are often uneasy or even annoyed.

In Chinese society, interpersonal relationships are vertical; that is, in almost all two-person relationships a difference in status exists. The basis for this status distinction may be any of several factors: age, sex, place of education, position in a firm, which firm, or even industry of employment. For example, the president of the number one firm in an industry holds a higher status position than the president of the number two firm in the same industry. The Chinese are very much aware of such distinctions and of their positions in the hierarchy. And for good reason—knowledge of their status positions dictates how they will behave during interpersonal interactions. Thus it is easy to understand the importance of exchanging business cards in China; such a ritual clearly establishes the status relationships and lets each person know which role to play. The roles of the higher-status position and lower-status position are very different, even to the extent that different words are used to express the same idea depending on which person makes the statement.

Such rules for conducting business discussions are difficult for Americans to understand. We can perhaps get by with our informal, egalitarian style when we're dealing with foreigners in the United States. However, we make things difficult for ourselves and our companies by asking executives in Shanghai, Tokyo, Paris, or London to, "Just call me Mary (or John)."

Pardon My French

Americans aren't adept at speaking foreign languages. Often we aren't even apologetic about it. We rightly argue that English is the international language, particularly with regard to technology and science. Wherever we go, we expect to find someone who speaks English. Often we do; but when we don't, we are left to the mercy of third-party translators.

Even when our clients, partners, or suppliers do speak English, we are at a disadvantage at the negotiating table. First, the use of interpreters gives the other side some subtle but very real advantages. For example, Chinese executives will sometimes use interpreters even when they have a good understanding of English. This permits them to observe our nonverbal responses. Alternatively, when we speak, the executives have longer to respond. Because they understand English, they can formulate their responses during the translation process.

Having to bargain in English puts a second very powerful negotiation tool in the hands of our opponents. On the face of it, bargaining in our first language should be an advantage, but even the most powerful argument fizzles when the other side responds, "Sorry, I'm not sure I understand. Can you repeat that please?" Bargainers listening in a second language have more freedom to use the tactic of selective understanding. It also works when they speak. Previous commitments are more easily dissolved with the excuse, "That isn't exactly what I meant."

A third disadvantage concerns our assumptions about those who speak English well. When facing a group of foreign executives, it is natural to assume that the one who speaks English best is also the most intelligent and influential in the group. This is seldom the case in foreign business negotiations. Yet we often direct our persuasive appeals and attention toward the one who speaks the best English, and thus we accomplish little.

Check with the Home Office

It is not always easy to identify the key decision maker in international business negotiations. Indeed, American bargainers become very upset when halfway through a negotiation the other side says, "I'll have to check with the home office," thus making it known that the decision makers aren't even at the negotiating table. In such a situation, Americans feel that they've wasted time or even been misled.

Having limited authority at the negotiating table is a common circumstance overseas and can be a useful bargaining tactic. In reality the foreign executive is saying, "In order to get me to compromise, you have to convince not only me but also my boss who is 5,000 miles away." Thus your arguments must be most persuasive. Additionally, such a bargaining tactic helps to maintain harmony at the negotiating table by letting the home office take the blame for saying no.

But such tactics go against the grain of American bargaining style. Americans pride themselves on having full authority to make a deal. After all, John Wayne never had to check with the home office!

Get to the Point

As mentioned earlier, Americans don't like to beat around the bush, but prefer to get to the heart of the matter as quickly as possible. Unfortunately, what is considered the heart of the matter in a business negotiation varies across cultures. In every country where we've worked, we have found business negotiations to proceed in the following four stages:

1. Nontask sounding
2. Task-related exchange of information
3. Persuasion
4. Concessions and agreement

The first stage includes all those activities that help establish a rapport. During this so-called small talk, executives sound (in the nautical sense) each other out and make quick but important judgments about competence, mood, and character. It does not include information related to the business of the meeting. The information exchanged in the second stage of business negotiations regards the parties' needs and preferences. The third stage involves their attempts to change each other's mind through the use of various persuasive tactics. The final stage is the consummation of an agreement, which is often the summation of a series of concessions or smaller agreements.

From the American point of view, the heart of the matter is the third stage—persuasion. We have a tendency to go through the first two stages quickly. We do talk about golf or the weather or family, but relative to other cultures, we spend little time doing so. We state our needs and preferences, and we're quick about that, too. We tend to be more interested in logical arguments than in the people with whom we're negotiating.

In many other countries the heart of the matter is not so much *information* and persuasion as the *people* involved. In China, much time is spent getting to know one another. Since the Chinese would prefer not to depend on a legal system to iron out conflicts, a strong relationship of trust must be established before business can begin. Americans new to the Chinese way are particularly susceptible to what we call the "wristwatch syndrome." In the United States, looking at your watch usually gets things moving along. In China, impatience signals apprehension and thus necessitates even longer periods of nontask sounding.

Lay Your Cards on the Table

Americans expect honest information at the negotiating table. When we don't get it, negotiations often end abruptly. We also understand that, like dollars, information must be traded. "You tell me what you want, and I'll tell you what we want." And there is an uncommon urgency to this request for reciprocity. Compared to the negotiation styles of managers in the 20 other cultures we have studied, Americans expect information in return almost instantly. We begin to feel very uncomfortable if something is not given in return that day. Reciprocity is important in all cultures, but because relationships tend to last longer elsewhere, foreign negotiators are willing to wait until later to see the cards of the people they're negotiating with.

Don't Just Sit There, Speak Up

Americans are uncomfortable with silence during negotiations. This may seem like a minor point, but we have often witnessed Americans getting themselves into trouble by filling silent periods.

The American style of conversation consists of few long silent periods—that is, 10 seconds or greater. Alternatively, in some parts of China the conversational style includes occasional long periods of silence, often in response to an impasse. We have found that American negotiators react to Chinese silence in one of two ways. Either they make some kind of a concession, or they fill the gap in the conversation with a persuasive appeal. The latter tactic has two counterproductive results: (1) the American does most of the talking, and (2) he or she learns little about the Chinese point of view.

Don't Take No for an Answer

Persistence is highly valued by Americans. We are taught from the earliest age to never give up. In sports, classrooms, or boardrooms, we are taught to be aggressive and to win. Subsequently, we view a negotiation as something to be won. We expect a negotiation to have a definite conclusion, a signed contract. Moreover, we are dissatisfied and distressed if we don't get the bigger piece of the pie. But even worse than losing a negotiation is not concluding a negotiation. We can take a loss—consoling ourselves that we'll do better next time. It's much harder for us to accept the ambiguity of no outcome.

Although we will see that persistence is important in some parts of China, the American competitive, adversarial, "persistence pays" view of negotiation is not necessarily shared by our foreign clients and vendors there. Negotiations are viewed in many countries as a means of establishing long-term commercial relations, which have no definite conclusions. Negotiations are considered a cooperative effort in which interdependence is manifest and each side tries to add to the pie.

One Thing at a Time

Americans tend to attack a complex negotiation task sequentially. That is, they separate the issues and settle them one at a time. For example, we have heard American bargainers say, "Let's settle the quantity first and then discuss price." Thus, in an American negotiation, the final agreement is the sum of the several concessions made on individual issues, and progress can be measured easily. "We're halfway done when we're through half the issues." However, in other countries, particularly in Eastern cultures, concessions tend to be made only at the end of a negotiation. All issues are discussed using a holistic approach, and nothing is settled until the end.

Because negotiators on the other side "never seem to commit themselves to anything," American executives invariably feel that little progress is being made during cross-cultural negotiations. Agreements are often unexpected and frequently follow unnecessary concessions by American bargainers.

A Deal Is a Deal

When an American makes an agreement, he or she is expected to honor the agreement no matter what the circumstances. But agreements are viewed differently in other parts of the world. W. H. Newman[6] put it well:

In some parts of the world it is impolite to openly refuse to do something that has been requested by another person. What a Westerner takes as a commitment may be little more than friendly conversation. In some societies, it is understood that today's commitment may be superseded by a conflicting request received tomorrow, especially if that request comes from a highly influential person. In still other situations, agreements merely signify intention and have little relation to capacity to perform; as long as the person tries to perform, he feels no pangs of conscience, and he makes no special effort, if he is unable to fulfill the agreement. Obviously, such circumstances make business dealings much more uncertain, especially for new undertakings.

I Am What I Am

Most Americans take pride in their determination and not changing their mind even given difficult circumstances. John Wayne's character and behavior were constant and predictable. He treated everyone and every situation with an action-oriented, forthright style. John Wayne could never be accused of being a chameleon—changing colors with changing environments.

Many American bargainers take the same attitudes with them to the negotiating table. Competition, persistence, and determination no matter what. But during international business negotiations, inflexibility can be a fatal flaw. There simply isn't a strategy or tactic that always works. Different countries and different personalities require different approaches.

Conclusion

Most Americans are not aware of a native negotiating styles. We tend to perceive bargaining behavior in terms of personality, such as the Texas "good ole boy" approach, or the Wall Street "city slicker" approach, or the California "laid-back" style. But when viewed through the eyes of our foreign clients and partners, we Americans have an approach to bargaining all our own. And this distinct flavor we bring to the bargaining table, this John Wayne style, is the source of many problems overseas. We must learn to adjust our behavior and gain an appreciation for subtler forms of negotiation.

Notes

1 This chapter is an updated and revised version of the *Harvard Business Review* article titled, "Negotiators Abroad—Don't Shoot from the Hip" by John L. Graham and Roy A. Herberger, July–August 1983, pp. 160–168.

2 This vignette is an amalgam of several similar incidents we have observed.

3 There are two hugely important books on this topic well worth the read on your next flight to and from China: Jared Diamond's *Guns, Germs, and Steel—the Fates of Human Societies* (New York: Norton, 1999) won a Pulitzer prize. Richard E. Nisbett's *The Geography of Thought—How Asians and Westerners Think Differently . . . and Why* (New

York: Free Press, 2003) is essential reading for anyone doing business in Asia. Use your jet-lag recovery days to read your reports, and the like.

4   We think this is the most often forgotten word in his sentence. He says "frequently," not "always" or even "most of the time." Through his use of the term "frequently," Smith granted that competitive behavior can have negative consequences for society and organizations, and cooperative behavior can be a good thing. This subtlety in his lesson is most often missed (ignored?) by our colleagues in the finance departments of our business schools and on Wall Street. Gordon Gecko actually should have said, "Greed is *frequently* good."

5   We note that this situation is improving as negotiation courses are now popular electives at many business schools around the world (e.g., The Merage School at the University of California Irvine and at Wharton). Some business schools have taken the bold step of requiring a negotiation course as part of the curriculum (e.g., George Washington and Harvard, the latter beginning in 1993).

6   W. H. Newman, "Cultural Assumptions Underlying U.S. Management Concepts," in *Management in the International Context*, James L. Massie, Jan Luytjons, and N. William Hazen (eds.) (New York: Harper & Row, 1972), p. 75.

THE CHINESE NEGOTIATION STYLE

A COMMON THREAD OF THINKING AMONG 1.4 BILLION PEOPLE?

How can we generalize about a billion-plus people? The geography, the culture, the political systems, the religions, the spoken languages and dialects, the economies—across greater China there are huge differences. Indeed, Westerners recently seem to enjoy the "hobby" of predicting when China will ultimately disintegrate, Soviet style. Can such a huge country with such a heterogeneous population possibly survive in an age of independent thinking and the Internet? Does just knowing that people refer to themselves as Chinese tells us anything about how they might behave at the negotiating table?

In fact, a thick thread of consistency does show itself in how Chinese businesspeople negotiate in commercial settings. This is because culture strongly influences behavior. Of course, so do individual experiences and personalities, but knowing people's cultural background is quite valuable in interpreting their behaviors and understanding their thinking. We know this to be true based on our years of studying and observing Chinese behaviors and listening to Americans reporting their beguilement in consistent ways.[1] Indeed, much of what we have to say here is forecasted well in a book written by an American missionary to China published in 1894! Arthur Smith's *Chinese Characteristics*[2] is still an interesting read.

Specifics about the distinctive aspects of the different regions of China and the diaspora are topics for Chapters 11 to 15. Here we discuss the aspects of culture that bind all Chinese people together, that have done so for some 5,000 years, and that will continue to do so for the foreseeable future.

The Roots of the Chinese Style of Business Negotiation

Land, Not Islands

As we said before, culture starts with geography. China is a continental country surrounded by the Gobi Desert, Siberia, the Tibetan plateau, and the seas. Even with their long coastline the Chinese had no maritime tradition of exploration and trade.[3] Instead, their closed harbors were opened only with European cannon during the nineteenth century. Their love was and is their land. Pearl S. Buck's 1930s classic, *The Good Earth*,[4] recognized the salience of their soil to the Chinese people.

Chinese philosophers have historically distinguished between "the root" (agriculture) and "the branch" (commerce). In such an agrarian society as China, social and economic theories and policies have always tended to favor the root and slight the branch. The people who deal with "the branch"—the merchants—were therefore looked down upon. They were the lowest of the four traditional classes of society, the other three being scholars, farmers, and artisans. A family tradition of "studying and farming" was something of which to be proud.[5]

For the last 1,000 years, the economic center of China has been the great alluvial plain between the last three hundred miles of the Huanghe (also called the Yellow River) and the Changjiang (Yangtze River), particularly that portion between Nanjing and Shanghai. Certainly other cities have been capitals, Xi'an and

Beijing are examples, but the population center of the empire has been here. The rich soil left by eons of flooding and the humid, subtropical climate combine to make rice cultivation ideal. Indeed, this region has always been one of the most densely populated areas of the world because of the productivity of the land. The Chinese refer to the region as the *Yu Mi Zhi Xiang* (鱼米之乡) (the land of rice and fish). And, historically, most of the fish have come from the rivers, not the seas.

Despite the burgeoning modern cities that represent the Westerners' views of modern China, some 70 percent of the Chinese workforce is still involved in the production of food and live in rural areas. More than half the food produced in China today is rice. Of course, historically rice was much more important than it is today; and this central activity of the people has left an indelible mark on the Chinese culture. Rice production requires community effort and cooperation. Irrigation, planting, and harvesting are most efficiently accomplished with the participation of small groups of people. In China these salient social units are primarily composed of members of extended families. Individual needs and desires were and still are deemphasized in favor of one's family. Loyalty and obedience to hierarchy are key elements that bind such groups together.

Relatedly, the crowding in "the land of rice and fish" made necessary a social system that promoted harmony and order. Living in close quarters with neighbors does not permit the aggressive individualism and egalitarianism so charactcristic in the United States, or in ancient Greece for that matter.

The Sages

Recall the importance of the teachings of Confucius as described in Chapter 2. With the goal of making peace in his land 2,500 years ago, he prescribed strict adherence to social hierarchy: rulers over ruled, husbands over wives, parents over children, and older brothers over younger. Thus, social hierarchy is a key in Chinese cultures and those influenced by Chinese culture even today.

Roughly contemporary with Confucius was Lao Tzu, the founder of Taoism. Pronounced "dowism," it provided a more religious view of the world. Fundamental was the notion of yin (the feminine, dark, cold, and passive) and yang (the masculine, light, hot, and active). The two forces oppose and complement each other simultaneously. They cannot be separated, but must be considered as a whole. See the familiar symbol here: ☯. The implications of this collision and collusion of yin and yang are seen to be pervasive, affecting every aspect of life from traditional medicine to economic cycles. According to Lao Tzu, the key to life was not synthesizing the two forces (in the Hegelian sense), rather it was to find "the Way" between them, the middle ground, a compromise. This philosophy allows that two people (negotiators) disagreeing can both be right. Different from their Greek contemporaries, both Lao Tzu and Confucius were less concerned about finding the truth and more concerned about finding the Tao, the Way.

The Language

The values of harmony and hierarchy are further promoted then and now in Chinese classrooms. Highly respected teachers deliver lectures. Students ask few questions and don't disagree. Memorization is the key pedagogy leading to the best scores on the historically all-important national exams. Moreover, much time is spent on learning to write the thousands of Chinese characters. Because these characters are pictorial in nature, the written language promotes an unusual concreteness in thinking. It's easier to represent pictorially flowers than philosophies. And because words are pictures rather than sequences of letters, Chinese thinking tends toward a more holistic, big-picture processing of information rather than the Western reductionism that breaks down problems into presumably solvable parts.

Over the years linguistics researchers have determined that languages around the world conform to family trees[6] based on the similarity of their forms and development. For example, Spanish, Italian, French, and Portuguese are all classified as Romance languages because of their common roots in Latin. Distances can be measured on these linguistic trees. If we assume English[7] to be the starting point, German is one branch away, Danish two, Spanish three, Japanese four, Hebrew five, Chinese six, and Thai seven.

Other work in the area is demonstrating a direct influence of language on cultural values, expectations, and behaviors.[8] Our own studies demonstrate that as linguistic distance from English increases, individualism decreases.[9] These studies are the first in this genre, and much more work needs to be done. However, the notion of linguistic distance appears to hold promise for the better understanding and prediction of cultural differences in negotiation styles.

Moreover, the relationship between spoken language and cultural values holds deeper implications. That is, as English spreads around the world via school systems and the Internet, cultural values of individualism and egalitarianism are spreading with it. For example, both Chinese Mandarin speakers and Spanish speakers must learn two words for "you" (*ni* and *nin*, and *tu* and *usted*, respectively). The proper usage of the two depends completely on knowledge of the social context of the conversation. Respect for status is communicated by the use of *nin* and *usted*. In English there is only one form for "you."[10] Speakers can ignore social context and status and still speak correctly. It's easier, and social status becomes a less important consideration.

Nisbett's New Ideas

Completely consistent with the differences described above are the recent findings reported by University of Michigan social psychologist Richard Nisbett. In his wonderful book, *The Geography of Thought*,[11] he broadly discusses differences in "Asian and western" thinking. He starts with Confucius (and the crowded farmland in which he lived) and Aristotle (and his island nation) and develops his arguments through consideration of historical and philosophical writings and findings from more recent behavioral science research including his own social-psychological experiments. While he acknowledges the dangers surrounding generalizations about Japanese, Chinese, and Korean cultures on the one hand, and European and American cultures on the other, many of his conclusions are consistent with our own work related to international negotiations, cultural values, and linguistic distance.

A good metaphor for his views involves going back to Confucius's picture. Asians tend to see the whole picture and can report details about the background and foreground. Westerners alternatively focus on the foreground and can provide great detail about central figures, but see relatively little in the background. This difference in perception—focus versus big picture—is associated with a wide variety of differences in values, preferences, and expectations about future events. For example, Nisbett's findings imply that while an American at the negotiating table will focus on the senior person on the other side, a Chinese will tend to be conscious of the entire team across the table, as well as her or his own team's feelings. Through the millennia Chinese people have learned to pay attention to all that is surrounding them. Because close neighbors have always hurt or helped them, the Chinese have developed a keen peripheral vision and insight. Nisbett's book is essential reading for anyone negotiating internationally, and particularly in China. His insights are pertinent to Chinese selling in Boston or Americans selling in Beijing.

Political History

Finally, the history that Chinese students read teaches a wariness of foreigners. As mentioned in Chapter 2, The Middle Kingdom has been attacked from all points of the compass—Chinese have died from Hun and Mongol arrows, and from Manchurian, Japanese, Russian, American, Vietnamese, and British bullets. But, the disruptions caused by these "barbarians at the gates" have been more than matched by internal squabbling, civil wars, and the ebb and flow of empires. The combination of famine, unstable political systems, and aggressive foreigners yields a cynicism about the rule of law and rules in general. Trust is invested only in family and a big bank account.

Elements of the Chinese Style of Business Negotiation

Guanxi 关系 (Personal Connections)

The English "personal connections" doesn't do justice to this fundamental concept of business negotiations with Chinese. Everyone knows about the importance of networking in the United States. But we also trust information and institutions. By comparison, the Chinese do not. For Chinese nothing is more important than one's place within his or her social network. The importance of *guanxi* has its roots in filial piety, but the notion is extended to include friends, friends of friends, former classmates, relatives, and associates with shared interests.

The medium of *guanxi* is reciprocity, or what the Chinese call *hui bao* (*回报*). But it's a reciprocity of a sort different from what most Americans are used to. Americans expect immediate reciprocity—"I make a concession, and I expect one in return at the table that day." For Chinese there's no hurry. Favors are almost always remembered and returned, the latter often not right away. This long-term reciprocity works well in the context of long-term personal relationships. In China, ignoring such reciprocity is not just bad manners; it's immoral. To be labeled *wang en fu yi* 忘恩负义 (one who forgets favors and fails on righteousness and loyalty) poisons the well for all future business.

Furthermore, cold calls and cold contacts with Chinese do not work. Potential Chinese business partners must be approached through their network, making use of *guanxi*. Even then, it takes time to be accepted and treated as an insider yourself, but the introduction by a mutually connected third party is requisite.

Guanxi also provides a source of influence during negotiations. Impasses can be addressed by consultation with influential connections. Indeed, mere references to one's *guanxi* bolster a negotiation position better than a mountain of technical information. Given the centrality of *guanxi* in the Chinese business culture, you should expect your Chinese counterparts to display their own connections. Where Americans value expertise, Chinese value *guanxi*. What some Americans might deride as "name dropping" isn't a matter of personal puffery for Chinese negotiators; it's a matter of necessity. And it's also a matter of important information for you, so pay attention.

Mianzi 面子 (Face or Social Capital)

It seems that all Asian cultures have some notion of "face": in Japan it is called *omoiyari*; in the Philippines, *pakikisama*; in Korea, *kibun*; and in Thailand, *krengchai*. The notion of face for the Chinese is closely associated with American concepts of dignity and prestige. *Mianzi* defines a person's place in his or her social network. It is the most important measure of social worth. Sources of face can be wealth, intelligence, attractiveness, skills, position, and, of course, good *guanxi*. But, while Americans think in absolute terms—she or he has dignity or prestige, or not—the Chinese think of face in quantitative terms. Face can be gained, lost, given, earned, or taken away.

Breaking promises, displays of anger, or other disreputable behaviors at the negotiating table can all cause you, or more importantly your client or business partner, to lose face. Public praise and social recognition are the means for giving a business partner face. However, going too far or praising too frequently can suggest insincerity. Care must be taken. You can also save your Chinese counterpart's face by helping him or her avoid an embarrassing situation, covering a gross technical error, for example. But, causing a Chinese business partner to lose *mianzi* is no mere faux pas. It's a disaster. It marks the end of negotiations. The only way to recover is to replace the "barbarian" on your side of the table. There are several ways to cause a loss of face. Casual kidding may do it. Insults, criticism, or a lack of respect for status will subtract substantially from your partner's *mianzi*. None of these is a good idea.

Shehui Dengji 社会等级 (Social Hierarchy)

The crowding and collectivism of Chinese culture provide fertile ground for hierarchy. Add in a little Confucian advice, and status relationships become central for understanding Chinese business systems. Recall that Confucius defined five cardinal relationships: between ruler and ruled, husband and wife, parents and children, older and younger brothers, and friends. Except for the last, all relationships were hierarchical. The ruled (wives, children, and younger brothers) were all counseled to trade obedience and loyalty for the benevolence of their ruler (husband, parents, and older brothers, respectively). Strict adherence to these vertical relationships yielded social harmony, that being the antidote for the violence and civil war of Confucius's time.

In Chapter 6 we list Americans as being the most individualistic folks on the planet, at least according the Geert Hofstede's studies of work values at IBM (see Exhibit 6.1). Hofstede also studied the importance of social hierarchy across cultures, measuring a dimension he called the power distance index (PDI). PDI measures the tolerance of social inequality, that is, power inequality between superiors and subordinates within a social system. Cultures with high PDI scores tend to be hierarchical, with members citing social role, manipulation, and inheritance as sources of power and social status. Those with low scores, on the other hand, tend to value equality and cite knowledge and respect as sources of power. Thus, people from cultures with high PDI scores are more apt to have a general distrust of others (not in their groups) because power is seen to rest with individuals and is coercive rather than legitimate. High PDI scores tend to indicate a perception of differences between superior and subordinate and a belief that those who hold power are entitled to privileges. A low score reflects more egalitarian views. As might be expected, Hofstede reports high PDI scores for Chinese (PRC at 80, Singapore at 74, Hong Kong at 68, and Taiwan at 58) and a low score for Americans (40).

So by all accounts, status is no joke among Chinese. Age and rank of executives and other status markers must be taken into account during business negotiations with Chinese. Chinese tend to address others by their official titles plus their family names, such as Director Li, Manager Zhang, or President Chen. American informality and egalitarianism, "Just call me Mary," will not play well on the western side of the Pacific.

When the Communists took over on the mainland, one of their first actions was to give women legal rights equal to those of men. Officially, women have equal pay and equal status in the workplace. Women hold important positions in factories, offices, ministries, and the military. However, old hierarchies die hard. Confucian male chauvinism lingers in the PRC and certainly in other areas among Chinese. Indeed, the scariest metric regarding current discrimination of women is the lopsided population statistics favoring men over women. In the United States there are about 95 men for every 100 women, while in China there are 107 men. Such numbers reflect a preference for sons operating at all ages and the new prevalence of imaging technologies before birth. The good news for foreign businesswomen is that they will be considered foreigners first and will not be subject to the same discrimination as Chinese women are.

Finally, the requisite benevolence of the superior in the Confucian social system opens up a negotiation tactic not so available among Americans. Begging can work in the context of the right kind of relationship and the right circumstances in China. So-called appeals to the heart (*ren qing*) can play an important role in commercial relationships with Chinese businesspeople.

Renji Hexie 人际和谐 (Interpersonal Harmony)

The Confucian grassroots approach to peace preached interpersonal harmony as key. The saying goes, "A man without a smile should not open a shop (人无笑脸不开店)." Harmonious relations between business partners are essential for successful commercial negotiations and relationships with Chinese. While respect and responsibility are the glue that binds hierarchical relationships, friendships and positive feelings hold horizontal relationships together. Thus politeness and indirect communication are paramount—direct refusals are rare. Rather than saying no, Chinese negotiators are more likely to change the subject, turn silent, ask another question, or respond by using ambiguously and vaguely positive expressions with subtle negative implications, such as *hai bu cuo* (还不错, seems not wrong), *hai hao* (还好 seems fairly all right), and *hai xing/hai ke yi* (还行/还可以 appears fairly passable). The subtlety of these expressions, however, is hard to translate and explain in English. Only native Chinese speakers can discern the differences during a formal negotiation session, through consideration of their moods and intonations, facial expressions, and body language. Hearing what one wants to hear may not promote efficiency in communications, but it does promote harmony, at least in the immediate context.

Expressions of negative emotions are most inappropriate in negotiations with Chinese. "Getting mad" may work with Americans, but it most often ends talks with Chinese. The notion of venting anger and emotions makes no sense to Chinese businesspeople. We know. We've tried to explain it many times with little success to our business associates in Beijing and Hong Kong. American arguments and aggressiveness cannot only cause a loss of face (for both the angered American and the chagrined Chinese), but they will also most certainly destroy *renji hexie* and the potential for creative commercial negotiations.

Qundai Guanxi 裙带关系 (Nepotism)

Qundai guanxi is really an innate in-group collectivism, which is a key part of the Chinese cultural. We've already made reference to the importance of family in Chinese society. The extended family is the basic social unit. This is as true today as it has been historically. Indeed, Gordon Redding in his excellent book *The Spirit of Chinese Capitalism* suggests that Chinese owned companies seldom grow beyond the bonds and bounds of the extended family. This explains the fundamental distinction of what he calls a fourth kind of capitalism—different from the kinds of capitalism found in the United States, Japan, and Europe.

The importance of family in Chinese culture also challenges one of the fundamental precepts of the most important book ever written on the topic of negotiation—Roger Fisher and William Ury's *Getting to Yes*.[12] The book has been read by more people around the world than any other on the topic and contains some very good ideas about creative bargaining. We recommend it to you. However, a key bit of its advice—"separate the people from the problem"—makes no sense at all in negotiations with Chinese family-owned companies wherein nepotism is the glue that binds the organization together. Americans often preface criticisms with, "Don't take this personally." However, when one's family welfare is at stake, everything is "taken personally."

Family businesses are autocratic with the father usually in charge. Squabbles can break out in family boardroom meetings, but a united front will always be presented to outsiders. Moreover, persuasive appeals composed of benefits targeting individual negotiators will be of little or perhaps negative consequence. Benefits offered should be directed toward the welfare of the company/family.

All of this sounds strange to Americans who often work in companies that have rules against nepotism. Our point here is that things are different among Chinese, indeed, very different. And negotiation strategies must take into account the strong social and family ties that are prevalent in the Chinese business system.

The social leveling of Communism reduced the importance of *qundai guanxi* in the Peoples' Republic. In fact, it must be noted that since the Communist revolution in 1949, most of the wealth and resources in China have been controlled by the Communist Party. As such, powerful party members, princelings of the ruling elite, classmates of outstanding universities such as Tsinghua and Peking University, and colleagues have been often more important than family relations. But, everywhere else—Hong Kong, Singapore, Taiwan, the United States, even Europe, and so on—the concept is key for understanding the Chinese. And, as Communism continues to dissipate on the mainland, the salience of the concept of *qundai guanxi* burgeons anew.

Zhengti Guannian 整体观念 (Holistic Thinking)

Michael Harris Bond, a cross-cultural psychologist at Chinese University of Hong Kong, has written perhaps the most important book on Chinese thinking, *Beyond the Chinese Face*. In it he well describes a fundamental cultural difference in thinking patterns. In a variety of psychological tests Chinese children are better at seeing the big picture, and American children are better at seeing the details of the parts. He states, "Apparently the stimulus as a whole has more salience for Chinese; the parts of the whole for Americans."[13] Surely this holistic thinking of the Chinese comes from the years of learning the thousands of ideographs or characters. Words for them are more like pictures rather than the sequences of letters learned by Westerners. Thus, people themselves must be evaluated in the context of their overall social relations or *guanxi* in China. Americans' identities are more defined by individual accomplishments. Indeed, had Socrates been Chinese, rather than, "Know thyself," his motto may have been, "Know thy place!"

The implications of these differences in thinking patterns hold significant salience for business negotiations with Chinese. Americans tend to take a sequential approach to problem solving, breaking up complex negotiation tasks into a series of smaller issues—price, quantity, warranty, delivery, and so on—settling them one at a time, and the final agreement is the sum of the parts so to speak. Alternatively, Chinese negotiators tend to talk about all issues together, skipping around the issues, and seemingly never settling anything. This difference in style presents two major problems for Americans bargaining with Chinese. First, Americans get frustrated because discussions seem quite disorganized. Second, Americans cannot measure progress in negotiations because nothing ever seems to get settled. In the States you're halfway through when you've discussed half the issues. But with Chinese "settled" issues keep coming up again. Americans are getting ready to call it quits and get on the airplane home when the Chinese side may be about ready to settle. Indeed, in our current studies of Americans bargaining with businesspeople in Hong Kong, this difference is the source of the greatest tension between negotiation teams.

Chiku Nailao 吃苦耐劳 (Endurance or "Eating Bitterness and Enduring Labor")

The Americans and Chinese are famous for their work ethic. More than 100 years ago Arthur Smith listed "industry" as the number three trait behind only "face" and "economy" in his guidebook of *Chinese Characteristics*. But, the Chinese take diligence one step farther—to endurance. Hard work, even in the worst conditions, is the idea. Indeed, because Chairman Mao's 18-month Long March was endured, he was endeared to the Chinese people. And, while communism ultimately did do damage to motivation on the mainland, the innate industriousness of the Chinese people is showing through bright and shiny as the planned economy evolves toward free enterprise. The hard work begins in school. Long hours, long weeks, and long school years are prevalent in Chinese cultures. Kids in China go to school 251 days a year, while American kids only 180. This early socialization yields a work ethic admired around the world today. Where Americans place high value on talent as a key to success, Chinese see endurance as much more important and more honorable.

Our own studies of businesspeople in Guangzhou, Hong Kong, Tianjin, and Taiwan confirm such differences. Where American managers list analytical skills as most important for bargainers, Chinese list persistence, determination, and preparation as key traits. And we see Chinese diligence primarily reflected in two ways at the negotiating table. First, the Chinese will have worked harder in their preparations for the negotiations. Much midnight oil gets burnt in Hong Kong, Shanghai, Singapore, and Taipei. Second, your Chinese counterparts will have expectations about longer bargaining sessions than you. Combine jet lag and late night business entertainment with long hours in negotiations and trips to the cities listed above can prove exhausting experiences. Your Chinese counterparts know to take advantage of this circumstance.

Jiejian 节俭 (Thrift)

As mentioned above, Arthur Smith commented on Chinese thrift and frugality even back in 1894. Today saving rates in China exceed those in both Japan and the United States. Of course, it's no accomplishment to beat the U.S. savings rate since during the recent years it's often been negative. However, the Japanese are famous for their high savings rate at over 30 percent, and the Chinese rate has consistently exceeded that. Such thrift is encouraged by the long history of economic and political instability. In the United States we haven't experienced real economic "rainy days" since the 1930s. Alternatively, in China disruptions of the magnitude of our "great depression" gripped the country about once a decade during the last century.

Price will often be the crucial issue. We see this quite directly in our work with Americans negotiating with managers in Hong Kong. Among all the issues involved including quantity, product options, service contracts, terms of payment, warranty, and so on, price ends up being the central point of disagreement. You should know that your Chinese counterparts will pad their offers with more room to maneuver than most Americans are used to. And the Chinese will make concessions on price with great reluctance and only after lengthy discussions. Moreover, the combination of American impatience and Chinese patience further strengthens their strongly defended price positions. Finally, Americans should not be put off by aggressive first offers by the Chinese. Chinese negotiators do expect concessions to be made by both sides, particularly on prices. Indeed, they expect that everyone pads prices as they do. This is a case in which American negotiators will do well to meet Chinese expectations.

Linghe Tanpan (Zero-Sum Negotiations)

In Chinese cultures cooperation and trust among family members is standard procedure. Reciprocity and creative business negotiations among friends and acquaintances result from the degree of interdependence that has been established and the face invested in them. However, business negotiations with outsiders and foreigners take on a very different character, one more akin to the notion of zero-sum negotiations. All who write about the Chinese comment on this clear east-west difference. Chinese distrust outsiders and expect competitive negotiations with them. The fundamental notion of expanding the pie before dividing it up common in the West is not shared by them. Indeed, they expect to be distrusted, and they expect competitive behavior from you.

To carry this notion further, negotiations with outsiders can be seen as a kind of warfare where all the tools of the trade introduced by Sun-tsu's *The Art of War* can come into play. And warfare is a familiar theme for the student of Chinese history. The Chinese aphorism, "*shang chang ru shan chang*," literally translates as, "The marketplace is a battlefield." Moreover, battlefields have spies, offensives, maneuvering, and so on, and are generally places of destruction, not creativity.

The management implication here is simple. Only well-managed, long-term relationships with Chinese partners will result in anything resembling creative, mutually beneficial business negotiations. Since initial negotiations are apt to be zero-sum, they should involve relatively small numbers of dollars. Once trust is established and insider status is confirmed, then, and only then can the best kinds of substantial commercial relationships be negotiated.

Jiao Ta Liangshi Chuan (Threatening to Do Business Elsewhere)

When the persuasion starts in your negotiations with Chinese, you can depend on hearing about your competitors. Everyone commenting on the Chinese negotiating style mentions this particular tactic—threatening to do business elsewhere.

According to Fisher and Ury in *Getting to Yes*,[14] the best measure of power in negotiations is one's alternatives. Specifically they advise knowing your "BATNA," that is, your best alternative to a negotiated agreement. Considering ahead of time if you have others you might deal with is key. When the list of alternatives is long, negotiators can be confident. Fisher and Ury also recommend letting the other side know about your BATNA when it is a good one.

The Chinese version of displaying one's BATNA is a bit more aggressive and carries the additional implication that their talks with your competitors have already begun. That is, a good alternative by definition is one already inside one's network where *guanxi* can be brought to bear.

Chinese seem to use this tactic with little regard for its aggressiveness as perceived by most Americans. Because American negotiators tend to be in a hurry and tend to focus on "one thing at a time," the development of a symmetrical set of alternatives begins only when troubles crop up with the focal business deal. So most Americans feel like they're being "two-timed" when the "there's-more-than-one-game-in-town" threat is delivered. Americans get mad when the Chinese are just pointing out what they believe should be obvious to everyone.

Conclusion

The differences we have described between the American and Chinese cultures and styles of business negotiations are large. We have summarized them in Exhibit 7.1. Indeed, in many ways the Western approach and the Eastern approach are simply incompatible. Languages, values, and negotiation processes are about as different as they can get. However, business still gets done, and commercial relationships thrive across the Pacific because the opportunities and economics of cooperation are great. Moreover, when both sides take into account the many predictable differ-

SUMMARY OF DIFFERENCES IN AMERICAN AND CHINESE NEGOTIATION STYLES

CATEGORY	AMERICAN	CHINESE
Basic cultural values/ ways of thinking	Individualism	Collectivism
	Egalitarianism	Hierarchy
	Information-oriented	Relationship-oriented
	Focus, foreground, object	Big picture, background, environment
	Reductionism	Holism
	Content	Context
	The truth	The way, compromise
Negotiation process		
1. Nontask sounding	Short	Long, expensive
	Informal	Formal
	Cold calls	Intermediaries
2. Task-related exchange of information	Full authority	Limited authority
	Directness	Indirectness
	"Cards on the table"	Intermediaries
	Proposals first	Explanations first
3. Persuasion	Aggressive, persuasive tactics (threats, promises, arguments, and logic), "You need this."	Questions, competing offers, delays
4. Concessions and agreement	Sequential Goal = "a good deal"	Holistic Goal = long-term relationship

Exhibit 7.1   Summary of Differences in American and Chinese Negotiation Style

ences in expectations, values, and behaviors, business can be conducted more efficiently and with more creativity and more mutual gain. The next few chapters provide specific advice for Americans at each stage of their negotiations with Chinese business associates. That is, a road map is provided for avoiding the obstacles that the cultural differences present.

Notes

1   John Graham began his systematic studies of Chinese negotiation styles in the early 1980s. He continues that work today with colleagues from Dalian, Hong Kong, and Taipei. Mark Lam began doing business with China in the mid-1980s and now focuses on Chinese-American commercial and legal activities with emphasis on high-technology and intellectual property matters. He is a University of California JD/MBA and is fluent in Mandarin, Cantonese, and Fukienese (a Chinese dialect widely spoken in the southeast coastal province of Fujian, most parts of Southeast Asia, and Taiwan).

2   Arthur H. Smith, *Chinese Characteristics*, 2nd ed. (New York: Revell, 1894).

3   There is an exception to this rule. Huge Chinese trading junks plied the oceans about 70 years before Columbus, and some argue that they visited the Americas at the time. See Gavin Menzies' *1421, the Year China Discovered America* (New York: Morrow, 2003) if you enjoy historical controversies.

4   The classic portrayal of the life of Chinese peasants Wang-Lung and O-Lan. Awarded the Pulitzer Prize for fiction in 1932 and the William Dean Howells Medal for the most distinguished work of American fiction published in the period 1930–1935 in 1935.

5   Fung Yu-Lan, *A Short History of Chinese Philosophy: A Systematic Account of Chinese Thought from Its Origins to*

the Present Day, reissue ed. (New York: Free Press, 1997), pp. 17–19.

6   For the most comprehensive representation of global linguistic trees, see Jiangtian Chen, Robert R. Sokal, and Merrit Ruhlen, "Worldwide Analysis of Genetic and Linguistic Relationships of Human Populations," *Human Biology*, August 1995, 67(4), pp. 595–612.

7   We appreciate the ethnocentricity in using English as the starting point. However, the linguistic trees can be used to measure distance from any language. For example, analyses using French or Japanese as the starting point have proven useful as well.

8   Lera Boroditsky, "Does Language Shape Thought? Mandarin and English Speakers' Conceptions of Time," *Cognitive Psychology*, 2001, 43, pp. 1–22.

9   Joel West and John L. Graham, "A Linguistics Based Measure of Cultural Distance and Its Relationship to Managerial Values," *Management International Review*, 2004, 44(3), pp. 239–260.

10 In English there was historically a second person form. That is, "thee" was the informal form up until the last century. Even in some Spanish-speaking countries such as Costa Rica, the "tu" is being dropped in a similar manner.

11 Richard Nisbett, *The Geography of Thought* (New York: Free Press, 2003).

12 The 1981 original (New York: Penguin) has been published in a second edition with a third author, Bruce Patton (Boston: Houghton Mifflin, 1991). In the second edition the second chapter is still "Separate the People from the Problem."

13 Michael Harris Bond, *Beyond the Chinese Face* (Oxford: Oxford University Press, 1991).

14 Roger Fisher, William Ury, and Bruce Patton, *Getting to Yes: Negotiating Agreement without Giving In* (New York: Penguin, 1991).

CHAPTER 8

PREPARATIONS FOR NEGOTIATIONS

James Sebenius and his colleagues at the Harvard Negotiation Program have most eloquently argued for the importance of preparation for negotiations.[1] Certainly we agree that whom you send, how your organize the meetings among the different partners, and when and where you meet can all have dramatic impacts on negotiation processes and outcomes, particularly in China. What happens before you get to the negotiation table must be managed adroitly. Indeed, even though this is perhaps the luckiest chapter in the book—number 8—it would still be most imprudent to depend on your luck at this stage!

Selecting the Best Negotiating Team

The initial step in business negotiations is often the selection of company representatives. Negotiators come from all ranks of firms, depending on the size of the firms involved and the size and importance of the transaction. Selection of the best representative can make or break a business deal. More than one American company has found that sending the wrong person to handle negotiations in China has led to failures.

Key Bargainer Characteristics

We have surveyed business people in four regions of Greater China to learn what traits they consider important for their *domestic* negotiations. We compare the Chinese opinions to what American managers have had to say in Exhibit 8.1.

A quick look at the exhibit suggests the following: Regarding their negotiations at home, the Chinese emphasize preparation and planning skills, and the Americans do not. Indeed, American negotiators generally do a poor job of preparing vis-à-vis their Chinese counterparts. Thus, we invest time later in the chapter on this key area. Alternatively, the Americans list analytical abilities and integrity, and the Chinese do not. Ability to win respect of negotiation partners is shared across cultures. Perhaps the American and Hong Kong lists are the most similar, emphasizing verbal expression and thinking clearly under pressure.

So, whom do we send to China? These survey results suggest the kind of negotiators you might see across the table in each of the regions of China. However, our wider reading of the literature on *international* negotiations, our continuing research on the topic, our interviews with experienced bargainers, and our own experiences as negotiators in Chinese-American business transactions all suggest a somewhat different list of bargainer characteristics to be particularly important in Chinese negotiations. They are:

1. Listening ability
2. Interpersonal orientation
3. Willingness to use team assistance
4. Self-confidence
5. High aspirations
6. Social competence
7. Influence at headquarters
8. Language skills

UNITED STATES	CHINA (TIANJIN)	CHINA (GUANGZHOU)	HONG KONG	TAIWAN
Thinking clearly under pressure	Ability to perceive and exploit power	Persistence and determination	Preparation and planning skills	Persistence and determination
Verbal expression	Ability to win respect	Preparation and planning skill	Thinking clearly under pressure	Ability to win respect
Analytical ability	Problem-solving skills	Judgment and intelligence	Reliability and industriousness	Judgment and intelligence
Ability to win respect	Preparation and planning skills	Ability to win respect	Self-confidence	Preparation and planning skills
Integrity	Attractive personality	Competitiveness	Verbal expression	Attractive personality

Exhibit 8.1 The Top Five Negotiator Traits

Representatives with these qualities should be sought to fill temporary or more permanent positions negotiating with Chinese. The eight key bargainer characteristics and the reasons for their importance are further described below.

Listening Ability

The ability to listen is crucial in any bargaining context. Negotiation is by definition joint decision making. And decisions should be made with as much information as possible, including information about the client's or partner's needs and preferences. In order to achieve the most favorable bargaining solution for both sides, bargainers must be alert to all the subtle indications of clients' real interests. Also, good listening is the initial step in persuasion. Before trying to change the minds of those across the bargaining table, it is best to determine, through good questions and attentive listening, what the other side needs to know. There is little point in extolling the virtues of one's product when one's potential customer already believes it is the best available or when quick delivery is foremost in his or her mind. Finally, in international transactions one's listening abilities are put to the most difficult test—ascertaining meaning in the context of less than fluent English and different nonverbal vocabularies.

Interpersonal Orientation

This characteristic includes two aspects. First, bargainers must attend to a client's or supplier's behavior; second, they must respond accordingly. Successful bargainers who have high interpersonal orientations adjust their bargaining approach according to the situation and the behavior of their bargaining partners. When clients take a competitive approach, bargainers behave competitively. When clients are cooperative, bargainers respond in kind. Because negotiation styles differ from country to country (and person to person), taking a flexible approach to negotiations, or "playing the chameleon," is important.

Willingness to Use Team Assistance

Willingness to use team assistance can make a crucial difference in international business negotiations Expertise in technical details, financial matters, cultural considerations, and the all-important maintenance of personal relationships is simply too much to expect of one person—even an American executive! Application engineers, financial analysts, interpreters, and foreign agents should be included and used when appropriate. The additional expense may be an important and worthwhile investment. Also, observation of negotiations can be a valuable training experience for younger members of an organization. Even if they add little to the discussion, their presence may make a difference.

Self-Confidence

The job of representative is one of the most difficult of all. Bridging the gap between companies and cultures can be exhausting work. Negotiations are being conducted not only with clients but also with the home office. Clients question your company's policies. Sales managers question the time and money you invest in building personal relationships, and so on. Self-confidence, or belief in one's own ideas, will be an important personal asset for those working in such situations of role ambiguity.

High Aspirations

High expectations regarding the business deal are key. One of the basic lessons of the hundreds of bargaining studies mentioned earlier is that bargainers who ask for more in the beginning end up getting more. Thus, given two otherwise equal executives, the one with higher aspirations is the better one to send.

Social Competence

The importance of personal relationships in business negotiations are very much a social activity, particularly in China. Social competence, the ability to get along with other people, not only smoothes the social contact points but also tends to encourage the flow of information from the other side of the table. Thus better, more informed decisions can be made regarding the business deal.

Influence at Headquarters

Having influence at home is particularly important in international negotiations. We mention above the difficulty of the international representative's job—breaking through both organizational and cultural barriers. Many representatives we have interviewed suggest that the toughest part of business negotiations is selling the agreement to headquarters. Moreover, there is danger in presenting the other side's point of view too well—your own management might trust you less. In choosing a representative for negotiations in a foreign country, influence at headquarters will be a criterion worth much consideration.

Language Skills

No bargainer characteristic is more important in China, yet more ignored, than the possession of Chinese language skills. Whenever we talk to groups of executives, we ask them what they're looking for in graduating business students. Almost always, the first thing mentioned is good communication skills. Letter and report writing and presentations to clients and internal groups are crucial parts of "making things happen" in the United States. In our business schools, we emphasize the development of such skills. We give our students instructions, practice, and feedback.

Now comes the paradox. As the markets of American companies become more global, why aren't managers asking for students with foreign language skills? In American industry, at the present time, there is still little payoff for fluency in Chinese or Spanish. In fact, the lockstep curricula in most business schools almost preclude mastery of the language necessary to make things happen in a foreign country.

Many American executives who lack fluency in foreign languages argue that English is the international business language. And when American firms dominated world markets in the 1960s and 1970s, this was true. But now the Chinese can choose between American, Japanese, German, and even Korean suppliers. Indeed, during the 1990s the Koreans spent millions of dollars on Chinese language lessons in preparation for their growing trade with the People's Republic of China. Their investment has paid off handsomely in China, particularly in the northern parts.

Management Implications

Hiring young executives with language skills and foreign living experiences is crucial. Business schools are burgeoning in Asia, and perhaps the best managers to represent your firm in China will be graduates of these new business and law schools. Also, folks that have immigrated from Chinese speaking countries will prove particularly valuable for both their language and cultural skills. But it's also never too late to gain something from language training yourself. As soon as you begin to study Chinese, you begin to have a greater appreciation for the deeper nuances of the culture. As soon as you learn that there is more than one way to say "you" in Chinese, you begin to understand how social rank influences not just conversational style but also all behaviors and thinking in China.

Other Factors

Patience is critical in China. Negotiations and decisions take longer—particularly the early stages of nontask sounding and information exchanges. Also, quiet men and women should be sent to China. By quiet we mean individuals who are good listeners, are comfortable with silence, and are generally respectful of other people.

Another concern is ethnocentrism. We all suffer from this to a degree. But even those with the broadest views will be put to the test in China. Individuals harboring chauvinistic cultural attitudes will almost always do poorly in China, where mutual respect and deference anchors all interpersonal contact. A curious mind, a genuine tolerance, and interest in how folks do things in different places will all be helpful. Finally, while China has five-star hotels, the fast-developing country itself is not a five-star hotel. So, a personal ruggedness will also make a difference.

American Women as Negotiators

The gender bias against women managers that exists in some countries, coupled with myths harbored by American managers, creates hesitancy among U.S. multinational companies to offer women international assignments. Although women constitute nearly half of the U.S. workforce, they represent relatively small percentages of the employees who are chosen for international assignments—only 18 percent.

A key to success for either men or women often hinges on the strength of a firm's backing. When a woman manager receives training and the strong backing of her firm, she usually receives the respect commensurate with the position she holds and the firm she represents. For success, a woman needs a title that gives immediate credibility in the culture in which she is working, and a support structure and reporting relationship that will help her get the job done.[2] In short, with the power of the corporate organization behind her, resistance to her as a woman either does not materialize or is less troublesome than anticipated. Once business negotiations begin, the willingness of a business host to engage in business transactions and the respect shown to a foreign businessperson grow or diminish depending on the business skills he or she demonstrates, regardless of gender. As one executive stated, "The most difficult aspect of an international assignment is getting sent, not succeeding once sent."

Finally, there is good evidence that gender discrimination may be less of a problem in China than in the United States. Recall our story about the critical effectiveness of GM's Shirley Young in

Chapter 1. Perhaps the most important accomplishment of Chairman Mao may have been the promotion of the slogan, "Women hold up half the sky." His recognition of the wastefulness caused by Confucius's sexist views has led directly to more gender equality in China. And then there is Xie Qihua, CEO of China's biggest steel company—*Fortune*[3] relates her story:

> *A fierce intellect and a strong interest in all things technical helped propel 61-year-old Xie Qihau to the top of Shanghai Baosteel, China's largest steel company. The highest-ranking female corporate executive in China, she graduated with an engineering degree from Beijing's Tsinghua University in 1968 and joined Baoshan Steel (a predecessor company) when it was founded in 1978. She climbed steadily through the ranks, becoming general manager in 1994, then president and chairman in 2000. Under her leadership the state-owned company has grown rapidly, earning a place on the* Fortune *Global 500 for the first time in 2003 (revenues $14.5 billion). She has initiated a series of sweeping changes at Baosteel to make it more competitive— including offering salaries as high as $48,000 to top executives— and has aggressively pushed the company's expansion outside China. A Shanghai native, Xie prefers to keep a low profile. She doesn't travel abroad much and dresses in conservative pantsuits. She is clearly in command at a company whose executives are predominantly men. "It doesn't matter that I am a woman," Xie says, "as long as they listen when I talk."*

Our point here? Chinese men will also listen to American women executives.

Composing the Team

The next considerations are how many negotiators to send and what levels of management are appropriate. The "I can go it alone" style of American bargainers suggests sending one negotiator (usually middle management) with authority to sign. However, decisions regarding negotiation team composition must be made with consideration of the Chinese side.

The first rule of negotiation team composition is to remember that in China talk flows horizontally across levels, not vertically between levels. Also, what is talked about varies from level to level. That is, when top executives are present, they talk to corresponding top executives about primarily non-task-related matters. Executives at other levels may be asked questions (with short answers expected), but the focus of such meetings is the development of personal relations at the top level. When only middle managers and operational staff are present, middle managers confirm decisions and commitments to corresponding middle managers. Or, middle managers listen while operational staff members exchange information and try to persuade one another. (Given these circumstances, it is our recommendation that an American negotiation team should reflect the composition and behaviors of the Chinese team.)

Our final comment regarding negotiation team selection concerns interpreters. As we mention earlier, very few Americans speak Chinese. Thus, despite the disadvantages of using an interpreter, they are often a necessity. Particularly when substantive discussions begin, having your own interpreter will be important for two reasons. First, you will need to brief the interpreter before discussions begin. Second, you will need to sit with the interpreter after the negotiations end each day to assess results and the interests of the Chinese side. Without your own interpreter neither option is open to you.

The best interpreters will be a help in the negotiations not only by translating, but by communicating the meanings intended. Interpreters can hurt or help you, and generally you get what you pay for. Their fees vary depending on the level of technical knowledge and competence you require. But you can never spend too much money on interpretation services. Interpreters should be briefed on the background and terminology of the deal but not necessarily on your strategies. It must be remembered that interpreters are third parties. Even though they are paid by you, they have different personal motives.

Negotiator Training

Many companies in the United States provide employees with negotiations training.[4] For example, through his training programs, Chester Karrass[5] has taught more people (some 400,000) to negotiate than any other purveyor of the service[6]—see his ads in almost all in-flight magazines of domestic American air carriers. However, very few companies provide training for negotiations with managers from other countries. Even more surprising is the lack of cultural content in the training of our government's diplomats. Instead, in most schools of diplomacy the curricula cover language skills, social and diplomatic skills, and knowledge specific to the diplomatic profession, including diplomatic history and international relations, law, economics, politics, international organizations, and foreign policies. Cultural differences in negotiation and communication styles are seldom considered.

Some multinational companies have added international negotiations training for their employees. We have worked with companies such as Allergan, Conexant, Honeywell, Intel, and AT&T in developing and delivering programs on international negotiations. In particular, with our consultation, Ford Motor Company has over the years offered its executives the widest array of international negotiation programs including courses on Japan, South Korea, and China.

Unfortunately, Ford is one of the only major American companies making such a commitment to training its executives. But even Ford's innovative efforts are really just a first step toward increasing effectiveness in its Chinese partnerships and operations. We have advised many of the best American firms to consider how their hiring practices—which, for example, place almost no emphasis on foreign-language skills—have not kept up with their increasingly global strategies. Training will help in the short run, but who will be running the global operations of American firms in 2020? In 2030?

We are currently developing a new international negotiations training program for another Fortune 100 firm that includes its European, American, and Chinese employees. The pedagogy of the week-long course will include videotaping of simulated negotiations and systematic feedback among the participants. That is, the Chinese managers will give the Americans advice for improvement, and the Americans will do likewise for the Chinese. We see this interactive approach to international negotiations training as the wave of the future.

Efficient Preparations

Any experienced business negotiator will tell you that there's never enough time to get ready. Given the typical time constraints of international negotiations, preparations must be accomplished efficiently. The homework must be done before bargaining begins. Toward the goal of efficiency in preparation and planning for bargaining with Chinese clients, we provide the following checklist

1. Assessment of the situation and the people
2. Facts to confirm during the negotiation
3. Agenda
4. Best alternative to a negotiated agreement (BATNA)
5. Concession strategies
6. Team assignments

Assessment of the Situation and the People

It is only common sense to learn as much as possible about a potential client or partner before negotiations begin. All kinds of information might be pertinent, depending on the nature of the contemplated deal. Various sorts of financial data and competitive information regarding American companies are available to other American firms. But similar data regarding Chinese firms will be either unavailable or unreliable. The first step in preparing for many such negotiations is mining the critical information from several resources. Of course, your key source of information will be your *zhongjian ren* (the intermediary) who introduced you to your client, partner, or customer in the first place. It should be clearly understood that knowing who you will be bargaining with in China is far more important than most Americans would assume. If you and your business associates step off the plane with no personal or professional perspectives on your Chinese counterparts, you can expect little success once the meetings begin.

Facts to Confirm during the Negotiation

No matter how careful the analysis and how complete the information available, all critical information and assumptions should be reconfirmed at the negotiating table. As part of the preparations, a list of such facts should be discussed among the members of the negotiation team, and specific questions should be written down. We have found again and again that surprises (both pleasant and unpleasant) often surface as part of this confirmation of facts.

Agenda

Most business negotiators come to the negotiating table with an agenda for the meeting in mind. We feel it is important to do two things with that agenda. First, write out the agenda for all members of your negotiating team. Second, don't try to settle each issue one at a time. The latter recommendation goes against the grain of the typical American sequential approach. However, in any bargaining situation it is better to get all the issues and interests out on the table before trying to settle any one of them. This will be particularly true when the other side consists of representatives from a Chinese company.

The Chinese side will seem less organized (even disorganized) with respect to an agenda. A Chinese agenda permits skipping around among selected topics. Perhaps most frustrating for Americans, the Chinese will often reopen issues that were seemingly closed. Indeed, consistent with the holistic approach described previously, for the Chinese nothing is settled until everything is settled. Patience will be key.

The Best Alternative to a Negotiated Agreement

Fisher and Ury, in their popular book *Getting To Yes*[7] point out that an often skipped crucial aspect of negotiation preparations is a clear definition of the best alternative to a negotiated agreement, or BATNA. They suggest, and we agree, that negotiators and managers must spend time considering what happens next if the deal doesn't work out. "Is there another Chinese firm to court, or should we just concentrate on our domestic business for now and try again later?" The BATNA sets the cutoff point at which negotiations no longer make sense. But it is more than a simple bottom line; it is a kind of contingency plan. Moreover, your list of viable alternatives defines your power in the negotiation. And be assured that you will hear about your competitors from your Chinese counterparts.

Concession Strategies

Concession strategies should be decided upon and written down before negotiations begin. Such a process—discussion and recording—goes a long way toward ensuring that negotiators stick to the strategies. In the midst of a long negotiation there is a tendency to make what we call "streaks" of concessions. We have found that the only way to avoid this is careful planning and commitment before negotiation.

Of particular concern is the American propensity to "split the difference." Never split the difference! Have specific reasons for the size of each concession you make.

Finally, you will notice very quickly that Chinese bargainers seldom make a concession without first taking a break. Issues and arguments are reconsidered away from the social pressure of the negotiating table. This is a good practice for Americans to emulate.

Team Assignments

The final step in negotiation planning is role assignments. We mentioned earlier the importance of the different roles in Chinese bargaining. Each American bargainer should understand his or her corresponding role. Other kinds of team assignments might include listening responsibilities or monitoring the agenda or concession strategies. And perhaps roles should be adjusted to circumstances or over time.

Manipulation of the Negotiation Situation

The next aspect of negotiation preliminaries is manipulation of the negotiation situation to your company's advantage. Some of the issues we raise in this section may appear trivial, but the most skilled negotiators and your Chinese clients always consider them. Particularly in a tough negotiation, everything should be working in your favor. If situational factors are working against you, it will be important before the negotiations begin to manipulate them. Also, management of situational factors may be important once the discussions have commenced. In the pages that follow we consider seven situational factors that we feel are particularly important. They are:

1. Location
2. Physical arrangements
3. Number of parties
4. Number of participants
5. Audiences (news media, etc.)

6. Communications channels

7. Time limits

All seven factors are ordinarily set before negotiations begin. All can and should be manipulated to your advantage. Any one of them can make the difference between success and failure in business negotiations with executives from China.

Location

The location of the negotiations is perhaps the most important situational factor for several reasons, both practical and psychological. The location of the negotiations may have a substantial impact on the legal jurisdiction if litigation is considered. But, just having the "home court" is an advantage because the home team has all its information resources readily available and all the necessary team members close by. Alternatively, the traveling team brings the minimum necessary resources, information, and players, and it stays in hotels. But perhaps a greater advantage the home team enjoys is psychological—a perception of power. If the other side is coming to you, that means you have something it wants. You are in control of the scarce resource, whether it be a product or service (you're the seller) or access to a key market (you're the buyer). Smart negotiators will always try to hold negotiations in their own offices. Short of this, a neutral location is best.

The location factor will be even more important when dealing with Chinese clients or partners, for it communicates power much louder in China. Thus, in business dealings between Chinese people, we see a strong emphasis on getting to a neutral location, such as a restaurant, karaoke bar (actually, we hope this is on the way out since neither of us can sing!), spa, or some other sort of off-site location.

The U.S. government's current restrictions on visas granted to Chinese executives deliver a big disadvantage to American firms. It will often be impractical to invite your Chinese counterparts to visit you given the frequent delays and denials of the American immigration officials. However, you may want to invite them to one of your offices in another country—recall from Chapter 1 that the General Motors negotiators arranged a visit to their Brazilian plant for their Shanghai Auto counterparts.

In the event that you do travel to China, there are some things that can be done to reduce the Chinese home-court advantage. One is to make arrangements for meeting facilities at your hotel (or your bank or a subsidiary's office) and invite the Chinese executives to call on you. You might argue, "I've already made the arrangements and everything is all set," or perhaps you need to wait for an important phone call. This may not help much, but it may help some.

Physical Arrangements

Once the negotiation site has been agreed upon, then comes the question of specific physical arrangements. American bargainers should understand that the physical arrangements of the bargaining room will be much more important and will communicate far more to Chinese executives than they would be to Americans. Americans value and feel comfortable with informality. Chinese value and feel comfortable with formality. If you travel to China, the Chinese will manage the physical arrangements of the negotiations (that is, unless you make the arrangements). The only advice we have for Americans in such situations is to ask the Chinese where to sit. They will have a specific arrangement in mind, and if you ignore their arrangement, they will feel uncomfortable.

If the Chinese are calling at your offices, then we recommend setting the physical arrangements to make them feel comfortable and more cooperative. If you wish to communicate that you are interested in the prospective business deal, then the most appropriate atmosphere will be a comfortable living room setting without desks or conference tables. Many chief executives have such furnishings in their offices, and for more reasons than one, a brief nontask encounter with the American CEO may be the appropriate first step. For companies that have frequent visits by Chinese clients, a specific room should be set aside and furnished as described.

Given that you wish to greet the Chinese visitors as honored guests, they should also be seated appropriately. But what appears to be the "best seat in the house" to an American may not be the best seat from the Chinese perspective. Two criteria are important to the Chinese: (1) distance from the door and (2) location of the center of focus in the room. The top Chinese executive will feel most comfortable seated farthest from the door and being framed by the focal object, which is usually a large painting or a window with a view. In most American meeting rooms these criteria are complementary; the focal point is farthest from the door. This attention to seating should also be paid to dinners and other business-related functions. We recommend place cards as an easy way to avoid a faux pas. Finally, if a couch is in the room, it will be best to seat the Chinese client there, by himself, because the size of the chair is another sign of status.

Number of Parties

In many trans-Pacific business deals, more than two companies are involved. Often, in addition to a buyer and a seller, there are other involved suppliers, engineering consulting firms, banks, trading companies, and government officials. Generally, the more parties involved, the more complex and more difficult the negotiations. Our American impatience often leads us to try to get everyone together to hammer out an agreement. Such attempts almost always end in frustration. It is our recommendation that negotiations include as few parties as possible—hopefully just representatives of the two primary companies. If more than one other party is involved, we recommend a lobbying approach, which includes meeting with the separate parties individually before calling everyone together.

Occasionally, there may be some benefit to meeting with all parties in the early stages—as when everyone except the client agrees with you. But such circumstances will be rare, particularly when other Chinese companies are involved. You should be aware that Chinese companies will try to use this approach. In response you should always ask who is going to be involved and why. If you learn that more than the principals will be involved and you feel the reason is insufficient, you might suggest that things may be "simpler" without additional people. Alternatively, if you plan to bring along a third party, you should let the Chinese know ahead of time and be prepared with a good explanation.

Number of Participants (people at the table)

In negotiations, Americans are almost always outnumbered by Chinese. We consider this to be a serious disadvantage. Earlier we mention the importance of finding out whom the other side is sending and then putting your team together in response. Moreover, you shouldn't hesitate to include additional members on your team such as financial or technical experts. The extra expense may be a wise investment.

In addition to bringing along extra team members, the relative numbers can be manipulated in other, sometimes unethical, ways. We have heard of Chinese negotiators who, when faced with large numbers of visiting negotiators, purposefully delayed progress. As a result, some of the other side's team members return home, and the difference in numbers is reduced. We don't suggest you use such tactics, but you should be aware that they may be used against you.

Audiences

In any particular business deal there might be a number of audiences that could exercise influence on the negotiation results. The Chinese National Overseas Oil Corp. (CNOOC) bid for America's number 9 oil company, UNOCAL, is a case in point. Consider how many audiences existed:

1. Other competitors—Chevron had also submitted a merger proposal to UNOCAL, as had other domestic and foreign oil companies.
2. Governmental agencies—FTC (antitrust), Congress (trade barrier saber rattling), Commerce Department, and the U.S. Trade Representative, a variety of security agencies.
3. The American public.
4. Petroleum industry unions.
5. The local and international media.
6. Other Chinese firms considering American acquisitions— e.g., Haier and Maytag.

Now consider how the two companies might have manipulated these various audiences to their advantage. All the audiences had an interest and a stake in the CNOOC-UNOCAL talks, and certainly some were manipulated through selective leaking of information.

We know such manipulations do occur in deals between Chinese and American companies. We are familiar with more than one case in which information was deliberately leaked to the news media to pressure the other negotiating party to agree to the terms of the proposal. It is difficult for the other party to say no to an already publicized agreement. However, extreme caution is advised in this area. Often, the action by one party may result in mistrust and a breakdown in the negotiations. In particular, trying to influence negotiations through leaking information to a foreign press (that is, Americans in China or vice versa) is quite risky.

You should anticipate that Chinese clients or partners may manipulate audiences for their advantage, particularly Chinese audiences with which they are more familiar such as local governments. You should also be aware of audience reactions that may help you, and you should know how to elicit such reactions when appropriate.

Channels of Communication

Face-to-face negotiations with Chinese clients are always recommended. Other channels of communication that might be used for negotiations in the United States simply are not effective or acceptable. As described earlier, the Chinese social system is built around almost continuous face-to-face contact. Too much of the important, subtly transmitted information can't be communicated in a letter, memo, fax, e-mail, telephone call, or even by teleconferencing. Moreover, it is much harder for Chinese bargainers to say no in a face-to-face situation. The social pressure and interpersonal harmony preclude negative responses, and these pressures are not as strong over the phone or in e-mail.

Time Limits

If location is not the single most important aspect of the negotiation situation, then time limits are. Generally, the side that has more time *and knows it* is in a stronger bargaining position. The side with less time is forced to make concessions in order to move the other toward agreement. The use of time can be a powerful bargaining tool.

Chinese bargainers have a big advantage when it comes to manipulation of time limits—an American's internal clock apparently ticks much faster and much, much louder. Impatience is perhaps our greatest weakness in international negotiations. We're interested in quick action and immediate results. In contrast, the Chinese executive tends to take a more careful approach to business transactions. It is much more difficult to rush a Chinese decision by imposing a time limit because (1) their more collective approach to decision making generally takes longer, particularly if the government is involved, and (2) the Chinese would often rather make no decision than a bad one. Alternatively, most Americans would rather risk a bad decision than let a potential opportunity slip by.

Americans in China can also manipulate the Chinese side's perception of their time limits by making hotel reservations for longer or shorter periods than expected. Most foreign clients will check the length of your hotel reservations as part of their prenegotiation preparation. Your reservations will influence their behavior. Upon your arrival, you will also be asked how long you expect to stay in China. Negotiators should be aware that something simple like a hotel reservation communicates much, and this channel of communication should be used to your advantage, not theirs.

Another factor related to the timing of negotiations is Chinese holidays. Negotiations might be scheduled to use their holidays (such as the Spring Festival around the Chinese New Year) as a lever. Such tactics are often used by foreign businesspeople against Americans—purposefully scheduling talks in mid-December, for example.

Finally, in some circumstances it may be possible to impose time limits on Chinese negotiators by setting deadlines. The imposition of time limits should be used only in extreme circumstances and should be accompanied by an explanation. Even a comment such as, "When can we expect to hear from you?" can translate into Chinese as inappropriate impatience. It is probably best to say nothing at all. American bargainers should understand the Chinese decision-making process, anticipate that things will move slowly, and plan accordingly.

Notes

1 James K. Sebenius, "The Hidden Challenge of Cross-Border Negotiations," *Harvard Business Review*, March–April 2002, pp. 76–82.
2 Nancy J. Adler, "Pacific Basin Managers: A Gaijin, Not a Woman," *Human Resource Management*, 26(2), summer 1987, pp. 169–191; and Nancy J. Adler, *International Dimensions of Organizational Behavior*, 4th ed. (Mason, OH: Southwestern College Publishing, 2001).
3 Annie Wang, "Holding up Half the Sky," *Fortune*, October 4, 2004, p. 174.

4 The Harvard Program on Negotiations provides a range
   of negotiations courses (www.pon.harvard.edu). Also,
   negotiations course are the most popular in MBA programs
   around the country: see Leigh Thompson and Geoffrey J.
   Leonardelli, "Why Negotiation Is the Most Popular Business Course," *Ivey Business Journal Online*, July/August
   2004, p. 1.

5 See Karrass's Web site for information regarding his
   programs: www.karrass.com. Other Web sites providing
   information about publically offered training programs
   and information on international negotiation styles are
   www.pon.harvard.edu, www.usip.org, www.iimcr.org,
   www.executiveplanet.com, www.etiquetteintl.com. See
   Marisa Mohd Isa, "Learning the Art of Refined Behavior,"
   New Straits Times, March 17, 2003, p. 23.

6 Lee Edison provides an interesting description of what he
   calls "The Negotiation Industry," in an article he wrote
   for *Across the Board*, April 2000, 37(4), pp. 14–20. Other
   commentators on training for international business negotiators are Yeang Soo Ching, "Putting a Human Face on
   Globalization," *New Straits Times*, January 16, 2000, p. 10;
   A. J. Vogl, "Negotiation: The Advanced Course," *Across
   the Board*, April 1, 2000, p. 21; and R. V. Veera, "MIT
   Preparing Students for New Millennium," *New Straits
   Times*, July 21, 2002, p. 5.

7 Roger Fisher, William Ury, and Bruce Patton, *Getting to
   Yes: Negotiating Agreement without Giving In* (New York:
   Penguin, 1991).

CHAPTER 9

AT THE NEGOTIATING TABLE

The most difficult aspect of an international business negotiation is the actual conduct of the face-to-face meeting.
Assuming that the appropriate people have been chosen to represent your firm and that those representatives are well prepared
and that the situational factors have been manipulated in your
favor, things can still go wrong at the negotiating table. Obviously, if these other preliminaries haven't been managed properly,
then things will go wrong during the meetings.

Nontask Sounding

Trust and connections can make a big difference in the United
States—indeed, sometimes all the difference. They're great to
have, but not essential. In China, they're essential. Getting started
in the States means: (1) a letter explaining your business purpose
and in it dropping a name or two if possible; (2) a follow-up call
for an appointment; (3) five minutes of small talk across the desk
(this is the nontask sounding); and (4) talking business. There are
a few more steps to the dance in China.

The Chinese are loath to use the legal system (attorneys and
courts) to clean things up if the business goes sour. They depend
on strong and trusting relationships between the people on both
sides to mitigate conflicts down the road. And, time and money

are *invested* in building those relationships *before* getting down to business. Five minutes of nontask sounding in the States can translate into five days, weeks, or even months of nontask sounding in China. There is no other way.

In the States we tend to trust until given reason not to. In China suspicion and distrust characterize all meetings with strangers. In China, trust cannot be earned because business will not even begin without it. Instead, trust must be transmitted via *guanxi*. That is, a trusted business associate of yours must pass you along to one of his or her trusted business associates and so on. So the key first step in nontask sounding in China is finding the personal links to your target organization or executive.

Those links can be hometown, family, school, or previous business ties. They cannot be just institutional—as in Japan where your banker can do the introductions. In China, the links must be based on personal experience. For example, you call your former classmate and ask him to set up a dinner meeting with his friend. Expensive meals at nice places are key. If things go well, his friend accepts the role of your intermediary (*zhongjian ren* 中间人) and in turn sets up a meeting with your potential client or business partner whom he knows quite well.

Often, your *zhongjian ren* or intermediary will then arrange a dinner the night before a visit to the client's offices. The intermediary will attend both. Your intermediary will insist that you spend big bucks on the dinner. This is important. Your sincerity will be gauged by the size of the check for this ritual sharing of food. That's why they have abalone as a $700 entree at the Peninsula Hotel in Hong Kong! Now for someone who grabs a sandwich at his or her desk for lunch, this will seem inefficient. However, $700 abalone may in fact be a great investment in China.

The talks at these initial meetings will range widely, even inanely from the American perspective. Even though your intermediary has "blessed" the relationship, your Chinese partner will still endeavor to sound you out in the broadest senses—trustworthiness, sincerity, integrity, competence, and so on. He or she will be looking for feelings of interpersonal harmony (*renji hexie*). And, there is no rushing this process. Indeed, this "empty questioning" may test your own *chiku nailao* (endurance). Moreover, you should take these questions as a sign of progress—they're interested.

At some point when you have "passed" the total-you test, the client or the intermediary will bring up business. This signals the end to nontask sounding in China. Only the client or intermediary can give this signal. We repeat—only the client or intermediary can give this signal. *Not you!* And even then, after brief discussion of business, your Chinese client may lapse back into more nontask sounding.

Most Americans make it through the dinner, but at the client's offices the next day they can't keep from making proposals. This is incredibly rude from the Chinese perspective. Even when they've been told by their own experienced staff to continue the small talk until the client broaches business, most high-powered Americans can't stand the "delays."

A vice president of a U.S. computer maker went to Beijing, hoping to close a deal with the Ministry of Education. The local sales team had been working with an intermediary on this case for more than six months. The intermediary arranged a dinner party with a deputy minister for the evening the vice president arrived. Many toasts to mutual cooperation were made at the dinner, and in accordance with his briefing, no business was discussed. The next day, the vice president paid a visit to the deputy minister. Sensing that the atmosphere was right from the previous night, but contrary to his briefing, the vice president asked a straightforward question, "So, when can we sign the contract?" The deputy minister politely replied, "Well, Mr. Vice President, you just arrived in Beijing; you must be tired. Why not take your time and see the city first?"

The management implications are clear. In China, always, *always* let the client or intermediary bring up business.

Other minor considerations: Business cards will be required, and small gifts (exchanged before leaving the offices) will be appropriate. For meetings in the United States, setting and formality will be marginally less important for operational-level executives, but not much less. Particularly when the Chinese firm is the one courted, more of a Chinese approach—long periods of nontask sounding including dinner at a very good restaurant or at your home—is advised.

Nontask Sounding for Top Executives

The role of top executives in Chinese negotiations is ceremonial. Ordinarily they are brought into negotiations only to sign the agreement after all issues have been settled by lower-level executives. On occasion, top executives are included earlier in the talks to communicate commitment and importance. In either case, their main activity is nontask sounding. Only vague statements should be made about the potential for a strong, long-lasting business relationship. Specifics must be left up to managers and staff.

All this can be hard on your liver. A chief of a major Post & Telecom bureau told a high-level sales manager, "You have to ask your boss to come, otherwise you are not giving me face! I am not going to deal with a small potato." On the eve of the negotiations, at the best banquet hall in the city the chief proposed a toast: "Let's drink to our friendship! We will have long cooperation! But if you aren't drunk tonight, there will be no contract tomorrow." The executive from the American firm matched him drink for drink and couldn't remember how he got back to his hotel. But, the next morning he was greeted with a big smile and a fat contract.

Getting top American executives to understand the importance of nontask sounding and to make the appropriate adjustments in their behavior may be difficult. One successful way has been to supply them with a list of appropriate questions to ask during the initial meetings with their high-level Chinese counterparts. Sports that are popular in China (such as soccer, table tennis, or basketball); family (especially if you know through the *zhongjian ren* that someone in his family has attained great distinction) and kids studying or staying overseas after attending graduate schools in the States are all good topics.

The American executives should be prepared with business cards in Chinese and should exchange them if the other side offers. However, when presidents of companies meet, business cards often are not required. Of course, American presidents should be well briefed about their Chinese counterparts in advance.

Finally, when high-level meetings are held in the United States, we recommend the Chinese approach. Top-level Chinese executives will not be prepared to bargain and will not be persuaded, even when in the United States. It's simply not their role. When American hosts wish to demonstrate the importance of the visit and the deal, we advise sending a limousine to pick up the members of the Chinese party at their hotel. The initial meeting between top executives should not be held across a boardroom table, and certainly not across the American executive's desk. Rather, a more comfortable living room or a private room in a high-class restaurant type of atmosphere is preferable. Remember, the key is to show sincerity or *cheng yi* (诚意).

Task-Related Exchange of Information

A task-related exchange of information implies a two-way communication process. However, when Americans meet Chinese across the negotiating table, the information flow is most often unidirectional—from the American side to the Chinese. Following are actions we recommend for American bargainers that will help them to manage efficiently the give-and-take of information.

Giving Information

The most obvious problem associated with providing information to Chinese clients will be the language. It is true that many more Chinese executives can speak and understand English than American executives can Chinese. English is, after all, the international language of business and technology. However, Americans should be careful of misunderstandings arising from the Chinese side's limited knowledge of English. Confusion can result when Chinese executives, because of politeness, indicate they understand when in fact they do not. When any doubt exists, Americans should use visual media (slides and brochures) and provide copious written support materials and an interpreter if the Chinese side doesn't have one. Even when the Chinese side does provide an interpreter, there may be critical stages of the negotiations in which your own interpreter should be included on your negotiation team. Also, be sure to talk to and listen to the executive on the other side of the table even when she or he speaks in Chinese. The interpreter should not be the sole focus of your attention.

Regarding written materials, imagine for a moment that you are a Chinese executive trying to choose between two competitive offers. One is written in your native language, and the other is written in a foreign language. Which proposal will you "like" better? Which company will you choose as a vendor? Proposals for Chinese clients should be written in the Chinese language. Perhaps you can get by with technical or engineering details in English, but the sections that will be reviewed and evaluated by upper Chinese management, particularly Party officials, must be written in their native language. We've heard more than once that translation of documents is expensive and takes time. But would you rather have your clients spending their time reading your proposal in their second language? And how expensive is losing the deal, much less, never establishing a business relationship?

Once you are comfortable with the language situation, you can turn your attention to more subtle aspects of giving information to the Chinese. The first of these has to do with the order of presentation. In the United States we tend to say what we want and explain the reasons behind our request only if necessary. That's why the task-related exchange of information goes so quickly. This isn't the Chinese way; they are used to long descriptions of background and context before specific proposals are made. Given this mode of operation, it is not surprising to hear the American executive's complaint about the thousands of questions the Chinese ask.

Clearly then, communicating your bargaining interests and your company's needs and preferences will take longer in China. Language problems and lengthy explanations will require more meetings, involving more of your people (technical experts) and more of theirs. We strongly recommend patience with this process and anticipation of increased time and money spent at this stage. But at some point American bargainers will have to terminate such questioning. While answering a thousand questions may be tedious but necessary, answering two thousand questions may not be productive. Our Mr. Shipwright from the Chapter 2 vignette had a variety of responses that may have worked better:

1. "Apparently delivery is a key issue for you. Can you remind me again why?"
2. Summarize your previous answer after something like: "I already gave that information to Mr. Chen yesterday, but to reiterate . . ."
3. Offer to write down the requested information so that it may be shared with all concerned Chinese executives.
4. Generally, a repeated question should be answered the second time in about three minutes. The third time it's asked the answer should be a one-minute summary. If the same question is asked a fourth time, it's probably a persuasive tactic and not information gathering. The appropriate response is then silence or a change of subject.

You should recognize one other thing about Chinese questions. The Chinese understand, and even expect, that some questions cannot be answered. But they will go ahead and ask them anyway. This is in sharp contrast to the American practice of asking only questions that will be answered. That is, if American managers ask a question and don't get an answer, they often are upset. This is not necessarily the case with the Chinese.

Finally, we recommend that American bargainers guard against the tendency to make concessions during this exchange of information. We have found that often American negotiators, impatient with the process, will actually make concessions during this second stage of negotiations, before they have even determined the Chinese negotiator's position, needs, and interests. It will take great patience indeed to avoid the natural urge to get to the third stage, persuasion, by making concessions in the hope that the Chinese will reciprocate.

Getting Information

Of course, getting information *before* negotiations begin is hugely important. James Sebenius advocated "mapping the players and the process" in international negotiations in an excellent *Harvard Business Review* article.[1] We agree, and your intermediary will be essential in this activity. Key information will be issues related to the larger context of your business—government or Party involvement and the larger economic plans of local, provincial, and/or even national authorities. Also crucial will be knowledge of the key decision makers. Often in family businesses it's almost always the patriarch, in state-owned enterprises it's the top Party official.

Hopefully, your Chinese clients will be courting your business. In such a situation they will be the ones making proposals and supplying you with more information than you probably want. But should your firm be initiating the contact or trying to make the sale, expect great difficulties getting feedback on your proposals. If you ask a group of Chinese executives what they think of your price quote and proposal, they will invariably say, "Let us *kan kan* (看看) or *yanjiu yanjiu* (研究研究)," which means, "Let us take a look," or, "Let us study (or do some research on) it."[2] They will respond in such a manner even if they think it stinks.

Let's review the reasons behind this seemingly unfathomable behavior. First, the Chinese executive wishes to maintain your face (*mianzi*) and interpersonal harmony (*renji hexie*). From his point of view a negative, albeit honest, answer at the negotiation would disrupt the harmony established. Finally, American executives are unable to read the subtle, nonverbal, negative cues that accompany the, "Let us study it." Another Chinese executive would read the nonverbal message that, "It stinks," but even the most experienced Americans won't be able to process this implied message.

In the United States, another key source of information regarding your client's reaction to your proposals is his or her facial expression. Most of us process such information unconsciously, but we all do pay attention to this channel. Indeed, many American executives report great frustration because of the Chinese negotiator's "poker face." Indeed, some Chinese managers report increasing their eye contact to demonstrate interest, but controlling their facial expressions to hide negative reactions.[3]

Indeed, the most efficient way to get feedback from a Chinese client is through the indispensable intermediary (*zhongjian ren*). For example, Chengdu Commercial Bank was interested in buying new transaction software from an American vendor. The sales manager did all the necessary groundwork including using the proper intermediary, and things had gone well. Finally, anxious why the final "yes" had not been given, the American seller engaged his intermediary to ask the head of the bank about the delay. The head of the bank disclosed to the intermediary that the deal was only in the planning stages and no decision to purchase was forthcoming. Ouch!

Persuasion

From the American perspective persuasion is the heart of a negotiation. In America we have a wide range of persuasive tactics that can be and often are employed to change our clients' minds. Among them are promises, recommendations, appeals to industry norms, providing more information, asking questions, and the more aggressive threats and warnings. We have observed Americans using all such persuasive tactics. However, the appropriateness and effectiveness of these approaches varies in China. Things are a bit more complicated.

Honeywell Bull had won negotiation rights for an order of 100 ATMs from the Bank of China. Toward the end of the negotiations, the Bank of China buyer asked for deeper price cuts. But to him it wasn't just a matter of thrift (*jiejian*). He appealed, "If the price isn't reduced further I will lose face." This is Chinese for, "The deal will be off, and we'll talk to your competitor." The Honeywell Bull executive responded that he had some room to move in the bid, but the lower price would not allow for training in the United States for the Chinese managers. The Chinese side then asked for a break and came back smiling in 10 minutes agreeing to all the terms. Some might conclude that for Chinese executives, seeing Harvard, UCLA, Hollywood, and Las Vegas is more important than a face-saving price reduction. However, the clever negotiator will understand that his staff's travel to the States gave much more *mianzi* to the Chinese executive than any mere price break.

As we mention in Chapter 8, when the persuasion starts in your negotiations with Chinese, you can depend on hearing about your competitors. Everyone commenting on the Chinese negotiation style mentions this particular tactic—threatening to do business elsewhere. The Chinese call this tactic *liangshou zhunbei* 两手准备 (or two-handed preparation). Of course, Americans do the same thing, but with more finesse perhaps.

The Chinese seem to use this tactic with little compunction. Because American negotiators tend to be in a hurry and tend to focus on "one thing at a time," the development of a symmetrical set of alternatives begins only when troubles crop up with the focal business deal. So most Americans feel like they're being "two-timed" when the "there's-more-than-one-game-in-town" threat is delivered. Americans get mad when the Chinese are just blandly pointing out what they believe should be obvious to everyone.

Another important factor in China is the context in which specific tactics are used. Aggressive influence tactics, which can only be used by negotiators in higher power positions (usually buyers), should be communicated through intermediaries and informally. And even then, only subtle and indirect threats, commands, and so on are appropriate. Getting mad ruins relationships. Loud voices and angry tones destroy even longstanding interpersonal harmony (*renji hexie*). So the intermediary is doubly important from the American perspective. First, he or she provides a method of more accurately reading Chinese clients, and, second, it makes available to American bargainers persuasive tactics that would be completely inappropriate during the formal talks.

To sum up, if an impasse is reached with Chinese clients, rather than trying to persuade in the usual American manner, we recommend use of the following eight persuasive tactics, in the following order and under the following circumstances:

1. *Ask more questions.* We feel that the single most important piece of advice we can give is to use questions as a persuasive tactic. This is true in not only China, but anywhere in the world, including the United States. In his book, *The Negotiating Game*, Chester Karrass suggests that sometimes it's "smart to be a little bit dumb" in business negotiations. Ask the same questions more than once—"I didn't completely understand what you meant. Can you please explain that again?" If your clients or potential business partners have good answers, then it's perhaps best if you compromise on the issue. But often, under close scrutiny, their answers aren't very good. And with such a weak position exposed they will be obligated to concede. Also, questions often put more information on the table providing leads toward more creative solutions. For all these reasons questions can elicit key information and can be powerful persuasive devices.

2. *Educate.* Condescension will kill this approach, so be careful. But, re-explain your company's situation, needs, and preferences. You might also make oblique reference to the "internationally recognized business practices" about which most Chinese managers are becoming more interested.

Some executives supply Chinese customers with information about their own competitors, again with the intent of education about the overall marketplace.

To make a tough sale of smart cards systems to Shanghai Pudong Development Bank, such education included not only delivery of the data sheets and proposals, but also a trip for the right bank vice president to Paris for a demonstration of the maturity of the technology. This convinced him, and today some 2 million smart cards are used in 1,000 ATM, 2,000 POS machines, and in all the taxicabs in Shanghai.

3. *Silence.* If you are still not satisfied with their response, try silence. Let them think about it and give them an opportunity to change their position. However, you should recognize that the Chinese are among the world's experts at the use of silence. If silence is a tactic you find difficult to use, you should at least be aware that your Chinese clients will use it frequently.

4. *Intermediary.* If tactics 1 through 3 produce no concessions, it will be time to change the subject or call a recess and put to work the intermediary. But rather than going directly to the more aggressive tactics, we recommend repeating the first three tactics using that important communication channel—the intermediary or *zhongjian ren*. The questions and explanations may expose new information or objections that couldn't be broached at the negotiating table.

5. *Aggressive influence* tactics may be used in negotiations with Chinese only at great risk and under special circumstances. First, they should be used only via the intermediary (*zhongjian ren*), and even then they should be used in the most indirect manner possible. Second, they should be used only when the American company is clearly in the stronger position. Even under these two circumstances, use of such aggressive persuasive tactics will damage the interpersonal harmony (*renji hexie*), which may in the long run be to your company's disadvantage. If power relations ever shift, the Chinese will be quick to exploit the change in events. However, if the

American side exercises restraint and maintains the *renji hexie*, then if and when power relations shift, the Chinese side will consider the American company's interests.

This point is difficult for most Americans to believe. But we have witnessed Chinese executives behave in this way several times. For example, a corporate vice president at Honeywell Bull threatened a senior executive at China Post with a lawsuit demanding final acceptance of a signed contract. The China Post executive responded, "Go ahead. You may win the case. But, you will be finished in the China market." At a subsequent meeting the Honeywell Bull country manager, schooled in the Chinese style of business negotiations and possessing a good relationship (*renji hexie*) with the China Post executive, was able to smooth things over by appealing to the interests of the long term. The customer responded, "This is the right attitude, I will see what I can do to expedite the final acceptance."

6. *Time.* If tactics 1 through 5 have not produced Chinese concessions, we suggest the use of time to enable the people you're negotiating with to consider new information and to reach a decision satisfying almost everyone involved on their side, from technical experts to Party officials. The Chinese rarely make concessions immediately following persuasive appeals without broader consultation. Indeed, the combination of collective decision making and social hierarchy (*shehui dengji*) can make things quite complicated on the Chinese side. Unfortunately, time is perhaps the most difficult tactic for American bargainers to use. We're in a hurry to solve the problem and settle the deal. "Letting things hang" goes against our nature, but it may be necessary. And hopefully, they will run into their time limits before you run into yours. Also, use of this tactic will require the cooperation and understanding of your home office.

Remember that the Chinese are skilled in the use of time as a persuasive tactic. Group decision making and the long-term approach to business deals seem to enhance the effectiveness of tactical delays for Chinese bargaining with Americans.

7. *Informal Arbitration.* The next persuasive tactic to use is asking the intermediary to arbitrate your differences. Let him or her call your clients and meet with them separately as a go-between. We have seen *zhongjian ren* successfully settle otherwise irreconcilable differences.

    A vice president of a New York–based software company went to Beijing to negotiate the distribution contract with China Post Research Institute. The appropriate meetings were arranged by an intermediary, a former senior executive at China Post. The first two days went well. Price, delivery, training, and warranty were no problem. During the third day, the discussion turned to intellectual property rights. The U.S. side insisted that any derivatives of the original software created by the Institute be owned by the U.S. company. The Chinese side disagreed, saying that the derivatives of the software were created by the Institute, so they should be owned by the Institute. In reality, the derivatives were useless without the original software that was owned by the New York–based company. Then the "face" issue kicked in, and the Chinese side ended the meeting. That night, the vice president and the China country manager met with the intermediary. The intermediary then called the head of the Institute and discussed other possibilities. The next day, both sides agreed that the derivatives were to be jointly owned, and the contract was signed.

8. *Top Executives.* Finally, if all else fails, it may be necessary to bring together the top executives of the two companies in the hope of stimulating more cooperation. However, such a tactic may fail, particularly if negative influence tactics have been used in the past. A refusal at this stage means the business is finished.

To conclude our discussion of persuasive tactics, we want to emphasize the importance of our recommendations. A mistake at this stage, even a minor one, can have major consequences for your Chinese business. American managers will have to be doubly conscientious to avoid blunders here because the Chinese style of persuasion is so different from ours and apparently ambiguous. Remember that the Chinese are looking to establish a long-term business relationship of mutual benefit. Threats and the like don't fit into their understanding of how such a relationship should work. You should also recognize that we are recommending adoption of a Chinese approach to persuasion when bargaining with Chinese clients and business partners. We realize that it takes longer, but in the end you and your company will benefit by such an approach. Finally, smart American negotiators will anticipate the Chinese use of the persuasive tactics just described.

Concessions and Agreement

The final stage of business negotiations involves concessions, building toward agreement. Negotiation requires compromise—as the Chinese say, "Finding *the way*." Usually, both sides give up something to get even more. But the approach used for compromise differs on each side of the Pacific.

American managers report great difficulties in measuring progress. After all, in America you're half done when half the issues are settled. But in China nothing seems to get settled. Then, surprise, you're done. Often, Americans make unnecessary concessions right before agreements are announced by the Chinese. For example, Tandem was eager to sell Non-Stop servers to China Telecom. The sales manager offered, "If you can take delivery next month, I will give you an extra 5 percent off." The purchasing manager responded, "We're not really in a hurry, but since you have some room, you might as well give us the price break." American bargainers in China should expect this holistic approach and be prepared to discuss all issues simultaneously and in an apparently haphazard order. Progress in the talks should not be measured by how many issues have been settled. Rather, Americans must try to gauge the quality of the business relationship. Important signals of progress will be:

1. Higher level Chinese executives being included in the discussions.
2. Their questions beginning to focus on specific areas of the deal.
3. A softening of their attitudes and position on some of the issues.
4. At the negotiating table, increased talk among themselves in Chinese, which may often mean that they're trying to decide something.
5. Calls for additional meetings, increased bargaining, and use of the intermediary;
6. They ask about things like overseas training.

As part of your team's preparations, it will be important to document concession strategies. When they're agreed to and written down before negotiations begin, it's easier for everyone on your side to stick to the "concession schedule," so to speak. Americans need to follow such schedules with care. Trading concessions with Chinese bargainers will not work because they view nothing to be settled until everything is settled. We advise making no concession until all issues and interests have been exposed and fully discussed. Then concessions should be made, on minor issues first, to help establish the relationship.

Finally, concessions should not be decided upon at the negotiating table. Rather, Americans are advised to reconsider each concession away from the social pressure of the formal negotiations. This again is a Chinese practice that Americans will do well to emulate. Having strategically limited authority can be an important check on runaway concession making.

Minor Distractions

Before closing our discussion of the process of business negotiations, it is important to mention briefly three Chinese behaviors that will seem rude to American bargainers but are nothing more than common habits for Chinese executives. First, the Chinese will often break into side conversations—in Chinese. Ordinarily, the purpose of a side conversation is clarification of something Americans have said, that is, getting the translation straightened out. Second, often Chinese executives will enter or leave negotiations in the middle of your comments. This reflects their busy schedule and a different view of "meeting etiquette." Finally, it can be particularly disturbing to be talking to a group of Chinese and discover that one, perhaps even the senior executive, is "listening while doing other things." Again, this shouldn't be taken personally; it simply reflects a different view of appropriate behavior at meetings. Further, busy senior Chinese executives can also be signaling that they are comfortable with how things are going—if they are not comfortable, they will remain quite attentive.

Conclusion

Implementing corporate strategies through business negotiations in China will remain one of the most daunting and interesting challenges facing American executives during the next few decades. Indeed, we might have said the same thing back in 1789 when Yankee clipper ships first plied the Pearl River passing Hong Kong on the way to Canton. Smart bargainers have always made money there. And the good news is that things are getting better fast in China. The Chinese themselves are working hard to catch up with and to compete with Western style enterprise. Despite the historical slighting of the "branch" (the merchant class), business schools are sprouting up all over the mainland. And Chinese students are flooding into the best MBA programs around the world and learning about concepts like corporate image, brand equity, and the ins and outs of intellectual property. The Internet is also making a difference, making efficient communication more available. While currently engineers and political persons usually lead companies, the future bodes well for the new business class. The two signs most telling of China's new direction have been their rewarded persistence about World Trade Organization membership and the invitations for Communist Party membership issued to private, capitalist entrepreneurs in 2005.

In a relationship-oriented culture such as China, there are huge advantages to moving first. Old friendships work their magic only when they are *old*! We recommend investing now in the Middle Kingdom, if only in a small venture. This activity will allow your executives and your organization to learn the game. You will be able to develop the *guanxi*, and your own staff will understand and grow the business there. Chinese language skills and cultural knowledge will continue to be crucial. This means selecting, promoting, and *trusting* the advice of your own Chinese-American staff and advisors.

Other than arrogance, condescension, and ethnocentricity, *time* has always been the American bargainer's biggest handicap in international business. Impatience will be your enemy once you get to China. But impatience is your friend when it comes to making the decision about whether to go or not. We counsel studied entry, but there is no better time than now to begin your work.

Notes

1 James K. Sebenius, "The Hidden Challenge of Cross-Border Negotiations," *Harvard Business Review*, March 2002, pp. 76–82.

2 There is a Chinese joke about yanjiu. In Chinese cigarette is yan (菸) and wine is jiu (酒). So, it means some smoking and drinking will be required over this one.

3 Please see Vivian C. Sheer and Ling Chen, "Successful Sino-Western Business Negotiation," *Journal of Business Communication*, January 2003, pp. 50–85.

CHAPTER 10

AFTER NEGOTIATIONS

Once verbal agreements have been reached, it is time to consider what follows the negotiations. In the United States executives talk of "concluding business deals." In China executives speak of "establishing business relationships." We've already discussed how such differing views influence negotiation processes. Now we turn to the subject of how they influence post-negotiation procedures.

Contracts

Contracts between American firms are often longer than 100 pages and include carefully worded clauses regarding every aspect of the agreement. American lawyers go to great lengths to protect their companies against all circumstances, contingencies, and actions of the other party. In a typical American commercial contract conditional phrases such as, "If . . .," "In the event . . .," and "Should . . .," are often used more than 50 times. The best contracts are the ones so tightly written that the other party would not think of going to court to challenge any provision. Our adversarial system requires such contracts.

In China, as in most other countries, legal systems are not depended upon to resolve disputes. Indeed, the term "disputes" doesn't reflect how a business relationship should work. Each side should be concerned about the mutual benefits of the relationship and therefore should consider the interests of the other. Consequently, in China written contracts are very short—two to three pages—are purposefully loosely written, and primarily contain comments on principles of the relationship. From the Chinese point of view, the American emphasis on tight contracts is tantamount to planning the divorce before the marriage. Simply stated, contracts in China do not fulfill the same purposes as they do in the United States.

So what form should a contract between a Chinese and an American firm take? There is no simple answer. It may have to be negotiated. It depends somewhat on the size and importance of the agreement and the size and experiences of the firms involved. Generally, larger deals justify the extra expense of including legal review by both Chinese and American lawyers. Large Chinese firms with histories of American contracts will understand the Americans' need for detailed contracts. Some Chinese, recognizing the increasing frequency of litigation between U.S. and Chinese firms, will specify the American approach. It is the executives of smaller Chinese firms, inexperienced in the ways of Americans, who may become suspicious when faced with lengthy, fully detailed contracts. In these cases, it will be particularly important to explain the necessity of the legal review and detailed contract. However, you should realize that, even with the most complete explanation, not all Chinese executives will understand.

An American style contract will also cause considerable delays in signing. Chinese lawyers will tediously consider every detail. One rule of thumb suggests that every clause takes an entire day. Thus, something your legal counsel ordinarily reviews in three days will take at least three weeks in Shanghai.

A California firm was selling training services for executives to First Auto Works, one of China's largest companies. All the prices, content, and other terms and conditions were agreed to, and the American firm sent the contract for signatures. However, the Chinese side balked at the "boiler plate" in the contract. The Chinese side simply hadn't seen such standard provisions, and it took another frustrating month before things were finally straightened out.

Thus, it is difficult for us to make general recommendations regarding contracts. Many American executives of even the largest firms have been satisfied with a "compromise" contract when strong, long-standing personal relationships are involved. But each case is different. It is important that you and your firm push for the kind of contract you feel is necessary. Of course, your legal counsel should be consulted on this issue.

The key here is to understand that trust and harmony are more important to your Chinese counterparts than any piece of paper. They'll actually be more interested in what James Sebenius and his colleagues call the "spirit of the deal."[1] In China contracts are for reference only and currently mean little. Yes, they are becoming increasingly important since China has joined the WTO, but catching up to the American legal system will take decades. In the meantime, your Chinese counterparts will depend on interpersonal harmony.

Signing Ceremonies

Informality being a way of life in the United States, even the largest contracts between American firms are often sent through the mail for signature. Here, ceremony is considered a waste of time and money. But when a major agreement is reached with a Chinese client or partner, the Chinese will expect the top executives involved to meet and sign the contract with ceremony. We recommend American firms accommodate these expectations.

Headquarters' Assessment of the Agreement

Often U.S. negotiators return to company headquarters with an agreement, only to receive a mixed greeting. Executives at several companies have told us, "The second half of the negotiation begins once I return to the home office." Headquarters, unaware of the requirements of business negotiations in China, will ask, "What took so long?" Ordinarily, all compromises and concessions have to be explained and justified in detail. Moreover, commitments requiring specific management actions must be delegated and ordered. All this can slow implementation and performance of the contract. In the worst cases, when negotiator and home office communications have been poor, negotiators have been required to renege and start over. When this occurs, the Chinese client or partner will either bypass this executive, who has lost face, and talk to those considered the real decision makers or decline further discussion, thus ending the relationship.

It has been the experience of American firms that once the first deal has been struck with a Chinese client or partner, successive negotiations tend to proceed quickly. Therefore, it is generally not necessary to send a complete negotiation team when new issues are to be considered. Clearly, then, it is best to start with a small, relatively simple business proposal. Once the relationship has been established, substantial and complex negotiations will proceed more smoothly. This is the approach used by Chinese firms entering the United States, and it is a sensible strategy when American firms court Chinese business.

Follow-Up Communications

Just as personal considerations are important during negotiations with Chinese clients, they are also important after the negotiations are concluded. Obviously, you will be in touch with your Chinese clients and partners regarding the business of the relationship. But it will be equally important to keep personal relationships warm.

A formal letter should be sent from your top executive to their top executive expressing happiness that the talks have been concluded successfully and confidence that the new relationship will be prosperous and long lasting. But even more important will be periodic personal visits with your Chinese counterparts. The best way to keep relationships warm in China is investing in what Americans call "face time."

One final consideration is crucial when doing business with the Chinese. Avoid switching executives managing your Chinese business relationships. In dealing with American clients this is not much of a problem. Here the economics of the business deal are more important than the personal relationships involved. Managers often shift positions within companies and between companies. But in China executives stay with the same company longer than they do here. Moreover, Chinese executives are given longer-term responsibility for managing intercompany relationships. After all, much was invested in building the personal relations that make business between the companies work smoothly. So when American companies switch key managers, Chinese clients get very nervous. Therefore, such shifts should be made with great care and should be accompanied by new efforts of nontask sounding and rapport building.

Dispute Resolution and Modifications to Agreements

During the course of almost all business relationships, changes occur in the environment or to either partner. In such situations in the United States the conflicts arising from the changing circumstance would be settled through the use of direct and confrontational legal channels or, as is now more often the case, arbitration.

In China, given the same set of changing circumstances, companies would ordinarily resolve the conflicts through conferral. Thus, Chinese contracts often include such wording as, "All items not found in this contract will be deliberated and decided upon in a spirit of honesty and trust." When differences can't be ironed out through simple conferral, then the next step is to express concerns through the all-important *zhongjian ren*, who hopefully can mediate a new understanding. Rarely will confrontational and legal approaches be used in China, because they would destroy the harmony and trust required for continued business dealings, and the fledgling legal system is plagued by favoritism and inefficiency. Even arbitration is viewed negatively in China.

Our recommendation is to include an international arbitration clause in your contract in case conflicts arise. For example, "Any controversy or claim arising out of or relating to this contract shall be determined by arbitration in accordance with the rules of the . . ." But even though such measures are included in the contract, we suggest a Chinese approach to conflict resolution. That is, approach the dispute from a cooperative standpoint and talk with your Chinese client or partner. If you have maintained the harmony and trust and since you have an honest mutual interest in the deal, problems can usually be resolved through simple conferral. The next option is *zhongjian ren* mediation.

The U.S. Department of Commerce[2] provides the following advice for circumstances in which neither negotiation nor mediation has been effective:

> *There are three primary ways to resolve a commercial dispute in China: negotiation, arbitration and litigation. Simple negotiation with your partner is usually the best method of dispute resolution. It is the least expensive and it can preserve the working relationship of the parties involved. In fact, most business contracts in China include a clause stipulating that negotiation should be employed before other dispute settlement mechanisms are pursued. When a foreign firm experiences difficulty in directly negotiating a solution to a dispute with its Chinese partner, companies sometimes seek assistance from Chinese government officials who can encourage the Chinese party to honor the terms of the contract. Companies should specify a time limit for this process. Unfortunately, negotiations do not always lead to resolution.*
>
> *Arbitration is the next preferred method. Unless the parties can agree on arbitration after the dispute has arisen (which is often difficult), the underlying contract or separate agreement must indicate that disputes will be resolved through arbitration. Agree-*

ments to arbitrate usually specify a choice of arbitration body, which may be located in China or abroad, and a choice of law to govern the dispute. There are two Chinese government-sponsored arbitration bodies for handling cases involving at least one foreign party: China International Economic and Trade Arbitration Commission (CIETAC) and, for maritime disputes, China Maritime Arbitration Commission (CMAC). For foreign-related disputes where CIETAC is the selected arbitration body, parties to the contract may specify the nationality of members of the arbitration panel in the contract; CIETAC has implemented contract clauses that stipulate that two of the three arbitrators, including the presiding arbitrator, must be non-Chinese. CIETAC does not have to preapprove any contractual stipulations on the nationality of the negotiators. CIETAC has published rules which govern the selection of a panel if the contract does not specify how the choice of arbitrators will be handled. CIETAC's list of arbitrators for foreign-related disputes, from which CIETAC's arbitrators must be chosen, includes many non-Chinese arbitrators. Although many foreign experts believe that some aspects of CIETAC need to be improved, it has developed a good reputation.

Companies should be aware when drafting a contract that, as an alternative to CIETAC or CMAC, they can specify an arbitration body outside China, such as Singapore, Stockholm or Geneva. In addition, Hong Kong—under one country, two systems—has a separate and well-regarded international commercial arbitration system.

A final way to resolve a commercial dispute in China is through litigation in Chinese courts. In China, foreign individuals and companies have the same ability to bring action in court as Chinese citizens and companies. There are three levels of courts in China. Every major city has basic courts and intermediate courts. Supervising these courts are the provincial high courts. The Supreme People's Court, located in Beijing, has appellate jurisdiction over all courts in China. Cases involving foreign interests can be filed in either the basic-level courts or intermediate courts, depending on their nature. Most observers agree that Chi-

nese courts are not up to international standards. For instance, most judges have minimal or no legal training and observers have stated those poorly trained court officials are susceptible to corruption and regional protectionism.

In China, arbitration offers many advantages over litigation. A major advantage is the finality of the rulings. Court rulings are subject to appeal, which means litigation may continue for years. As indicated above, judges in China are often poorly qualified, while arbitration panels are made up of a panel of experts, which improves the quality of the hearing. In addition, the proceedings and rules of arbitration are often more transparent than litigation.

Many observers have noted that it is often difficult for parties to enforce and obtain payment on court judgments and arbitral awards in China. While courts are required to receive approval from the Supreme People's Court prior to refusing to enforce a foreign arbitral award, courts have occasionally circumvented this requirement by employing delaying tactics when local interests are adversely affected by the arbitration rulings. The Supreme People's Court has issued new guidelines to limit the ability of local courts to delay enforcement and this appears to have had a positive effect.

The Role of the U.S. Government in Commercial Disputes

The U.S. government also offers the following advice.

American companies involved in a dispute often approach the Department of Commerce and other U.S. agencies in China or the United States for assistance. The department can provide companies with assistance in navigating China's legal system, provide a list of local attorneys, and share basic information on potentially applicable trade agreements and relevant Chinese business practices. The department is not able to provide American companies or individuals with legal advice.

American companies that have disputes with private firms often request U.S. government intervention with Chinese authorities on their behalf. Such intervention is rarely appropriate unless the company has exhausted all remedies under China's legal system. The Commerce Department's efforts in assisting with commercial disputes are aimed at achieving a fair and timely resolution in accordance with Chinese law and in advancing both countries' interests in adequate legal and judicial protection for all parties. When a dispute is in the Chinese court system, embassy officers will intervene on behalf of an American company only in extremely limited circumstances and in accordance with U.S. government guidelines.

Disputes Involving the Chinese Government

When a U.S. firm has a dispute with the Chinese government, a Chinese state-owned enterprise, or a government-subsidized project, the most effective initial step is to quietly raise the issue with the entities involved, citing the importance of foreign companies' investment in China. The firm should explain its situation to the Chinese entity and offer to work with it to resolve the problem amicably. This allows for a more aggressive approach at a later date, if necessary. The Commerce Department can work with companies in considering the best strategy. While China is obligated to fully implement the terms of its trade agreements, including the WTO once it is a member, differences over implementation may arise. In such circumstances, the department is committed to working with firms and the Chinese government to ensure full compliance. Generally, U.S. embassy staff and Washington agencies will work directly with concerned companies, or the industry association, to identify solutions and formulate strategies. If appropriate, the embassy will advocate on behalf of the American companies with Chinese officials.

If the dispute cannot be resolved at this level and additional U.S. government support is appropriate, the U.S. involvement will usually entail increasingly senior level officials of the appropriate U. S. agencies. If compliance with WTO obligations underlies the dispute, the U.S. government will examine the possible use of WTO dispute settlement procedures. In reaching a dispute resolution strategy, a firm should consider all possibilities, including negotiation, arbitration, mediation, or litigation, and the time and expense that it may take to resolve the problem.

We note that CIETAC has been the busiest commercial arbitration institution on the planet during the last few years. Regarding fairness, in some years foreign firms have won the majority of cases. Still foreign criticism has been leveled at CIETAC procedures, particularly related to the difficulty of collecting awards. One Hong Kong party that received a $400,000 award by CIETAC so far has been able to collect a mere $20,000. Most recently, in response to criticism from foreign companies, the Chinese authorities have made two significant changes to CIETAC arbitration rules.[3] First, now arbitrators can be appointed from outside the commission's own panel, including foreigners. Second, the arbitration period has been shortened from nine to six months. These adjustments suggest that Chinese authorities are interested in advancing CIETAC's services to international standards—but work still needs to be done.

Conclusion

Many "old China hands" report that, even with a signed contract, negotiations are actually never really completed; and what Americans call "careful follow-up" is really just the continuing maintenance of an ever-evolving business relationship. We must caution that most recently litigation is being used as a business tool in a new way by some in China. Indeed, some foreigners complain that a new class of lawyers is abusing the fast-changing legal system as a kind of extortion. So be careful out there!

Notes

1   Ron S. Fortgang, David A. Lax, and James K. Sebenius, "Negotiating the Spirit of the Deal," *Harvard Business Review*, February 2003, pp. 66–73.
2   Susan Hamrock and Fewick Yu, "Dispute Avoidance and Dispute Resolution in China," *Export America*, U.S. Department of Commerce, April 2003.
3   Toh Han Shih, "Reforms of China's Trade Arbitration System Welcomed," *South China Morning Post*, May 2, 2005, p. 3.

REGIONAL DIFFERENCES IN CHINESE BUSINESS SYSTEMS AND BEHAVIORS

CHAPTER 11

THE MAINLAND
AND ITS DIVERSITY

During the industrial revolution in the nineteenth century, Lancashire, in the northeast of England, was known as "the workshop of the world." The city once possessed more machines than the rest of the planet combined. Today, another workshop of the world is being created to the west of the Pacific. It stretches down the eastern coast of China, from Dalian in the northeast, to Beijing and Tianjin in the north, to Shanghai and Suzhou in the south, and then further south to Guangzhou and Shenzhen bordering Hong Kong.

The historic transformation from an isolated Communist regime to the exporter of toys and footwear and further on to the world's high-tech foundry could not be more obvious. Driving through the skyscraper-decorated Pudong New Area across from the Bund in Shanghai, you will find spanking new factories as far as the eye can see. Intel is making high-end chips. Further down the road is Corning, producing sophisticated photonics and ceramic casings for catalytic converters. Then there is Japan's Matsushita making delicate liquid crystal display screens. Alcatel is producing practically everything in its arsenal—from digital switching systems to videoconferencing equipment. The company has also moved its Asia-Pacific headquarters to Shanghai because it could not think of anything Alcatel could not make in China.

For a global economy, it simply means that you have to have a major manufacturing presence in China because your competition is already there. The ability to make nearly everything in China with high quality and at a reasonable price and then sell it to customers both near and far is having a big impact in the corporate suites in every corner of the planet.

Moreover, multinationals have found China's labor force not only vast and cheap but also educated and disciplined. The country has a huge growing pool of young business and engineering talent from which companies can draw. More and more Chinese students studying abroad are returning to their homeland today than did 10 years ago. At U.S. universities, the largest numbers of foreign graduate students in engineering and scientific disciplines are from China. More than ever business graduate students are flocking from China to American and European business schools, with deepening globalization of China's economy calling for more talent with internationally recognized management insights and skills.

Remarkably, today's China is divided into mutually competitive, yet complementary economic "warring states," just as it was 2,000 years ago before being united in the Qin dynasty. Among these "warring states," the four subeconomies stand out from the north to the south of the country:

- The longtime industrial heartland in northeast China, with the coastal Dalian city, its hub among three provinces of Liaoning, Jilin, and Heilongjiang.
- The Beijing-Tianjin Information Technology (IT) corridor in north China.
- The Yangtze River delta known as the Greater Shanghai area, with its emerging IT manufacturing center of Suzhou.
- The Pearl River delta, containing Hong Kong, Macau, Guangzhou, and Shenzhen, as the world's manufacturing base of the IT industry.

While northeast China is gaining momentum in becoming the fourth pole of Chinese economic development for real, the other three zones already have become the fundamental engines driving the national economic progress. With just 7.53 percent of the nation's population and 1.24 percent of the nation's territory, the combined GDP of these three regions is over 30 percent of the nation's total GDP, and the utilized foreign investment is 73 percent.

Northeast China: Longtime Industrial Heartland

In the old, planned economy, northeast China used to be the most industrially and technologically advanced part of the country. It had a petrochemical, steel, and heavy industry base with a large number of state-owned enterprises. Liaoning province was once the largest industrial center, after Shanghai. Northeast China, however, remains an important subeconomy of the country although it is lagging behind the dynamic economic growth of the other three subeconomies.

The three provinces in northeast China—Liaoning (41.2 million persons), Jilin (26.1 million), and Heilongjiang (38.1 million) extending from south to north—have historically prided themselves on being an integrated whole in culture, economy, and geopolitics. Indeed, nowhere else in the vast Chinese territory could you possibly see such a close-knit interdependency among separate provinces. As a matter of fact, the Chinese people always refer to these three provinces as *dongbei*, meaning northeast, or *dong sansheng*, meaning northeastern three provinces, instead of referring to each province individually.

With such blurred, almost nonexistent, provincial borders, these three provinces complement one another with distinct features and influences. Each is also directly connected economically with its adjacent foreign neighbors. Roughly speaking, Liaoning province has the closest economic ties with Japan, Jilin province with South Korea, and Heilongjiang province with Russia. Northeast China is indeed a geopolitical and socioeconomic melting pot that blends everything together to become one of the most important subeconomies of China.

Unlike the rest of the country, many high school students in the region study Japanese or Russian in foreign language class, instead of English. Korean is also a widely spoken language, with about 2 million minority Koreans residing in this area. The Chinese dialect spoken in this region is one of the most similar to Mandarin, with just a slight twist of *dongbei* accent.

Northeast China/Liaoning Province and Japan

The Japanese influence of northeast China can be traced back to the 1930s when the Japanese imperialists proclaimed the puppet Manchukuo (Manchurian State), with the last emperor Puyi as the puppet emperor. The Japanese economic influence has resumed since the 1980s when China adopted an open-door and economic reform policy.

Japan is one of the top foreign trade partners of China. One-third of all Japanese investments in China, however, is concentrated in the Dalian area. Dalian, a coastal city at the southern tip of Liaodong Peninsula in Liaoning province, serves as a port of entry to northeast China. It is one of the world's largest container ports with more than 60 million tons of annual transportation volume. Interestingly, this port contains a twist of a Singaporean logistics management system amid numerous Japanese invested companies. See Chapter 14 for details.

While other parts of *dongbei*, such as the Liaoning provincial capital of Shenyang, are plagued by bankruptcies of state-owned enterprises in traditional heavy industries developed under the old centrally planned economic system, Dalian stands as one of the most internationalized economies in China. In the list of the best commercial cities on the Chinese mainland of the year 2005, published by *Forbes* (Chinese edition), Dalian was surprisingly ranked fourth, ahead of Beijing (fifth), and after Hangzhou (first), Wuxi (second), and Shanghai (third). With a population of 5.5 million, Dalian's GDP in 2004 amounted to nearly $12.5 billion, to which 800 high-tech companies contributed more than half. This city is the fastest growing economy in the Bohai Bay Rim region and is expected to fast become the software outsourcing center of northeast Asia, claims *Forbes*.

The development of Dalian from the old, backward, and filthy industrial port city to one of the most prosperous and beautiful metropolises in Asia today may largely be attributed to its mayor Bo Xilai. The charismatic and forward-looking mayor, who is the son of the veteran Communist Party revolutionary leader Bo Yibo, made every endeavor to promote Dalian to the rest of the country and the world during his eight-year tenure. He has succeeded in transforming the city into what may be considered the best city in China, with a well-maintained environment, superior investment climate, and the highest standard of living in the country. Mayor Bo, who was later promoted to the governor of Liaoning province and today is the Minister of Commerce, once claimed that "Dalian, together with Shanghai, is one of the economic pillars of China."[1] No wonder the fifth annual Asia-Europe Meeting (ASEM) Economic Ministers' Meeting (EMM) was held in Dalian in July 2003.

Dalian, described by Kenichi Ohmae as a city with beautiful environment, gorgeous buildings, and dirtless streets as that of pre-automobile-era French cities, boasts a high-tech development park with three national technological development institutions and over ten universities and research institutes. Most recently in Dalian, there were over 12,000 foreign enterprises, of which over 4,000 are Japanese-invested companies.[2] Foreign investments in Dalian are estimated to be about over half the total investments in the province of Liaoning.

With just a four-hour flight from Japan and a large Japanese-speaking population—more than 70,000 people speak Japanese fluently in Liaoning Province—it is no wonder that Japanese investors have been flocking to the city of Dalian. Some Japanese managers explain that Dalian is to Japan what Mexico is to the United States, "a cheap industrial zone near the main office." They attribute their decision to invest in Dalian to the quality of workforce, lower cost of real estate, and cheap labor costs. As a result, more than 100,000 highly trained workers are employed in Japanese high-tech companies in Dalian. And thousands of Japanese managers live in Dalian. Major Japanese employers include such big names as Mabuchi Motor, Canon, Matsushita, Toshiba, and Marubeni.

The productivity of the backroom logistics departments is hard to beat in labor-expensive Japan, which is considered a major obstacle in maintaining and improving corporate competitiveness. The Japanese language advantage and Japanese cultural ties of Dalian and Liaoning Province, however, have helped bewildered Japanese enterprises resolve the issue. Outsourcing the labor-intensive and low-value-added businesses to Dalian, such as Japanese language database input and administration and telephone customer service centers, has proven successful.

With such close Japanese ties, Liaoning, particularly Dalian, has a huge potential to become China's driving force in marketing and sales to Japan, the world's second largest market.

The Dalian Container Terminal

Dalian is one of the four international deep-water transshipment ports designated by the Chinese government in 1989. A twist in this largely Japanese-invested economy is a Singaporean-managed container transportation port in Dalian. Singapore enjoys the reputation of being one of the most effective and efficient port management entities. Equipped with Singaporean expertise and advanced IT technology know-how, the harbor of Dalian now boasts a higher level of container management and transportation efficiency than that of Japan.

The city established the joint venture Dalian Container Terminal Co., Ltd. (DCT) with PSA Corporation Ltd. of Singapore in July 1996 with a total investment of $500 million. In 1997, DCT introduced the advanced container integrated terminal operation system from PSA, which enabled DCT to handle containers at the most efficient level in China. In August 2000, PSA launched an electronic cargo shipping service, a computerized system that is more advanced than that in Japan, that enables DCT to complete

the tedious routine containers transportation and vessels administration procedures within as short a time as 30 minutes.

As the best gateway for northern China to the world, with five
container berths—1,459 meters in length and 14 meters in depth—
DCT can accommodate the fourth and fifth generation container
ships. The annual handling capacity has exceeded 1.5 million TEU's
(twenty-foot containers equivalent unit).

Currently, DCT has more than 40 international service destinations covering Japan, Korea, Hong Kong, Taiwan, Southeast
Asia, the Middle East, the Red Sea, the Mediterranean, Europe,
and the East and West Coast of the United States. Over 170 vessels call at DCT from all over the world. More than 40 container
shipping lines' vessels call at DCT and have set up branch offices
in Dalian.

The Software Industry in Dalian

With more than 40 percent of the city space covered with grass
and trees today, Dalian has transformed itself into a green city
from a seriously polluted heavy industry base. The growth of a
software industry partially contributed to this dramatic change.
Dalian High-Tech Industrial Park has witnessed an output value
of $40 million in the software development businesses outsourced
from Japanese and South Korean companies. Since its founding
in 1998, the Dalian Software Park, one of 11 state software industry bases declared by China, has enrolled 140 companies, of which
32 percent are foreign funded. The park realized $96 million in
output value and $25 million in export income in 2002. Built
strategically close to many universities and research institutes, it
has become a magnet for software development, business process
outsourcing, and IT-enabled services. Sixteen Global 500 corporations, including IBM, GE, HP, Dell, SAP, NEC, Matsushita,
Sony, Toshiba and Accenture, have established R&D centers there
for north Asia and/or the world. The park has the goal of becoming the largest software export base in China. To provide main-
frame training, Dalian Software Park, in a move supported by

the Chinese government, turned in 2004 to IBM to develop a *workforce development solution*. The training certificate program, created and managed by IBM Global Services, will produce somewhere between 1,600 and 5,000 graduates by 2010. At that point IBM will hand over management of the program to the Dalian Software Park.

Bohai Bay Economic Rim

Dalian and Liaoning are part of the greater Bohai Bay Economic Rim, which comprises parts of the provinces of Liaoning, Shandong, Hebei, Shanxi, the Inner Mongolia Autonomous Region, and the two megacities of Beijing and Tianjin. It has 240 million inhabitants—20 percent of the population of China—and covers an area of more than 1 million square kilometers—12 percent of the Chinese territory. It takes one fourth of the country's total economic and foreign trade volumes. About 20 major cities cluster around Bohai Bay's 5,800-kilometer-long coastline, including four large ports—Dalian, Tianjin, Qingdao, and Qinhuangdao. Of the over 60 various-sized ports, four have been on the agenda to be further developed into modernized international harbors—Yingkou, Jingxi, Huanghua, and Tangshan.

The Bohai Bay area, comparable to the Baltic Sea in Europe, offers a strategic opening to the Pacific Ocean for all of northern China and forms the central part of the Northeast Asian Economic Zone. The deltas of the Yangtze River and the Pearl River have drawn worldwide attention for their astoundingly fast economic growth. One must wonder, "So what is going on at the much neglected delta of the other "mother river" of China—the Yellow River?" After the other two deltas in the south, the Bohai Bay Economic Rim has fast become a third "pole" of China's economic development and an engine driving the economy of north China. Its subsoil contains 40 percent of the country's coal, oil, and iron ore reserves. The region handles 40 percent of all cargo shipped out of China.

In 2002, Texaco China, a subsidiary of U.S.-based Chevron Texaco, discovered an oilfield in Bohai Bay. Located 150 kilometers southeast of the Tianjin port, it covers an area of 218 square kilometers and is one of the largest oilfields in Bohai Bay with oil and gas reserves estimated at 210 million cubic meters. China National Offshore Oil Corp (CNOOC), the nation's third largest oil company, has reached an agreement to jointly develop this oilfield, marking the first time for CNOOC to work as an operator in developing an oilfield that was discovered by a major foreign company.

The economic integration is developing fast in the Bohai Bay Rim. Since 1992 when the Bohai Bay Economic Alliance was first established, the 29 member cities have reached complementary agreements on more than 1,400 economic cooperation projects, totaling nearly $4 billion. The airports, harbors, and customs and tariff ports in Beijing and Tianjin, two of the most important ports in the rim, have been put under a single traffic-flow management system, functioning as the two complementary parts of the same port. The railway connecting various major cities surrounding the Bohai Bay Rim will be completed soon, with two thirds of the construction project done in 2003. This rail artery starts with Shanhaiguan in Liaoning province in the north—which coincidentally happens to be the eastern terminus of the Great Wall stretching across north China for 4,500 miles—and ends at Yantai in Shandong province.

Northeast China and Korea

Liaoning province shares a border with North Korea. It has historically been the entry gateway to the Korean Peninsula. Therefore, there is a great deal of Korean influence in northeast China in addition to the Japanese and Russian influences.

China is home to over 2 million minority Koreans who immigrated to China within the last several hundred years and earlier. Of them, 97 percent live in these three provinces in northeast

China; more than 60 percent live in Jilin province alone. In Jilin, some 70 percent inhabit the Yanbian Korean Autonomous Prefecture. There are approximately 500,000 and 230,000 minority Koreans living in Heilongjiang and Liaoning provinces, respectively.

In 2002, China for the first time became the largest investment country for South Korea, registering $2.7 billion, up by 26.4 percent over the previous year. Indeed, the trade volume between China and South Korea increased by almost 800 percent over the past 10 years. Because of the traditional cultural and language ties between Korea and northeast China's minority Koreans, the bulk of South Korean investment in China is concentrated in northeast China.

To attract South Korean investments, the Liaoning provincial capital of Shenyang has gone so far as to present an annual Korea Week. South Korea's investment in Shenyang first started in 1989, three years before Beijing established formal diplomatic relations with Seoul. As of today, more than 1,100 South Korean-invested enterprises in Shenyang have had a total foreign direct investment of $660 million, about 10 percent of the total foreign direct investments in the city. This ranks third among the 78 countries who invested in Shenyang. Of all the South Korean invested companies in Shenyang, 46 have invested more than $5 million. Over 10,000 South Korean citizens live in Shenyang today. A January 2003 poll showed that more than 60 percent of the 80,000 member companies of the South Korean Medium and Small Enterprises Association hope to relocate their businesses from South Korea to China. Liaoning province is expected to share a considerable amount of these investments.

Jilin Province and Northeast Asia's "Golden Triangle"

In the early 1990s, China, Russia, North Korea, and Mongolia launched an ambitious initiative to develop the Tumen River region, said to be the last economic frontier on the Asian continent. The Tumen Project has won the support of the United Nations Development Program despite the fact that the economic potential of the Tumen region has been hindered by the regional political situation that continues to remain unclear. The four areas that form the Tumen Region are:

- Yanbian Korean Autonomous Prefecture (China)
- Rajin-Sonbong Economic and Trade Zone (DPRK)
- Eastern Mongolia
- Primorsky Territory (Russian Federation)

Heilongjiang Province and Russia

China shares a border of 4,600 miles with Russia. Of the Chinese provinces neighboring Russia, Heilongjiang has the bulk of this border, with the borderline rivers of Heilongjiang and Wusulijiang running in its north and east, respectively. Heilongjiang, meaning Black Dragon River, is referred to as the Amur River in Russia.

Harbin: "Little Moscow" in the Far East

Harbin, the capital city of the northernmost province of Heilongjiang, historically an important gateway from China to Russia and Europe, may surprise visitors because of its Russian appearance. For centuries, this "ice and snow capital," China's closest megacity of the Arctic, has demonstrated its Russian influence and legacy, even including Russian culinary traditions. Typical Heilongjiang foods are a mix of Chinese dumplings and Russian-styled bread and sausages. The Harbinese, like the Russians, are arguably China's biggest drinkers of vodka and *baijiu*, a Chinese drink comparable to vodka. Apparently they also inherited their love of ice cream from the Russians long before ice cream had become a popular snack in other parts of China since the 1980s.

Remarkably, almost every Chinese you meet on the streets of Harbin speaks basic, if not fluent, Russian. This city is known as "Little Moscow" in the Far East. The Russian influence in Harbin, including a continuing large Russian population there, is no better felt than by walking around the streets of the Daoli district—the old Russian city center known as Pristan. Here there is an outdoor museum of prewar Russian architecture in all European styles, especially neo-Baroque, neoclassical, and art deco. These buildings, thanks to China's newly gained wealth, are better preserved and maintained than their counterparts in the Russian Far East.

Among the many Orthodox churches and Russian style facades in this district, the Byzantine-styled St. Sophia Orthodox Church, completed in 1907 by the Russians, stands as the biggest Orthodox church in the Far East. Under the bright sun, the church, together with the square around it, may remind people, bizarrely, of Red Square in Moscow. As more evidence of the Russian influence, there are still hundreds of followers of the Russian Orthodox religion in Harbin. The number is expected to grow with China's increasing openness.

Chinese northeasterners share an enthusiasm with Russians for skiing and snowboarding which are still considered exotic sports in the rest of the nation. With the country's biggest and best Yabuli skiing resort—which used to be a royal hunting ground in the Qing dynasty, 194 kilometers east of Harbin—Heilongjiang province hosted the 1996 Asian Winter Games, and bid for the hosting right of the 2010 Olympic Winter Games—only to be defeated by Vancouver, Canada. To develop the local tourism industry and promote the province's little known ice and snow sculpture festivities and skiing resorts, Heilongjiang has produced an apt slogan hoping to boost its international image—"China's 'Cool' Province."

Russian Suspicion of Chinese Expansionism

As a result of wave after wave of tsarist expansions into the Far East in the nineteenth century, Russia annexed the Chinese territory to the east of the Wusuli River, which today serves as the Russian-Chinese border, depriving Heilongjiang and Jilin provinces of access to the sea. The historical trend is reversed now. Today the Russians fear a Chinese penetration into and annexation of the Russian Far East. They fear that China is systematically expanding into the Russian Far East with its trading activities, export of cheap labor, and demographic penetration (both legal and illegal Chinese immigrants).

Chinese-Russian Energy Cooperation

China became a net oil importer in 1993. In 2002, China surpassed Japan to become the world's second largest oil importer of 70 million tons, only after the United States. The Paris-based International Energy Bureau forecasts that by the year 2030, imports will increase from 34 percent in 2002 to over 80 percent of the total oil demand in China. By then, Chinese oil imports will be close to 10 million barrels per day, equivalent to that of the United States in 2000.

Despite mutual suspicions and wariness between these two Far Eastern giants, China and Russia see a need to cooperate, particularly in the energy field, with Siberia's rich oil reserves and China's increasing hunger for energy to fuel its economic growth. Heilongjian province's Daqing city was once considered the oil capital of China, but it has been fast drying up after 40 years of exploitation. Thus, export of Russian oil to China in 2006 will be 1.5 times greater than in 2005, up from 10 to 15 million tons.

The trend of rising Russian oil exports will continue in the future. In 2006, Russian President Vladimir Putin finally approved an oil pipeline project from Siberia to Daqing, following 12 years of marathon talks on the project between the two nations. This pipeline stands as a branch line extending into China from the main Russian line. Originally, both sides agreed to bring oil from east Siberia to Daqing, with one-third of the pipeline to be built within the Chinese territory. But plans changed when Japan stepped into the equation. At the end of 2002, Russia reportedly gave up this route and decided to construct a new line ending at the port city of Nakhodka in the Sea of Japan. The current route served as a compromise to combine the two pipelines—to China and to Japan—into one, while priority was given to the construction of the China line.

The cost of the 4,130-kilometer pipeline is estimated at between $11 billion and $16 billion. The annual capacity of the pipeline is likely to be 80 million tons of oil. China will purchase up to 5.13 billion barrels of Russian oil, worth $150 billion, between 2005 and 2030 supplied via the pipeline. This deal means that the Russian government may have put off, indefinitely, the rival Japan project, despite intense bidding from Tokyo to pull the oil its way. The Kremlin said that the 3,800-kilometer Japan line stretching from Siberia to the port of Nakhodka in the Sea of Japan could be built only after more oil reserves are found and the Chinese market has been served.

While Japanese-Russian negotiations reached an impasse, China made a breakthrough on the construction of an oil pipeline with its oil-rich western neighbor Kazakhstan, another former Soviet republic. The first phase of the 960-kilometer pipeline connecting Kazakhistan and northwest China's Xinjiang province was completed in 2005, with a designed annual oil transmission capacity of 10 million tons. Its second phase is expected to be finished in 2010, creating a delivery capacity of 20 million tons.

Chinese-Russian Economic Cooperation and Trade

Trade volume between China and Russia reached a record high of $29.1 billion in 2005, a surge of 37.1 percent. China is now Russia's fourth-largest trade partner, and Russia is China's eighth-largest trade partner.

Most of China's exports to Russia remain apparel and footwear. Renowned Chinese companies, such as the home-appliance maker TCL and the telecommunications firm Huawei, have witnessed the increasing market share of their products in Russia.

Russia's exports to China consist mainly of energy sources, such as crude oil, which is mostly transported by rail, and electricity exports from neighboring Siberian and Far Eastern regions. In the near future, exports of both oil and electricity are set to increase, as Russia is finishing up the giant pipeline to the Pacific Ocean with a branch to the Chinese border, and the Russian power grid monopoly UES is building some of its hydropower stations with a view of future exports to China.

Russia and China complement each other with their geopolitical closeness and complementary needs for one another's resources, markets, high technology, and investment. Several China-Russia science and technology cooperative bases have been set up in China. And the foundation of a China-Russia science and technology park is underway in Moscow. With its geographic closeness to Russia and unique Russian legacy, Heilongjiang province is bound to continue its role as the key link between Chinese and Russian trade.

Northeastern Negotiators

Certainly, eating wheat, rather than rice, makes you taller. Perhaps it also makes you more forthright. Such is the stereotype of the businesspeople in the northeast held by their southern neighbors. Negotiators from the three northeastern provinces above the Yangtze are certainly industrious, competent businesspeople. They are generally honest and plain spoken to the point of being uncouth. They are also not known for their risk-taking propensity or creativity. And, their uncomplicated food well reflects their local culture.

Beijing and Tianjin—China's Research and Development Center

On the midsummer night of July 13, 2001, amid the boiling heat wave, residents of the Chinese capital city of Beijing, along with the rest of the nation, spent a sleepless night celebrating winning the 2008 Summer Olympic Games with exuberance and extravagance—traditional dragons and lions dancing at Tiananmen Square, colorful fountains lighted by fireworks shows in the dark skies in various city plazas, people honking their car horns and waving flags and T-shirts in the streets around town, and top politicians lining up yelling their welcome to world athletes.

Beijing is now embarked on an impressive program of construction and investment in preparation for the games. Beijing plans to spend a total of $34 billion on the Olympic Games in the years preceding of 2008, including $22 billion for modernizing the Chinese capital's civic and transport facilities. Such a grand plan has certainly promised great potential for world investors.

Unlike the spontaneous development of the economic and urban clusters in the deltas of the Yangtze and Pearl Rivers, the Beijing-Tianjin economic region (more than 26 million persons) takes its shape with the assistance of the current political and sociopolitical systems, which enabled the nationwide and even worldwide resources to gather around in the capital city area. The development of the central business district (CBD), Zhongguancun (China's Silicon Valley), and the Olympic village have all benefited from the unique political and cultural background of Beijing as the Chinese capital.

R&D Center and High-Tech Industry

Unlike the deltas of the Yangtze and Pearl Rivers, which are hyped as "the world's workshop," the Beijing-Tianjin area is thought to have the potential to become "the world R&D center." The Beijing-Tianjin area is known as China's IT corridor, with Beijing the R&D center and Tianjin the industrialization and production base. China's developing version of Silicon Valley, *Zhongguancun*, is home to almost 5,000 Chinese high-tech companies, including big names like Lenovo, and more than 1,000 international IT companies. It is an amazing confluence of high IQ and entrepreneurial drive, with over 70 universities, including Peking University and Tsinghua University, China's equivalent of Harvard and MIT.

These universities educate social elites and leaders who have defeated numerous other high school graduates through a series of rigorous examinations from the moment they stepped into the elementary school and have been chosen from within an extremely competitive Chinese university recruiting system. "Speaking of talent resources, this is a place with the most concentrated intelligence powers and the most dynamic R&D activities of all China," says social sciences professor Liu Shiding of Peking University. Approximately 500,000 research and technical personnel work in Zhongguancun, a district the area of a small town. Many of them are employed by more than 200 science and technology research institutions in Zhongguancun, including such high-caliber entities within the Chinese Academy of Sciences as the Institute of Electrical Engineering, Institute of Electronics, Microelectronics R&D Center, Institute of Semiconductors, Computer Network Information Center, Institute of Software, and Institute of Computing Technology.

These academic institutions have all established their own companies to industrialize and commercialize their research findings and achievements. In 1980, Chen Chunxian, a researcher with the Institute of Physics of the Chinese Academy of Sciences, was among the very first to *xiahai* [or jump into the sea], a modern Chinese term referring to the act of giving up a more stable position in the public and nonprofit sector and entering the sea of more volatile businesses. Chen, later called "the Father of Zhongguancun," registered a small company and opened a new era by setting an unprecedented example of scientists engaging in product R&D and industrialization in China.

Several years later, another scientist from the Institute of Computing Technology of the Chinese Academy of Sciences, Liu Chuanzhi, followed suit and launched his business "Computers Company," which would develop into the country's largest computer producer, Lenovo, in the future. The country's second largest computer producer, Founder, is affiliated with Peking University. Tsinghua University has its own IT companies as well, such as UNIS and Tongfang.

Foreign investors, drawn by the high-caliber Chinese scientists and engineers, also flocked into Zhongguancun and set up their R&D institutions, such as IBM, Microsoft, Intel, Motorola, Nokia, Siemens, Panasonic, Hitachi, Fujitsu, and Acer. Since Motorola set up the first foreign R&D lab in China in 1993, the number of such facilities in the country has increased to more than 700.

Remarkably, Motorola is the largest foreign corporate investor in China, the world's largest mobile phone market, ahead of the United States. In 2001, Motorola's sales reached $4.9 billion to replace German's Volkswagen as the number 1 foreign-invested company in China. Motorola has invested $4 billion in China since 1986 and has a staff of about 15,000 there. Motorola has plans to increase annual production to $10 billion and accumulated investment in China to $10 billion. The company will boost its local purchasing in China to $10 billion.

CBD (Central Business District), a Work-in-Progress New Attraction of Beijing

In China, different parts of the country are often competing fiercely against one another for the attention of world investors and export opportunities. In 2002, Beijing unveiled an ambitious plan of building "a world class central business district (CBD)" in its core business area. Beijing officials boast that, "Beijing's business district is to have the allure of Shanghai's Pudong New Area so as to compete with it for domestic and foreign investments."

Although the CBD concept first appeared in the United States in the early 1920s, Beijing finally feels it is ready to build one of its own, like that of midtown Manhattan in New York City, La Defense in Paris, and Shinzuku in Tokyo. The CBD will be a zoned business space where offices, apartments, technology centers, traffic networks, and communications facilities are constructed for financial, commerce, and trade service agencies, allowing for highly profitable and productive business activities.

The designated location of Beijing CBD is in the eastern downtown area outside Beijing's old city, with a total area of four square kilometers. With fewer historic restrictions protecting the capital's architecture and flexible zoning laws regarding building heights, the district is able to provide the maximum potential to meet the growing needs of its investors. The district to be developed into the CBD currently accommodates 70 percent of the foreign-related resources of the whole city as well as the three foreign embassy districts. Over 60 percent of the city's foreign agencies and over 50 percent of the five-stars hotels are conveniently located within the district and its surrounding areas, such as the Hilton, Sheraton, Shangri-la, Holiday Inn, St. Regis, Hyatt, and Marriott.

The total number of enterprises in the CBD is about 1,750, with 457 multinational corporations, 570 foreign representative offices, 150 foreign-funded banks, insurance companies and agencies, as well as 192 intermediary services. There are more than 3 million square meters of the existing business infrastructure facilities, including China World Trade Center, Motorola Plaza, the Kerry Center, and Hewlett Packard Plaza, which accommodate hundreds of multinational companies and financial agencies, such as Motorola, Hewlett Packard, Ford, Samsung, BNP Parisbas Group, UBS AG. Currently, 160 of the global top 500 enterprises have their operations in Beijing. More than 120 have set up offices in the CBD and its surrounding areas.

Tianjin

The coastal city of Tianjin is one of the four provincial-level municipalities directly under the central government, along with Beijing, Shanghai, and Chongqing, and is an integral part of the Bohai Bay Economic Rim. The nominal GDP for Tianjin was $45.8 billion in 2005, a year-on-year increase of 14.5 percent. Per capita GDP was approximately $8,000. Tianjin municipality also has deposits of about 1 billion tons of petroleum, with Dagang district containing important oilfields.

As China's third largest industrial city after Shanghai and Beijing, Tianjin had the fastest GDP growth (12.0 percent) in 2001 among all provinces and municipalities. Its industrial output ranked the third among all cities in China in the first three quarters of 2002. Its pillar industries include automobiles, electronics, metallurgy, and petrochemicals.

In recent years, Tianjin witnessed the fast development of high-tech industries, mainly in the areas of information technology, biotechnology, medicine, new materials, and new energy. Output of high-tech industries accounted for about one-third of the municipality's total industrial output.

Tianjin is becoming the biggest mobile phone manufacturing base in China thanks largely to investment from Motorola in the Tianjin Economic and Technology Development Zone. It is estimated that half the cell phones used in China are manufactured in Tianjin. Reportedly, Motorola will invest another $1.9 billion in the next few years to build a semiconductor chips manufacturing center and its Asia's telecommunication product center in Tianjin.

Negotiating in and around the Capital

Negotiators from the Beijing area are known for their unusual (within China) bureaucratic sloth and imperialist perspective, both yielding a relatively uncommon lack of creativity or "thinking outside the box." Indeed, since they have defined the box in the first place, they are not used to thinking of ways to escape it. From our own studies of the Beijing/Tianjin negotiation style, we see an unusually heavy emphasis on questions. Also distinctive is their frequent use of silent periods and a very indirect communication style including few uses of the word "no" and "you" compared to almost all other cultures around the world. The one note of caution about these generalizations is the growing cosmopolitanism of managers working in and around the capital city.

Shanghai

Shanghai and Hong Kong are both well known internationally as leading business and economic centers in Asia. Shanghai's reputation was established primarily before World War II when it was one of the most open and secure cities in a land of unending turmoil; it became known to some as an "adventurers' paradise." Hong Kong emerged onto the international scene after World War II as one of Asia's greatest economic miracles and the world's freest economy. In some ways, Hong Kong's rise was partly a consequence of Shanghai's decline since the 1950s after China embarked on a course of Communist experimentation.

However, Shanghai's impressive economic achievements in its efforts to become a regional economic and financial center have been nerve-wracking for the forward-looking Hong Kong economists who research the impact of Shanghai's development—along with WTO membership—on Hong Kong's economic position. Their angst exists even though Hong Kong's GDP is nearly three times that of Shanghai; per capita GDP is more than six times that of Shanghai, and foreign direct investment flow into Hong Kong in 2001 was five times that of Shanghai. Hong Kong's economic accomplishments today are being achieved with a population of less than 7 million, while Shanghai has over 16 million.

Shanghai, the host of the World Expo 2010, is one of the four provincial-level municipalities directly under the central government and historically a commercial and financial center of China. With a population of only 1.3 percent and a land area of 0.1 percent of the national total, Shanghai contributes 5 percent of the nation's GDP and 8 percent of the nation's total industrial output value. Shanghai has China's largest container port which handles 10 million TEUs annually.

Shanghai's economy increased by 11.1 percent (outpacing the national figure of 9.9 percent) to US$114 billion in 2005, the 14th straight year of double-digit growth. Shanghai has become the world's busiest port in terms of cargo throughput, handling a total of 443 million tons of cargo.

Shanghai has been undergoing major industrial restructuring over the last decade. The share of low value-added manufacturing has decreased significantly, particularly the textile and heavy-equipment manufacturing industries because many firms have relocated outside of Shanghai. Although low and medium value-added industries still account for the vast majority of Shanghai's industrial employment, Shanghai has made significant progress in developing its automobile assembly industry and other high-tech industries, such as computer, telecommunications equipment, and integrated circuit manufacturing.

China's sustained economic growth and accession to the WTO have advanced Shanghai's position as a regional trade and financial center. Half of the city's GDP is attributed to financial services industries such as banking, retail, finance, trade, insurance, and real estate development.

Shanghai is a major destination for foreign direct investment. It ranked at the top in attracting foreign direct investment (FDI) in China. Hong Kong is the largest source of overseas direct investment in Shanghai.

Other major investors in Shanghai were from Japan, the United States, South Korea, and Germany. Many world leading multinationals such as General Motors, Mitsubishi, Exxon, General Electric, Toyota Motor, Siemens, Hitachi, Sony, Fiat, Toshiba, BMW, Samsung, Bosch, Volvo, Alcatel, Cannon, Xerox, and LG have established their presence in Shanghai.

Shanghai found new opportunities for success in the 1990s with the opening up and developing of Pudong New Area. In just a decade, Shanghai has successfully reshaped itself from a traditional manufacturing-based city to a modern business center. The Lujiazui, Waigaoqiao, and Jingqiao development zones are now names representing finance, trade, and manufacturing centers, respectively.

2010 Shanghai World Expo
Spells Business Opportunities

Total investment in Shanghai's 2010 World Expo projects is estimated at $3 billion, of which 43 percent will come from government sources, 36 percent from companies, and 21 percent from banks. The 240-hectare Expo site will house a China pavilion, other national pavilions, corporate pavilions, a convention center, and an integrated hall. The key exhibition venues will occupy an area of 3.4 square kilometers in Pudong.

A Gallup poll estimates that visitor arrivals in Shanghai including sightseeing and business travelers will reach 70 million during the Expo period from May to October 2010. If 2 percent of these visitors are from overseas, the demand for flights will be for 2.8 million passengers. If 20 percent of the domestic visitors travel by air, it will translate into 26.8 million passengers. Based on these two projections, Shanghai's airports will have to handle close to 30 million travelers during that six-month period. In order to cater to this demand, yet another expansion of the recently completed international airport at Pudong will be speeded up.

The Expo is likely to generate similar business opportunities for world businesses as the 2008 Beijing Olympics, including project construction and management, project finance, tourism, hotel investment and management, retail, and environmental protection, and so on.

The Yangtze River Delta (YRD): The Greater Shanghai Economic Circle

While approximately two-thirds of the population still lives in rural areas, China's urbanization level has reached one-third today. With 30 percent being the internationally recognized benchmark as an accelerated quality urbanization trend, China is well on its way to becoming a fully industrialized and urbanized economy.

After two decades of unprecedented economic growth, China has witnessed the emergence of the three metropolis clusters that have developed complementary economic resources and interdependent divisions of labor and tasks among each member city within the clusters. These metropolis clusters also function as the driving engines for their respective regional economic development. The greater Beijing metropolis cluster contains the double megacity of Beijing and Tianjin and a total population of 40 million. The greater Pearl River delta metropolis cluster is centered around Hong Kong and Guangzhou and has a total population of 21 million. The largest metropolis cluster is the greater Shanghai area in the Yangtze River delta, with a total population of 70 million, including numerous various-sized cities in the neighboring Zhejiang and Jiangsu provinces.

The Yangtze River Delta metropolis cluster is among the world's top six megacity clusters, along with New York City-Boston-Washington, D.C., in the northeastern United States, Toronto-Chicago in the Great Lakes area, Tokyo-Yokohama-Osaka in Japan, London-Manchester in the United Kingdom, and Amsterdam-Ruhrgebiet-Paris in northwestern Europe.

The greater Shanghai area is divided into four concurrent circles, with downtown Shanghai being the common center and the driving time from different regions in the Yangtze River delta to the center being the four radiuses:

- The half-hour drive radius zone, covering basically each and every district of the Shanghai municipality, including Pudong New Area.
- The one-hour drive radius zone, covering the neighboring cities of Suzhou in Jiangsu province (71.1 million persons) and Jiaxing in Zhejiang province (41.1 million persons).
- The two-hour drive radius zone, covering the cities farther away—Nantong, Wuxi, and Changzhou in Jiangsu province, and Hangzhou and Ningbo in Zhejiang province.
- The four-hour drive radius zone that includes the Jiangsu provincial capital of Nanjing.

These four concurrent circles cover the total population of 70 million in the entire delta of the Yangtze River. While Shanghai has China's highest per capita GDP, the combined GDP of Shanghai, Jiangsu, and Zhejiang amounts to over one-fifth of that of the country—over $240 billion—and the combined utilized foreign direct investment of Shanghai, Jiangsu, and Zhejiang is as high as one-third of that of the country—$12 billion.

The Pudong New Area

Pudong, with an area of 533.44 square kilometers and a population of 1.68 million, is located on the east bank of the Huangpu River that runs through the urban part of Shanghai. Just like the Shenzhen miracle—which transformed a fishing village into a metropolis within just a decade, Pudong, in its 15-year history, has surprisingly progressed in its economic strength and urban development. The Pudong New Area has become the epitome of Shanghai's modernization and even the symbol of China's reform and drive for openness.

In 1990, at an early stage of the development of Pudong, the local GDP was a mere $750 million. The estimate for 2005 was over $25 billion. The number of overseas-funded projects in Pudong New Area had increased to 8,000, bringing in a total investment of $40 billion.

"Infrastructure first" has been a strategy followed by Pudong since the very beginning of the development. Since 1990, a total amount of $25 billion has been injected into the infrastructure sector. A package of major projects like bridges, tunnels, metro lines, a deep-water port and an infoport as well as energy projects have been completed. The investment environment in Pudong has been greatly improved.

Between 2001 and 2005, Pudong developed "three ports" (deep-water port, airport, and infoport), "three networks" (rail network, urban highway network, and cross-river transportation network), and "three systems" (power supply system, natural gas supply system, and central heating system) as the core of infrastructure construction.

Phase I of the Pudong International Airport was completed and opened to traffic in October 1999. The project, which cost $1.5 billion, involved a 4,000-meter main runway and a passenger terminal of some 250,000 square meters in gross floor area. The current handling capacity of the airport is 20 million passengers and 750,000 tons of cargo. According to plan, the airport will eventually have four runways and an annual handling capacity of 70 million passengers.

As the cornerstone of the Shanghai Info-Port, the Pudong International Info-Port will be a hub for collecting, processing, storing, exchanging, and transmitting information in Shanghai. Using multimedia, optical fiber communications, computer technology, and telecommunications satellites, the Pudong Info-Port will provide intelligent and round-the-clock global communications and business information services. Phase I of the project, the Info-Port Complex has been completed. The building is 180 meters high, with a total floor space of 80,000 square meters. The equipment installed in the building is an integral part of the information facilities in west Shanghai and for the rest of the country as well as those for global communications, thus laying the foundation for the Shanghai Information Highway.

The Waigaoqiao new harbor area in Pudong New Area (now under construction) will be the centerpiece of the new Shanghai port in the future. Waigaoqiao harbor has enough room to accommodate 49 ten-thousand-ton berths and a number of small and medium-sized berths in addition. The full annual handling capacity is planned to be 50.4 million tons of cargo, of which 5.25 million tons is container handling capacity. The development is divided into four phases and is scheduled to be completed by 2020. At this stage, the development of the port has entered Phase IV, and the throughput has reached 3 million TEUs.

Shanghai CBD—"Manhattan of the East"

Shanghai has decided to turn the Lujiazui area into a well-equipped central business district (CBD) within a decade. The total investment is expected to exceed $12.5 billion. Plans were drawn up from architects from the Richard Rogers Partnership of UK, Dominique Perrault Associates of France, Toyo Ito & Associates Architects of Japan, and Massimiano Fuksas Associates of Italy. The best elements of each plan will make up the final blueprint of the CBD.

Lujiazui CBD's development concept is plain to see from its orientation toward the financial services industry. It will be made up of seven national-level markets—securities, real estate, futures, talents, property rights, diamonds, and publishing. In the long term, Shanghai's stock exchange appears to have the potential to become much stronger than those of Hong Kong and Shenzhen, because Shanghai has a much broader variety of industries, complementary economic resources from the Yangtze River delta, even the entire Yangtze River Valley area that extends deep into China's hinterland, and powerful backing from Beijing.

Suzhou

Suzhou, an hour's drive west of Shanghai, is quickly emerging as one of China's hottest manufacturing centers. It has replaced the provincial capital Nanjing, a two-hour ride away on the Shanghai-Nanjing expressway, to become Jiangsu province's number one economic and foreign trade center. Since the turn of the century, overseas investors, especially tens of thousands of Taiwanese firms making everything from consumer goods to high-tech products, have flocked into what was once a quiet silk-making town.

The cost and quality advantages of Suzhou have definitely contributed to the astounding growth of the manufacturing sector of Suzhou. Philip Chen, the chairman of Taiwanese electronics maker Avision—maker of scanners and optical equipment for top companies such as Canon, HP, and Brother—relocated his company from Hsinchu near Taipei to Suzhou, because he can squeeze cost savings of 8–10 percent for its higher-end products by building a manufacturing plant in Suzhou. And the traffic and logistical snarl near Taipei is worse than in Suzhou.

Suzhou has been reborn as a high-technology outpost in the global economy and has been constantly ranked in the top 10 of the Chinese Cities Comprehensive Competitive Powers Ranking. The Swiss company Logitech International assembles more than a third of the world's mice for personal computers in Suzhou. But that is just the tip of an iceberg of what Suzhou manufactures for the world IT sector. The city boasts nearly every computer component making facility, from the circuit-etched silicon wafers at the heart of computer chips to the molded plastic shells that house most pieces of electronic gear. Logitech has encouraged its Taiwanese suppliers to move to Suzhou. It now buys most of its plastic mouse cases, integrated circuits, and cable wire locally in the Yangtze River delta area. And a recent poll by the Taipei Computer Association found that 90 percent of Taiwan-based high-technology companies have invested or plan to invest in the mainland. There are already about a half-million engineers, managers, and their families from Taiwan living in the Shanghai-Suzhou area at any one time. Presently, Taiwanese printed circuit board (PCB) manufacturers have concentrated their investment on Kunshan and Suzhou in Jiangsu province.

Beware Getting Shanghaied

The negotiators from the Shanghai area are renowned in China for shrewdness. They are outgoing and big talkers and big spenders. They will try to impress you in ways and to extents you won't see anywhere else in China. For them, anything is possible—they are very creative thinkers. Folks that grow up speaking the Shanghai dialect are quite clannish and cunningly political. Some in China describe them as calculating, even devious. But, more than anything else, they are successful, really the dominant business group on the mainland. Be careful. It will serve you well to the take the title of Chapter 1 to heart.

The Pearl River Delta (PRD)

The Greater Pearl River area, including Hong Kong and Macau, is an area covering 47,000 square kilometers with a population of 21 million people, one-third that of the entire province. By the beginning of the twenty-first century, the delta had had three cities with populations of more than 5 million: Hong Kong, Guangzhou, and Shenzhen; five cities with more than 1 million inhabitants: Zhuhai, Huizhou, Foshan, Zhongshan, and Dongguan; and a number of cities each with approximately half a million: Macau, Zhao-qing, Shunde, Panyu, and Nanhai.

The Pearl River delta region within the province of Guangdong (70.0 million persons) has become the world workshop of the IT industry and one of the most important manufacturing bases of the world. The PRD economic zone is the province's economic hub, accounting for over 80 percent of the province's GDP. Many cities in the PRD, such as Shenzhen and Dongguan are among the Chinese cities that have generated the most foreign exchange revenues.

Guangdong's manufacturing industries develop rapidly as a result of foreign investment, particularly in the PRD economic zone. It is noteworthy that Guangdong is a major export-processing base for foreign investors mainly from Hong Kong and Taiwan. Guangdong ranked at the top in attracting foreign direct investment (FDI) among all provinces and municipalities. Guangdong accounted for one-third of China's total utilized FDI. Foreign investments in Guangdong are mainly in manufacturing industries (70 percent of utilized FDI), including computer accessories, computers, biological products, mechanical and electrical products, refined chemicals, and traditional industries such as toys and garments. Foreign-invested enterprises are playing an important role in Guangdong's economy, accounting for 60 percent of Guangdong's gross industrial output and exports.

Hong Kong is the largest source of foreign direct investment in Guangdong. Other major investors in Guangdong are from Taiwan, Japan, South Korea, Singapore, and the United States. Many world leading multinationals such as IBM, Intel, Hitachi, Samsung, Nokia, Sony, General Electric, P&G, Amway, ICI, Ericsson, Siemens, Panasonic, Bosch, Toshiba, Sanyo, Nestle, Pepsi, Coca-Cola, and Mitsubishi have established their presence in Guangdong.

Shenzhen

Shenzhen, a boomtown bordering Hong Kong and a fishing village just 20 years ago, has replaced the provincial capital

Guangzhou to lead the local economy. In 1980, Shenzhen was designated as China's first special economic zone. The permanent resident population in Shenzhen in 1980 was only 300,000. Today's population has reached 7 million, reflecting the significance and attractiveness of the city as a manufacturing and transportation base.

Shenzhen's GDP totaled over $120 billion in 2005, up by 15 percent over the previous year. Its economy grew by 16.3 percent yearly from 2001 to 2005 on average. The Shenzhen port ranks as the world's fourth largest container port, having an annual throughput of 13.6 billion containers.

While Shenzhen is a manufacturing base for a number of traditional industries, new and high-tech industries development has been designated as one of the focuses of the city's economic construction since the mid 1990s. New and high-tech products account for nearly half the city's total industrial output, ranking first among Chinese cities. Shenzhen's exports of new and high-tech products account for 20 percent of the national total, higher than other major Chinese cities. Electronics and telecommunications equipment account for over 90 percent of the total output of Shenzhen's new and high-tech industries.

Proximity to Hong Kong, an international service center, is one of the advantages of Shenzhen. As a manufacturing base for a wide range of industries, Shenzhen can use Hong Kong as a trade platform to expand its global market. On the other hand, foreign enterprises can supply industrial products to Shenzhen through Hong Kong.

Negotiating in the Dynamic South

Chinese in the south have always been the closest to foreign influences. This has yielded a special entrepreneurship and creativity. Negotiators are reputed to be relatively honest and forthright. They are less calculating than folks in Shanghai. But they are excellent traders and particularly interested in making a quick buck.

They share with their Hong Kong cousins Cantonese, the rough sounding, vulgar, dialect as rich and complicated as their food.

The Other 800 Million Chinese

So far in this chapter we have talked about one-third of the population of China—the coastal, industrializing, relatively rich folks. There is also the rural China few Westerners ever see. This is the part of China that doesn't yet participate in the global economy. The central government has not paid much attention to these people until recently. These 800 million people received about 9 percent of the central government budget, that is, some $42 billion in 2005. That amounts to about $55 a head for rural roads, water and power supplies, and schools and hospitals. Recent tax cuts for these folks also added up to about $19 per person.

Unrest in the countryside flares up as the economic divide widens and communication technologies display the gap. The problems of development for this two-thirds of the population are daunting, and the scale of the potential social frictions are truly frightening. The opportunities for American companies there may be very different from those on the bustling east coast.

Development in the central and western regions is focused on the large cities such as Chongqing, Wuhan, Changsha, Chengdu, and Kuming. China's World War II capital of about 31 million today, Chongqing is 1,500 miles up the Yangtze River from Shanghai. The average income for a Chongqing resident was about $1,000 last year, compared with that of his rural neighbors at about $250. But the government is not spending much in the area. Instead, we find multinational companies funding the development. For example, British Petroleum is building a $200 million chemical plant in the area, Volvo has begun producing its small S40 series there, and Yamaha has a motorcycle plant nearby as well. Much, much more work needs to be done. But, as wages rise along with the recent labor shortages along the east coast, the "market" will pull development westward.[3] "How fast" is the question of the day. Already labor-intensive industries such as textiles and consumer electronics have been moving westward. Provinces in central China such as Hunan, Hubei, and Jianxi are the sizes of France, Italy, and Spain, respectively. The infrastructures are developing there, and the workforces are well educated.

We find it encouraging that despite the immense difficulties that China faces, President Hu and Premier Wen are taking a genuine interest in improving the lot of the other 800 million Chinese. It appears that the focus on developing the coastal region has now shifted to developing the hinterland, and with a new sense of urgency. Whether China succeeds depends on how foreign investors react to various factors such as lower costs and wages, as well as government incentives.

Notes

1 Willem van Kemenade, *China, Hong Kong, Taiwan, Inc.:
   The Dynamics of a New Empire* (New York: Random House,
   Vintage Books edition, 1998), p. 315.
2 Kenichi Ohmae, *The China Impact* (Taipei: Common
   Wealth Magazine Co., Ltd., Complex Chinese edition,
   2002), p. 131.
3 Yao-Hwa Shen, "Chinese Industries Will Move Upward
   and Westward," *Business Weekly* (Taipei), August 1, 2005,
   pp. 92–93.

CHAPTER 12

HONG KONG— THE PEARL OF THE ORIENT AND ITS LUSTER

Hong Kong captures the world's imagination like no other place on the face of earth. From an outpost used by the British opium traders (see James Clavell's famous novels *Tai-Pan* and *Noble House*) to a colony which became Great Britain's crown jewel to a haven for tourists and shoppers the world over to a locale of Bruce Lee (*Enter the Dragon*) and Jackie Chan (*Shanghai Noon*) films to a financial center known as the Morocco of Asia, Hong Kong has long enjoyed its fame as the Pearl of the Orient.

However, as June 30, 1997, loomed near and Hong Kong was to be returned to China, many began writing obituaries for Hong Kong, the most famous of which is the cover story of the June 1995 issue of *Fortune* titled, "The Death of Hong Kong."

Since 1995 Hong Kong's experience can be aptly signified by two similar acronyms—SAR and SARS. First, since 1997 Hong Kong has been officially designated not as a country or a province but instead as a "Special Administrative Region," or SAR. As a condition of returning Hong Kong to China and for ensuring certain civic liberties, the British, with Chris Patton as their mouthpiece, managed to extract from China a promise that Hong Kong would be ruled under the concept of "one country, two systems" for the first 50 years after its return to China. Hence, the term SAR was born.

After Hong Kong's handover to China in 1997, Hong Kong could do no right. The new airport which was supposed to showcase Britain's gift of Hong Kong to the world malfunctioned upon its opening, causing great embarrassment to many and inconvenience to many more travelers. Tales of woe and lost luggage abounded.

The Asian financial crisis which ravaged many Asian countries such as Indonesia and South Korea also descended upon Hong Kong, causing tremendous financial loss and emotional pain for many. In 1998, Hong Kong's economic growth was −5.1 percent; the HangSeng Stock Index dropped to 6,643; housing prices dropped by almost 50 percent; and the unemployment rate reached 6.3 percent, the worst it had been in 19 years.

The Hong Kong economy stayed decidedly downbeat for the next seven years. Cabdrivers who used to brag about their winnings in the stock and property markets were talking about how they were lucky to have a couple pieces of "mantou" (the Chinese steam bun) per day. The long queues for taxis virtually disappeared, contrary to the earlier part of the decade when it was extremely difficult to get a cab.

Then in 2003 the second acronym demanded the attention of the planet. Early that year, a mysterious disease known as severe acute respiratory syndrome (SARS) hit Hong Kong. Confidence in Hong Kong sank to a new low. It looked as if *Fortune*'s prediction about Hong Kong was spot on—Hong Kong was doomed to an inexorable decline in its economic fortunes. Even the tagline of an all out marketing campaign by the Hong Kong government—Hong Kong, It Takes Your Breath Away—had the most unintended and negative consequence imaginable. It literally took people's breath, as well as their lives, away.

Just as it looked like Hong Kong was becoming less than "just another Chinese city," an apparent miracle happened, and Hong Kong's economy turned on a dime. In 2005, Hong Kong's economy grew by 8.1 percent; the HangSeng Index reached its highest level since February 2001; housing prices went up by 90 percent between 2004 and early 2006. What appeared to be the most immediate trigger to Hong Kong's rebound was the Chinese Central Bank's decision to revaluate the Chinese yuan. But, two far more fundamental reasons—Hong Kong as the world's freest economy and China's unwavering support and backing—best explain the dramatic recovery.

Overall Development[1]

Hong Kong's economic strength can be seen with a glance at the following economic highlights:

- The world's freest economy.
- The world's most service-oriented economy (services sectors accounting for 90 percent of GDP).
- The world's second highest per capita holding of foreign exchange reserves.
- The world's seventh largest foreign exchange reserves holding.
- Asia's highest per capita GDP.
- The second largest source of outward foreign direct investment (FDI) in Asia.
- The second largest FDI recipient in Asia.
- The second largest stock exchange in Asia.

Exhibits 12.1 and 12.2 demonstrate the late 1990s slowdown for Hong Kong and the most recent revival. Hong Kong's real GDP rose by 7.3 percent in 2005, following an impressive 8.6 percent growth in 2004; and overtook Japan's for the first time in the last 30 years. This solid expansion has been underpinned by a buoyant performance of the external sector and a sustained growth of private spending and investment. Growth is expected to moderate to 4 to 5 percent in the near term.

Trade

Total exports posted a remarkable 11.4 percent gain in 2005, with domestic exports and reexports growing by 8 percent and 11.7 percent, respectively. The vibrant export growth was underpinned by

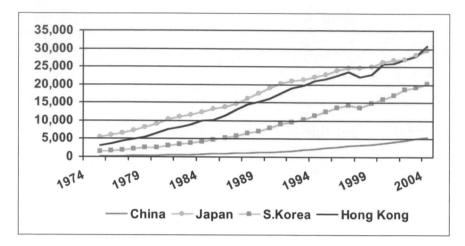

Exhibit 12.1   GDP per Capita PPP (Current International $)
(*Source: World Development Indicators*)

the Chinese mainland's hearty appetite for industrial inputs for export production, notably electronics parts and components resulting from stronger than expected global demand for electronics products and sustained consumer demand from the United States and the European Union, especially for garments amid quota re-

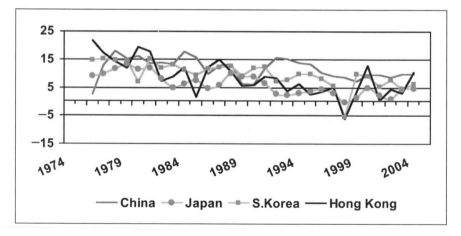

Exhibit 12.2   GDP per Capita PPP—Percent Change (Current International $) (*Source: World Development Indicators*)

moval. In addition, firmer unit values of Hong Kong exports, up by 1.3 percent in 2005, further contributed to the robust export performance. Hong Kong's major export markets are the Chinese mainland, the United States, the European Union, and Japan. They respectively made up 45 percent, 16 percent, 15 percent, and 5 percent of Hong Kong's total exports in 2005.

Hong Kong's trade performance is in part fuelled by outward processing activities in Guangdong where the majority of Hong Kong companies have extended their manufacturing base. In the first nine months of 2005, 38 percent of Hong Kong's total exports to the Chinese mainland were related to outward processing activities; the figure was 56 percent for domestic exports and 37 percent for reexports.

Investment, Finance, and Banking

According to the United Nations World Investment Report 2005, Hong Kong ranked as the second largest recipient of inward FDI in Asia and the seventh in the world. While world FDI inflows only grew by 2 percent in 2004, inflows to Hong Kong surged by 150 percent to $34 billion in that year. Hong Kong was the largest source of outward FDI among Asian economies and the seventh in the world in 2004. In terms of cumulative amount on approval basis, Hong Kong was the largest investor in the Chinese mainland and was among the leading investors in Indonesia, Taiwan, Thailand, Vietnam, and the Philippines.

Hong Kong's stock market ranks as the second largest in Asia and the ninth largest in the world in terms of market capitalization. In 2005 there were 1,124 companies listed on the stock exchange, including 202 companies on the growth enterprise market (GEM). The total market capitalization of Hong Kong's stock market reached $1 trillion in 2005. Hong Kong is also the second largest venture capital center in Asia, managing about 27 percent of the total capital pool in the region.

Hong Kong is an important banking services and financial center in the Asia Pacific region. In 2005 there were 201 authorized banks and 86 representative offices in Hong Kong; and the total loans provided by the authorized banks to finance international trade amounted to $18.4 billion, and other loans for use outside Hong Kong totalled $28.1 billion. According to the Bank for International Settlements, Hong Kong is the third largest foreign exchange market in Asia and the sixth largest in the world.

International Center of Commerce

Hong Kong is a popular venue for hosting regional headquarters or representative offices for multinational companies to manage their businesses in the Asia Pacific, particularly the Chinese mainland. Based on a government survey, the European Union as a whole has the largest total number of regional headquarters and offices in Hong Kong with 1,033 companies, followed by the United States (868), Japan (741), and the Chinese mainland (267).

Hong Kong is also a favorite place in the world to do business and host major conferences. Over 300 international conventions and exhibitions are held in Hong Kong each year. To name a few, Hong Kong hosted the 2001 Fortune Global Forum in May 2001, the 16th World Congress of Accountants in November 2002, and the "Luxury 2004: The Lure of Asia" Conference organized by the *International Herald Tribune* in December 2004. More recently in December 13–18, 2005, Hong Kong hosted the sixth session of the World Trade Organization's ministerial conference at which a Hong Kong declaration was concluded.

Information/Telecommunications

Hong Kong is a leading telecommunications hub for the Asia Pacific region. At the end of September 2005, there were 3.8 million telephone lines and 420,997 fax lines in Hong Kong. IDD telephone services are available to over 230 overseas countries/areas and 2,200 Chinese mainland cities, with the total international telephone traffic growing at an annualized rate of 8 percent to 6 billion minutes between 2000 and 2004. There are more than 8 million mobile phone subscribers, even outnumbering Hong

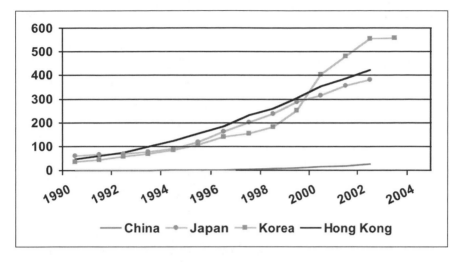

Exhibit 12.3   Personal Computers (per 1,000 People)
(*Source: World Development Indicators*)

Kong's total population! The penetration rate of broadband Internet reached 64.6 percent among households in September 2004. See Exhibits 12.3 and 12.4, which present the fundamental indicators of the information/telecommunications infrastructure.

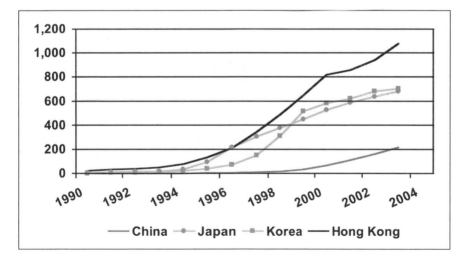

Exhibit 12.4   Mobile Phones (per 1,000 People)
(*Source: World Development Indicators*)

Tourism

Hong Kong has long been known as one of the world's most popular destinations for tourism and shopping. A total of 23.4 million visitors, or 3.4 times the size of the local population, came to Hong Kong in 2005, representing a 7.1 percent surge in arrival numbers from a year earlier.

Effective January 2002, the quota system for mainland tourists under the Hong Kong group tour scheme was abolished. Accordingly, the number of mainland tourists travelling to Hong Kong has soared. In 2005, visitor arrivals from China and rest of the world rose by 2.4 percent and 13.1 percent, respectively. Mainland visitors (13.4 million in 2005) now account for more than half of total tourist arrivals. About 5.5 million or 44 percent of mainland visitors came to Hong Kong under the individual visitor scheme, marking a growth of 30 percent in arrivals.

The brand-new Hong Kong Disneyland is expected to further boost tourism. Indeed, when plans were first discussed for the new amusement park, the mantra was, "Half the population of the planet lives within five hours of the new airport." However, an article from the *Wall Street Journal*[2] demonstrates that nothing is ever easy in China:

Li Zeng, a 14-year-old Chinese tourist, wandered Hong Kong Disneyland yesterday—and left after two hours. Mr. Li isn't that familiar with Mickey Mouse and his companions, and he and his father didn't take any rides, buy souvenirs, or eat food. "We don't understand this park," said the teenager, waiting for his tour bus. "We gave up looking at the map."

Five months after Walt Disney Co. opened its Hong Kong theme park in a bid to tap the booming Chinese market, the cultural divide that separates Mickey and Mr. Li is still a major challenge. It is one that the company is trying hard to bridge, though with mixed results.

The need to adapt was on display here last week. After Disney underestimated the number of people who would visit during mainland China's weeklong Lunar New Year holiday, vacationing crowds poured in, filling the park to its maximum capacity. Disney officials ordered the gates shut, and hundreds of angry guests from China who held valid tickets found themselves unable to enter. Some engaged in shouting matches with park staff, and at least one excluded family tried to pass a child over the park's wrought-iron fence.

Before last week, Disney's problem wasn't too many visitors, but the flak it was getting for having too few. It drew public rebuke over low attendance from local politicians, who questioned the wisdom of the Hong Kong government's 57% stake in the park. Local retailers said they didn't get the sales boost they were expecting from the new tourists Disneyland had promised to draw.

The company is "still learning" about Chinese culture, said the park's managing director, Bill Ernest, on Saturday during an emotional public apology for last week's ticket fiasco.

Jay Rasulo, the head of Disney's theme-park division, notes it is early days yet and stresses the need to put such criticism in "context." He says overall guest experiences at the park are "some of the best in the world," with over 90% of the visitors Disney interviewed last week saying they had a positive time. "Part of the way we make people happy is that we listen, learn and adjust as necessary," said Mr. Rasulo.

These lessons are crucial for Disney as Chief Executive Robert Iger holds what he calls "ongoing negotiations" to open another Asian park in Shanghai and seeks to build the company's consumer products, movie and television business in China. Disney has trumpeted its attempts to accommodate Chinese culture, some of which later drew fire. Conservationists blasted the company for planning to serve environmentally unfriendly shark's fin soup, and Disney later decided to forgo the practice. Efforts to woo local celebrities backfired when some complained of mistreatment by visiting American Disney executives. Disney designed the park for Chinese tourists, who the company said preferred photo opportunities over roller coasters. Many visitors now criticize the park for being too small.

Chinese travel agencies also have noted some visitor befuddlement. "Many customers complain they do not know how to enjoy Disneyland," says Chen Mei, the international tours manager of the Ju Cheng agency, which brings groups to the park from the city of Zhongshan in southern China. Some mainland tourists show up at the park only to walk aimlessly around Main Street U.S.A. and snap a few photos with Marie the Cat—a minor character from the 1970s film The Aristocats. Marie is familiar to some from the movie's repeat showings in southern China. She also happens to look like another Asian favorite, Hello Kitty.

Even before last week's incident, Disney was changing the way it does business at the park. Disney invited in more Chinese celebrities and made sure they got VIP treatment. It cut the cost of tickets for local residents during a low period for tourists, and added a local promotion, artificial snow, to Hong Kong's subtropical climate. Disney also now produces marketing that includes the testimonials of real people who have visited the park, instead of just slick studio shots.

To help confused visitors, since November Disney has started producing special "one-day trip guides" in Chinese, beyond the basic maps, to explain in clear terms exactly how to enjoy Disneyland—and why it is enjoyable. "You can get together with family to relax and improve communication and relationships with the people you love," reads the guide. Disney hands out the fliers inside the park, and at other Hong Kong tourist attractions. Perhaps most significantly for park attendance, Hong Kong Disneyland is changing the way it works with Chinese travel agents.

Most mainland Chinese still take vacations through package tours, and they make up about 50% of the Chinese visitors to the park. The guides who direct these tours frequently select hotels, restaurants, shopping stops and even tour destinations based on where they share in the profits. Because of lucrative deals with tour operators, one Hong Kong transvestite cabaret brags that its five-times-a-day $20 show draws more Chinese tourists on a regular basis than Disneyland. Mr. Ernest says Disney, which doesn't have much experience with such financial arrangements, *now realizes that changing something as simple as how it offers dinners can make a big difference to the local travel industry. Many tour packages for visitors from China include pre-arranged dinners. Tour operators typically get a cut of the meal costs. Without group dinner deals and significant commissions, Disney wasn't offering guides much financial incentive to funnel tourists into the park. Now Mr. Ernest says he is considering starting a "dining with Disney" program. Special group breakfasts with Disney characters are another option, he says.*

Disney is reaching out in other ways. When the Ju Cheng agency publicly threatened to sue over last week's ticket problem, Disney offered a conciliatory tone—and refunds for people who couldn't come back on another day. "We are probably as critical on ourselves as anybody is with us," says Mr. Ernest.

To build relationships, Disney is giving Chinese travel agents a 50% personal discount if they come visit its park and hotels. The company also beefed up incentives for tour operators to build a Disneyland visit into packages by increasing the margin it offered them to about $2.50 per adult ticket. And it changed its sales packages to include open-ended instead of just fixed-date tickets so operators wouldn't have to eat the cost of returned tickets.

It was the old ticketing system combined with unexpected crowds, says Disney's Mr. Ernest, which created the overcrowding problems last week.

Disney declines to release specific attendance figures. When legislators in the Hong Kong government demanded some public accountability in late November, two months after the park's mid-September opening, Disney said that it had hosted more than one million guests. While that figure suggests that the park is behind its 5.6 million forecast for the opening year, Mr. Rasulo says the park still expects to reach that level.

In the wake of the changes, Disney officials say overall attendance is "ramping up," particularly among mainland Chinese tourists, whose attendance during the Lunar New Year period more than doubled compared with another weeklong Chinese holiday in October.

Understanding the peaks and troughs of attendance is another thing Disney concedes it has yet to master. Mr. Rasulo noted that Disney once suffered through some overcrowding at the EuroDisney park based in Paris: after the first summer in 1992, the park was inundated in September with locals who had been putting off their trips to avoid the early wave of tourists.

Li Ka-shing

Finally, one must also appreciate the past, present, and future influence of Li Ka-shing's financial/industrial empire on the economic development of Hong Kong. Toward that end we excerpt[3] the following information about the man and his institution:

Li Ka-shing is the wealthiest person in Hong Kong and East Asia. According to Forbes, *he is also the richest person of Chinese descent in the world. Presently, he is the Chairman of Cheung Kong Holdings. A Harvard Business School article summarized Li's career: "From his humble beginnings in China as a teacher's son, a refugee, and later as a salesman, Li provides a lesson in integrity and adaptability. Through hard work, and a reputation for remaining true to his internal moral compass, he was able to build a business empire that includes: banking, construction, real estate, plastics, cellular phones, satellite television, cement production, retail outlets (pharmacies and supermarkets), hotels, domestic transportation (sky train), airports, electric power, steel production, ports, and shipping."*

Considered one of the most powerful figures in Asia, Li was named "Asia's Most Powerful Man" by Asiaweek *in 2000. On March 9, 2006,* Forbes *ranked him as 10th richest man in the world at $18.8 billion. In spite of his wealth, Li has a reputation for leading a no-frills lifestyle, and is known to wear cheap shoes and plastic watches.*

Li is also a noted philanthropist; his 1981 donations resulted in the founding of Shantou University, near his hometown of Chaozhou. After the 2004 Indian Ocean Earthquake disaster, he *reportedly pledged a total of US$3 million. In 2005, Li announced a $128 million donation to the University of Hong Kong, which provoked controversy over the public status of the university. The Li Ka-shing Library at the Singapore Management University is also named in his honor after a $11.5 million donation to the higher education institution.*

For many years, Li was also a member of the boards of directors of the China International Trust and Investment Corporation (CITIC). CITIC is China's largest conglomerate and is 42 percent owned by the government of China. It serves as the chief investment arm of China's central government and holds ministry status on the Chinese State Council. Li is often referred to as "Superman" in Hong Kong because of his business prowess.

Li Ka-shing was born in Chaozhou in the Guangdong Province, China, in 1928. In 1940 the Li family fled to Hong Kong as the Japanese invaded China. Li's family stayed at the home of his wealthy uncle. The arrogance of Li's uncle and immense wealth ignited Li's determination to make a place for himself in the world. Not able to find work on his own, the young Li reluctantly accepted his first job selling watches at his uncle's store, Li's intensity and intelligence soon made him the best salesman in the shop at age 17, and general manager at age 19. Soon after, Li jumped to another company to sell metal wares door to door. He worked 16 hour days: during the day, he would visit customers and close deals; at night he would be at the factory, following up on orders and learning the manufacturing business. His commission paycheck as a salesman is said to be seven times the amount the second best salesman took home. Li, determined to do business with the powerful British, found a private tutor to teach him English every night.

Li's businesses are dominant in every facet of life in Hong Kong, from electricity to telecom, from real estate to retail, from shipping to the Internet. It is often said that for every dollar spent in Hong Kong, 5 cents goes into the pocket of Li Ka-shing. At the end of 2005 the flagship firms in which he controls, Cheung Kong Group and Hutchinson Whampoa, had a market capitalization *of over $150 billion (US dollars). His firms operate in more than 51 countries and employ over 210,000 staff worldwide. Li's two sons control major parts of his financial and industrial empire.*

Economic Relations with the Chinese Mainland

Hong Kong is the most important entrepôt for the Chinese mainland. If reexports to and from the Chinese mainland are included, about 22 percent of the mainland's foreign trade was handled via Hong Kong. Hong Kong is also the largest source of overseas direct investment in the Chinese mainland. By the end of 2004, among all the overseas-funded projects registered in the Chinese mainland, 47 percent were tied to Hong Kong interests.

The Chinese mainland is one of the leading investors in Hong Kong. According to the Hong Kong SAR Census and Statistics Department, the mainland's cumulative direct investment in Hong Kong was US$ 130.8 billion or 29 percent of Hong Kong's total stock of inward direct investment at the end of 2004. Over 100 mainland-backed and state-owned enterprises are listed on the main board of the Stock Exchange of Hong Kong and its growth enterprise market (GEM).

There are currently 26 Chinese banks and seven representative offices operating in Hong Kong. The Bank of China is now the second largest banking group in Hong Kong after HSBC Group. In addition, China's other three specialized banks—the Industrial and Commercial Bank of China, the Agricultural Bank of China, and the People's Bank of Construction of China—also opened branch operations in Hong Kong. Some other mainland commercial banks such as the Shenzhen Development Bank, China Everbright Bank, and China Merchants Bank also have representative offices in Hong Kong.

Hong Kong is also a key offshore capital-raising center for Chinese enterprises. By the end of 2004, a total of 301 mainland companies (including H-shares, red chips, and other overseas registered Chinese companies) were listed in Hong Kong with a total market capitalization of US$ 256 billion or 30 percent of Hong Kong's total market capitalization. In the past 11 years, total funds raised by these mainland companies amounted to US$ 102 billion. The listing of two Chinese insurers, PICC and China Life, is a major recent success.

CEPA: A Free-Trade Agreement between Hong Kong and the Chinese Mainland

In effect since 2004, the closer economic partnership arrangement (CEPA) between Hong Kong and the mainland is the first bilateral free-trade agreement (FTA) for both the Chinese mainland and Hong Kong. CEPA is designed to ensure that Hong Kong will be "economically interlocked" with the mainland and that smaller Hong Kong companies will benefit from the opening up of and liberalization on the mainland beyond China's commitments in its WTO accession.

Opportunities in Trade in Goods

With CEPA, 90 percent of Hong Kong domestic exports to the mainland will eventually enjoy zero tariffs. This will allow almost all of Hong Kong domestic exports to the mainland in 2007 to enter duty-free. The annual savings in tariffs are estimated to be HK$ 750 million.

Apart from zero tariffs enjoyed by products made in Hong Kong, products made by Hong Kong and/or trade by Hong Kong will also benefit from CEPA in other ways. Upon China's WTO accession, many Hong Kong manufacturers with production on the mainland would like to develop China as their domestic market. However, their market penetration efforts have been somewhat hindered by the underdeveloped distribution system on the mainland. Many hazards in developing the China market such as payment problems and intellectual property rights protection now facing Hong Kong manufacturers can hopefully be alleviated as more Hong Kong players will be allowed to engage in distribution business on the mainland under CEPA.

A longer-term effect of the zero-tariff agreement is the potential for attracting more high value-added manufacturing activities to be located in Hong Kong and promoting development of brand products made in Hong Kong to emerging middle-class consumers on the mainland.

Capitalizing on the advantage of Hong Kong in intellectual property rights protection, the free-trade and investment environment, and its reputation for cosmopolitan design, Hong Kong is in a good position to develop high intellectual property (IP) value industries that target the mainland market.

For high-end products such as designer clothing and personal accessories, and industries that involve proprietary technology (since the intellectual property input accounts for a much larger share than labor and other inputs in the total cost structure), production in Hong Kong may still be justifiable. Since the high IP value industries are knowledge-based and would not be massive in scale, the effect of job creation in Hong Kong, especially for unskilled workers, would be only moderate.

Opportunities in Service Industries

CEPA provisions on market access cover a total of 17 service industries. These include: management consultant services, exhibitions and conventions, advertising, accountancy, construction and real estate, medical and dental services, distribution services, logistics services, freight forwarding and agency services, storage and warehousing services, transport services, tourism, audiovisual, legal services, banking, securities, and insurance. Although the special liberalization varies from industry to industry, China has taken into account the special niche of Hong Kong as CEPA commitments go beyond the country's WTO accession protocol, for example, the opening-up of exhibition business to Hong Kong companies.[4]

Besides the exhibition industry, Hong Kong's niche in the audio-visual industry is well recognized. With the quota free access to the mainland of Chinese language films produced in Hong Kong and the relaxation on the coproduction requirements, CEPA paves the way for the recovery of Hong Kong's film industry by creating great potential in the mainland market. More important, it provides a very good avenue for Hong Kong to post itself as a modern and dynamic metropolis before mainland consumers.

Along with Hong Kong products and Hong Kong companies, Hong Kong professionals and residents will benefit from CEPA. Hong Kong professionals in the securities and insurance industries can apply to practice on the mainland, and Hong Kong permanent residents are permitted to take the legal qualifying examination on the mainland. Moreover, Hong Kong permanent residents are formally permitted to engage in retail activity in Guangdong. All this suggests that in the future more Hong Kong people are likely to seek employment and business opportunities on the mainland.

The Culture and Behavior of Chinese Managers in Hong Kong

The business culture in Hong Kong is distinct from the general descriptions in Chapters 7 to 10 in important ways. Almost all the Chinese people you deal with in Hong Kong will be bilingual, at least speaking English fluently. Indeed, their English is probably better than yours. John remembers fondly a banquet hosted by a Chinese colleague who recited from memory the chorus from *Romeo and Juliet* in perfect, British-accented English to open the festivities. Those British accents sound so intelligent!

As Hong Kong executives have learned English, they've also absorbed British culture in a deep way. At bus stops they actually queue, for example. For most their first language is Cantonese.

Among English speakers worldwide, the British are the most reserved, the stuffiest sounding, communicating hierarchy with tones of voice that Americans often miss. Among Chinese speakers around the world, Cantonese is the roughest dialect. It almost always sounds like an argument is going on, and the swearing possible and practiced in Cantonese is legendary—incredibly vulgar at times. Cantankerous Cantonese is also more complicated than the fast-encroaching mellow mainland Mandarin—the former uses nine tones and the latter only four. While your Chinese counterparts may appear to be arguing among themselves on the other side of the negotiating table, that's really just the style of talk. Moreover, they'll often seem strangely calm when they turn back to you to talk in English. And, complicating matters even more for Americans, managers in Hong Kong do not understand and/or appreciate the American notion of venting emotions and then getting back to business. If you get angry with them, face is lost on both sides of the table, and usually the deal is dead. Finally, humility and indirection are more emphasized in southern than in northern China as well. Relatedly, another contrast in behavior is well described in *Hong Kong Business*:[5]

> *[Hong Kong] Chinese can be the most courteous people in the world toward their friends. When a friend visits a friend, every detail of his or her stay may be prearranged, and the guest may not be allowed to spend money even on the smallest items. For individualists from the West, this form of courtesy can be overwhelming. However, when Chinese in Hong Kong deal with strangers, they are often rude or uncaring. Such behavior is a psychological necessity in a city as densely packed as Hong Kong (or New York or Paris). Crowds everywhere push and shove; no apologies are given, and none are expected.*

The Janus face of Hong Kong negotiators comes up in another peculiar way. The Hong Kong business culture is known for its efficiency and speed. Big decisions are often made on the spot, based more on an intuitive, almost speculative feel for the situation, by those at the top of the family hierarchy. Contrarily, an often reported negotiation tactic used in Hong Kong is strategic delays. So you will have to be ready for both speeds.

Hong Kong's Future

Given Hong Kong's glittering past as the pearl of the orient and its roller coaster ride in the last 10 years, what does the future hold for Hong Kong?

It would be presumptuous for us to predict the long-term future of Hong Kong, as its fate is so intertwined with the future of so many countries—especially those of China and Taiwan. However, we think that Hong Kong has managed to find its niche in the greater China region and is likely to maintain its place for the next 10 years based on a few well reasoned observations.

Because of Hong Kong's colonial past, it has a well-developed Anglo-American–based legal system. Generally, it takes quite some time to develop a well-functioning legal system which facilitates commerce and ensures predictability and the sanctity of contracts. Since the Anglo-American legal paradigm is generally regarded as the most important, if not the most widely used or admired, legal system in the world because of the dominance of Great Britain and the United States in the twentieth century, Hong Kong benefits from being a colony of Great Britain for over 100 years.

Furthermore, Hong Kong has the freest economy in the world. The Hong Kong government does not put capital or policy requirements on either foreign subsidiaries or branches. It boasts an extremely simple tax system—it only taxes corporate profits, individual incomes, and property incomes; it does not impose sales tax, capital gains tax, dividend tax, and other hidden taxes. It offers an extremely free labor market—no minimum wage requirement. It has no foreign currency control, unlike many other countries, particularly those in the greater China region—China and Taiwan. Hong Kong has ranked as the freest economy in the world for the past 10 years in Heritage Foundation's ranking of the world's freest economies.

Most importantly, during the past 10 years, a most difficult period in Hong Kong's economic history, Hong Kong has managed to find its niche in the face of its much better endowed neighbors—China and Taiwan. While Taiwan has excelled in capital and technology-intensive R&D and manufacturing and is anchored by high tech, information technology, and petrochemical industries (roughly 30 percent of its total publicly listed companies), Hong Kong's representative industries are finance, tourism, and retail, consisting of roughly 40 percent of its publicly listed companies. Of course, China has come to be known as the world's factory.

It is interesting to note that despite the relocation and outsourcing of practically all manufacturing activities in Hong Kong, it has been able to leverage its past and carve out rather important and unique niches—financial and legal services and tourism. Moreover, it has even become a major logistics center. It has the world's busiest airport for international cargoes, and it boasts the world's second largest container port.

Aggregately, Hong Kong's companies fared better than Taiwan companies in recent years in both revenue and profitability. Whether Hong Kong will be able to consolidate and strengthen its competitive position depends very much on Taiwan's response. In the next chapter, we examine Taiwan—known as Silicon Valley East—its unique past, its uncertain present, its future, and its impact on Hong Kong's future.

Notes

1 The source for much of the material in this section is the Hong Kong Trade Development Council Web site, www.tdctrade.com.
2 Geoffrey A. Fowler and Merissa Marr, "Disney and the Great Wall," *Wall Street Journal*, February 9, 2006, pp. B1, B2.

3 www.wikipedia.com.

4 China did not make any commitment to open up the
exhibition industry in its accession to the WTO. Foreign
exhibition companies have to cooperate with the 200-plus
appointed organizations to organize international exhibitions
in China. The exhibition license, however, is allocated to a
Chinese company. Foreign exhibition companies face the
uncertainties of ownership of the names and logos associated
with exhibitions. The plan for allowing joint venture exhibition companies has yet to be implemented.

5 Christine A. Genzberger et al., *Hong Kong Business*
(San Rafael, CA: World Trade Press, 1994), p. 129.

CHAPTER 13

TAIWAN—SILICON VALLEY EAST AND THE ENGINE THAT DRIVES CHINA

If Hong Kong captures the world's imagination like no other place on the face of earth, Taiwan is "the hidden center of the global economy"[1] and "the powder keg" which many say might lead to a military confrontation between China and the United States.

From an island which was occupied by the seafaring Dutch, to a base used by Chinese rebels who resisted the rule of the Manchu government, to a Japanese colony from 1895 to 1905, to a refuge used by Chiang Kai-shek and his government after he was driven out by the Communists in 1949, to an authoritarian police state for over 30 years, to a fledging democracy which boasts a freer press than that of the United States, to a de facto independent political entity the Chinese government called the "renegade province," to a region known as Silicon Valley East which has been a major player in the global high-tech boom in the last two decades,[2] Taiwan is a study in contrasts and of tremendous importance—both in terms of its crucial role in the global economy and in geopolitics.

Confusing? Indeed. While most people could very clearly think of Hong Kong with specific characteristics, Taiwan has no clear identity in either business or politics. At various times people have seen and used lots of "Made in Taiwan" products with or without knowing them, ranging from shoes and umbrellas to bicycles to tennis rackets to personal computers, peripherals, and monitors to the latest and the greatest rage—iPods. In a span of three decades, Taiwan has gone from an agrarian society to a low-tech manufacturing base to a high-tech mecca. Without it, personal computers and many other electronic gadgets would not have been so inexpensively produced and popularized. And Bill Gates would not have become the richest man in the world. However, most people have no way or reason to know this, as Taiwan has quietly gone about doing its own thing and has become "the little engine that could" and probably the best kept secret in the world for its immense contribution.

While Hong Kong is decidedly high profile and marketing-driven, Taiwan is just the opposite—always under the hood. Perhaps this is best illustrated by the fact that few people in the world know that Taiwan boasts the tallest building in the world—the 101 Tower in Taipei.

What has made matters even more confusing is the ambiguity that surrounds its political status—is Taiwan a country, a renegade province (and part of China), a city state, or a place under the sphere of influence of the United States? Many even have mistaken Taiwan for Thailand! Taiwan held its first democratic election in 1996, and Lee Teng Hui was elected. This was the first time in Chinese history that a democratically elected leader ruled its citizenry. President Lee embarked on a mission of calling the world's attention to Taiwan as an independent country. What ensued was tremendous tension between the mainland Chinese government and the de facto independent Taiwan government.

In an attempt to intimidate Taiwan voters and to change the outcome of the election in 1996, China fired missiles into the Taiwan Strait. The action backfired as Taiwan voters not only were not intimidated, but they overwhelmingly voted for Lee. This Chinese action also provoked a strong response from the United States as President Clinton sent a Seventh Fleet aircraft carrier battle group to the coast of Taiwan to warn China that the United States would not condone any further provocation.

In 2000 and 2004, a pro-Taiwan independence president Chen Shui-bian was elected. His tough stance on Taiwan's independent status did not make him a friend of Beijing. His administration also took actions to prohibit Taiwan companies from investing heavily in China as well as place restrictions on Chinese tourists and visitors. The relationship between the two governments is at a low point despite continual increases in their business and commercial ties. This has had an important impact on the Taiwanese economy in the last five years. Taiwan came out of the 1990s looking and smelling like roses and on top of the world, with its economic growth in full throttle, and it was scarcely affected by the Asian financial crisis that crippled many other Asian countries including South Korea. But the Taiwanese economy has been in a funk for the last half decade. What happened?

A Little Geography, History, and Politics

Located about 100 miles off the southeast coast of the China mainland, Taiwan is approximately 245 miles long (north–south) and 90 miles across at its widest point. The largest city, Taipei, is the seat of the government of the Republic of China, which is the official name of Taiwan. In addition to the main island, the Taiwan government also has jurisdiction over 22 islands in the Taiwan group and 64 islands to the west in the Pescadores Archipelago, with a total area of some 13,900 square miles.

Taiwan is bounded to the north by the East China Sea, which separates it from the Ryukyu Islands, Okinawa, and Japan; to the east by the Pacific Ocean; to the south by the Bashi Channel, which separates it from the Philippines; and to the west by the Taiwan (Formosa) Strait, which separates it from the China mainland. It literally sits in the most strategic location of East Asia—the heart of East Asia.

From the mid-1660s to 1895 Taiwan was administered by the Imperial Chinese government, after which (until 1945) the island was ruled by the Japanese as a colony. In 1945 Taiwan reverted to China, and in 1949 it became the last territory controlled by the Kuomintan Party (KMT) government which had lost the civil war to the Communists and withdrew from mainland China to Taiwan. The KMT has continued to claim jurisdiction over the Chinese mainland, whereas the government of the People's Republic of China (PRC) on the mainland claims jurisdiction over Taiwan; both governments are in agreement that the island is a province ("sheng") of China.

Taiwan was known to the Chinese as early as the third century AD, but settlement by the Chinese was not significant until the first quarter of the seventeenth century after recurrent famines in Fukien province encouraged emigration of Fukienese from the mainland. Before then the island was a base of operations for Chinese and Japanese pirates. The Portuguese, who first visited the island in 1590 and named it Ilha Formosa ("Beautiful Island"), made several unsuccessful attempts at settlement. The Dutch and Spaniards established more lasting settlements with the Dutch finally seizing the Spanish settlements in 1646. The Dutch were expelled in 1661 by Cheng Ch'eng-kung, a man of mixed Chinese-Japanese parentage and a supporter of the defeated Ming dynasty, who used the island as a center of opposition to the Ch'ing (Manchu) regime.

Imperial Chinese Rule

In 1683, 20 years after Cheng Ch'eng-kung's death, the island fell to China and became part of Fukien province. Meanwhile, sizable migrations of refugees and Ming dynasty supporters had increased the population to about 200,000. By 1842 the population was estimated at 2.5 million, and both rice and sugar had become important exports to mainland China.

Japanese Rule

In 1895, China ceded Taiwan and the Pescadores Islands to Japan after it lost the Sino-Japanese War. The Japanese occupied Taipei in June of that year over the violent opposition of the Taiwanese population. For several months a Republic of Taiwan was in existence, but it was overcome by Japanese forces. Taiwan was developed as a supplier of rice and sugar for Japan. Irrigation projects, agricultural extension services, and improvements in transportation and power supplies led to rapid increases in Taiwan's GDP. Then the Japanese policy was oriented toward the Japanization of the Taiwanese; Japanese was the language of instruction in a widespread basic educational system, and even after the end of World War II Japanese remained a lingua franca among the various Chinese dialect groups. During World War II, Taiwan was a major staging area for Japan's invasion of Southeast Asia.

The Republic of China (1945 to 1970)

As a result of the Cairo agreement of 1943, Taiwan was turned over to the Chinese KMT government in 1945, after the defeat of Japan. Many Taiwanese welcomed liberation from Japanese control, but much to their chagrin, the KMT government's objectives toward Taiwan were essentially to maintain Japanese colonial institutions—substituting Chinese mainlanders for Japanese, but only more corrupt, inept, and ruthless—and to exploit the island for its dream of retaking China. When in early 1947 the Taiwanese urban middle class protested, the mainlanders massacred ten of thousands Taiwanese—many of them were among the well-educated elite of Taiwan. This unfortunate episode is generally known as the 228 Incident in Taiwan or the March 1 Massacre. To this date, this incident still draws the demarcation between the KMT or the mainlanders and the Taiwanese. Although it was said that 30 years would pass before a new generation of Taiwanese political leaders emerged and mass Taiwanese resentment subsided, the 228 Incident leaves an irreparable scar on an older generation of Taiwanese which precludes its members from ever trusting or embracing the mainland Chinese.

In 1949–1950, following the victories of the Chinese Communists on the mainland, a stream of KMT troops, government officials, and other refugees poured into Taiwan. They survived, not knowing when the end would come, until the outbreak of the Korean War.

When North Korean troops invaded South Korea in 1950, U.S. President Truman interposed the U.S. 7th Fleet between Taiwan and the mainland and increased U.S. economic and military aid to Taipei. In the first of several major crises over Quemoy and Matsu following the Korean War, the United States incorporated Taiwan into its Pacific defense system. A mutual defense treaty signed in December 1954 pledged the United States to the defense of Taiwan and the neighboring Pescadores Islands.

U.S. support was important in the consolidation and rejuvenation of the KMT government. There was a dramatic increase in industrial and commercial construction on Taiwan and a significant improvement in communications and educational facilities. The KMT began incorporating members who were younger, better educated, more widely traveled, and much less likely to have been selected because of political connections alone.

In its first two decades on Taiwan, the KMT, the ruling party which lost China to the Communists, believed that its presence on the island would be temporary—at least this is what was made public. As younger mainlanders and Taiwanese rose to positions of authority, however, Taiwan itself became more the focus of attention.

During the 1960s an increased American demand for Taiwanese goods transformed Taiwan from an aid recipient of the United States to a trading partner. The economic boom also aided the KMT in that the growing Taiwanese interest in collective political demands—including a secret separatist movement that was actively suppressed by the KMT—was transformed into a pursuit of individual economic advancement. Moreover, the KMT continued its corrupt ways of redistributing most of the resources it controlled to selected groups comprising mostly of military personnel, teachers, and bureaucrats who either came with the KMT from China or were descendents. Thus, the great majority of the Taiwanese population had to draw on its own resources and became entrepreneurs in order to make ends meet.

It should be noted that the Taiwanese represent roughly 80 percent of the 23 million people who live in Taiwan. While they are ethnically Chinese, speak both the Fukien dialect and Mandarin, the Taiwanese are in many ways more tradition-bound (Confucian) than their counterparts in China. Because of the 228 Incident, the KMT government's relative corruption compared to that of the Japanese, the KMT's inattention to developing Taiwan for the first 25 years of its occupation, and its policies of favoring the mainlander Chinese over the Taiwanese, many Taiwanese feel a much stronger sense of kinship and connection to either Japan or the United States than to China.

Taiwan since 1970

Domestically, the transition in the 1970s from Chiang Kai-shek to Chiang Ching-kuo as president was accompanied by a gradual shift from a more autocratic to a more populist style of authoritarianism. The younger Chiang was also more interested in developing Taiwan than in dreaming about the KMT's return to China. Thus, he began to implement policies that would build the foundation for Taiwan's economic miracle.

Between 1969 and 1971, U.S. restrictions on trade and travel by Americans to China were eased. Meanwhile, a number of countries severed diplomatic relations with Taipei, and in 1971 Taiwan was ousted from the United Nations, and the People's Republic of China (PRC) replaced the Republic of China (Taiwan) as a permanent member of the U.N. Security Council. President Nixon visited Beijing in 1972, and the following year the United States established quasi-diplomatic relations with the PRC.

On January 1, 1979, the United States established formal diplomatic relations with the PRC. In the normalization agreement the United States accepted an end to all official U.S. defense ties with Taiwan and acknowledged the position that there is but one China and that Taiwan is part of China. It thus precluded itself from any future support for an independent Taiwan. Subsequently, however, the U.S. Congress passed the Taiwan Relations Act, authorizing continued social and economic ties with Taiwan. The

United States also unilaterally stated that it would continue to sell defensive arms to Taiwan, a move that complicated U.S.-China talks concerning greater defense cooperation.

Chiang Ching-kuo opened communications with the Chinese Communist mainland amid domestic political opposition in 1985. The opposition formed the Democratic Progressive Party (DPP) in 1986, and in 1987 the KMT lifted martial law, which had been in effect since 1949. The government began permitting visits to the Chinese mainland; scholars, journalists, businesspeople, tourists, and people visiting relatives were allowed to travel to the PRC.

For other important reasons 1987 was a watershed year. Not only did the KMT government lift martial law, but it also lifted currency control. This had the effect of bringing Taiwan into the global economy and allowing the prices of assets in Taiwan to reflect their true value. During the 1970s and 80s, the Taiwanese people had focused their energy on export-oriented business and manufacturing, and the Made in Taiwan (MIT) products had become ubiquitous. Meanwhile, Taiwan had continued to rake in more and more foreign currency reserves. The lifting of currency control allowed Taiwan companies and businesspeople to then participate in the global economy much more efficiently.

In January 1988 Chiang Ching-kuo died. His chosen successor, Vice President Lee Teng-Hui, became Taiwan's first Taiwan-born president. Despite the struggle between conservatives and progressives within the KMT, political democratization continued. Meanwhile, the DPP became a stronger opposition party.

With the collapse of Soviet Communism in the early 1990s and the resulting dramatic changes in world diplomacy and the balance of power, Taiwan's relations with the United States improved to some extent. Taiwan asserted its de facto autonomy through a pragmatic diplomacy, but it also began normalizing relations with the PRC by establishing organs for managing ongoing economic and social intercourse and for negotiating possible eventual reunification. Political liberalization in Taiwan focused renewed attention on social problems and fostered a cultural renaissance. As a result, Taiwan boasts one of the freest, if not the freest, press in the world. This is in striking contrast to what existed only a few years earlier and represents one of the most remarkable events in human history, for in the annals of Chinese history, there was no such thing as a free press.

The election in March 2000 of Democratic Progressive Party (DPP) presidential candidate Chen Shui-bian ended the KMT's half-century monopoly. The inexperience of the new DPP administration combined with the determination of the KMT to make things difficult for its political opposition made this unprecedented experiment a series of ugly partisan political skirmishes. Former president Lee Teng-Hui, who had resigned as head of the KMT after his handpicked candidate, Lien Chan, was crushed in the March 2000 election, threw his support to a new political party, the Taiwan Solidarity Union (TSU), which favored the maintenance of Taiwan's de facto independence from China.

Meanwhile, the KMT endorsed the novel concept of confederation with China as a way out of the half-century impasse between the PRC and Taiwan. In the December 1, 2001, parliamentary elections, the KMT suffered a crushing defeat, dropping from 110 to 68 seats, while its share of the vote plummeted from 46 percent to 31 percent. The DPP increased its seats from 66 to 87, and its vote share from 30 percent to 37 percent, making it the largest party in the 225-seat legislature. The fledgling People's First Party led by James Soong picked up 46 seats, and the TSU 13. Overall, this created a stalemate as the opposition parties—KMT and People's First Party—combined held a majority in the legislature. Thus, President Chen had difficulty pushing legislation through, which rendered his government ineffective.

The 2004 Taiwan presidential election created even more controversy than the 2000 U.S. presidential election. Lien Chan of the KMT and James Soong of the People's First Party teamed up in an attempt to unseat President Chen. It looked certain that Chen was to go down in defeat right up until the election. However, on the eve of election, an attempted assassination on President Chen was made, which invoked an outpouring of sympathetic votes, enabling Chen to win by the narrowest of margins. Allegations that the assassination was staged by Chen and/or his party flew, creating an air of illegitimacy surrounding Chen's second term, thus rendering his government even more impotent than it had been in his first term.

More importantly, prominent businesspeople who supported Chen in 2000 had practically all deserted him as Chen's government issued stringent regulations which prohibited Taiwan companies from making major investments in China. Under heavy pressure from the government, Formosa Plastic Group and other prominent businesses had to scuttle planned projects in China. It is said that Chen's unenlightened China policy had cost Taiwan industries to miss a major window of opportunity as well as marginalizing Taiwan's economic prospects. Many Taiwan originated investments are now made via Hong Kong or British Virgin Island (BVI) registered companies, thus benefiting Hong Kong and sapping Taiwan of its vitality. Recently, major Taiwan companies have sought and succeeded in raising capital in the Hong Kong Stock Exchange. The most notable was Hon Hai Precision Industries, one of the kingpins of the Taiwan Stock Exchange. Its affiliate company, Foxconn International Holding, went public in the Hong Kong Exchange in February 2004 and became one of the hottest companies on the Hong Kong Stock Exchange. Its price has risen from roughly HK$4 to over HK$25 per share. Many others are eagerly following in Hon Hai's footsteps and are planning to list their companies on the Hong Kong Stock Exchange.

Silicon Valley East and Its Future Prospects

You may wonder why we spend so much time and effort in detailing Taiwan's geography, history, and politics. Taiwan has played a crucial role in the economic boom of China in at least the last decade. It is impossible to understand the dynamics and growth of China without understanding Taiwan's critical roles in providing not only the needed capital, but also the technical know-how, managerial discipline, "whatever it takes to get it done" attitude, and marketing connections that Taiwan companies have worked so hard to build for over a quarter century (1970–1995). Taiwan has played an incredibly integral role in China's becoming the world's factory. In fact, it is impossible to look at China's economic growth without taking into consideration Taiwan's contribution, much the same way that the global economy couldn't function without Taiwan.

Taken together, the revenues of Taiwan's 25 key tech companies equalled more than $125 billion in 2005. These companies little known to the Western public, including but not limited to Asustek Computer, Quanta Computer, Taiwan Semiconductor Manufacturing Co., and Hon Hai Precision Industry, supplied everything from chips to iPods to laptops to Sony's PlayStation 2 to Nokia phones to virtually all the PCs and servers to the likes of Apple, Dell, Qualcomm, Nvidia, and Sony.

Taiwan's success is also China's, even though few know about this because of the much reported political tension. As much as everyone in the know acknowledges how important Taiwan is in driving the Chinese manufacturing sector, no one knows for sure what percentage of China's exports in high-tech, information, and communications hardware is made by Taiwanese-owned factories. The estimates run from 40 percent to 80 percent. Taiwan's involvement is not only in high technology, but also in traditional industries such as textile, shoe, bicycle, and tennis racket and golf equipment manufacturing. As many as 1 million Taiwanese work and live in China, with perhaps over 500,000 in the Shanghai area. "All the manufacturing capacity in China is overlaid with the management and marketing expertise of the Taiwanese, along with all their contacts in the world," comments Russel Craig of technology consultant Vericors, Inc.[3]

Some Key Measures of Taiwan's Economic Prowess

Taiwan first gained recognition on the economic front as one of the four Asian Tigers (Dragons). Up until the last few years, Taiwan had been rated consistently as one of the fastest-growing economies in the world. Its economy was so robust that even the Asian financial crisis, which ravaged many Asian economies, did not seem to make a dent in Taiwan's economy. It boasts one of the highest foreign reserves of any country in the world at about $250 billion. It is consistently rated as one of most productive and entrepreneurial economies in the world. The broadest measures of Taiwan's growth during the last decade are shown in Exhibits 13.1 and 13.2. You will notice that Taiwan avoided the major decline in 1998 following the financial crisis in Southeast Asia. But, because of its strong ties to Silicon Valley, it suffered a major economic downturn in 2001. Since then growth has returned to the island, but at a somewhat slower pace.

Please note that for Taiwan we do not use statistics from the reliable World Bank. The Bank ignores Taiwan for political reasons. So you will not be able to compare the analyses here with those in the chapters on China (11), Hong Kong (12), and Singapore (14). In particular, the GDP per capita statistics reported in the exhibits do not include the "purchase price parity" (PPP) correction, and thus understate the economic performance of all four

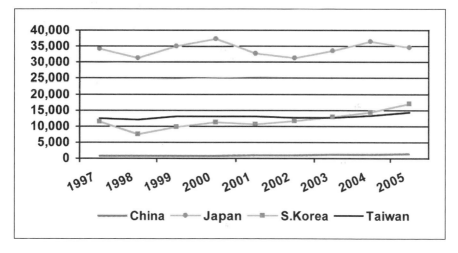

Exhibit 13.1   GDP per Capita (Current $) (*Source: Euromonitor*)

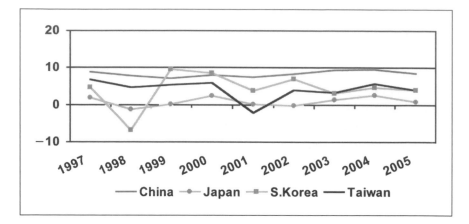

Exhibit 13.2   GDP per Capita—Percent Change (Current $)
(*Source: Euromonitor*)

Asian countries vis-à-vis the World Bank data reported in the other chapters. The two obvious examples of the importance of the PPP correction are: (1) the understatement of per capita income of Chinese in the PRC, about $1,500 without the correction and over $5,000 with it and (2) the manifest declines in Japanese per capita incomes during both 1998 and 2002. In both countries the purchase price of a market basket of consumer goods has been falling dramatically (deflation in Japan), and PPP takes this factor into account. But, this is neither an economics nor a statistics class. Just be careful not to compare these data with those in the other chapters.

On the all-important communications infrastructure dimension, Taiwan does well on PC ownership and dominates cell phone connectedness. See Exhibits 13.3 and 13.4.

Perhaps most important still is that the statistics do not measure the true output of Taiwan, because many of its manufacturing operations have been shifted to China to take advantage of the lower wage costs and to supply the demand of the huge Chinese domestic market. Again, no one knows what the true numbers are

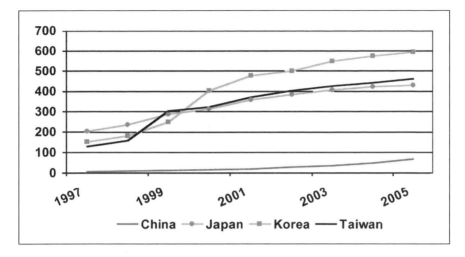

Exhibit 13.3   Personal Computers (per 1,000 People)
(*Source: Euromonitor*)

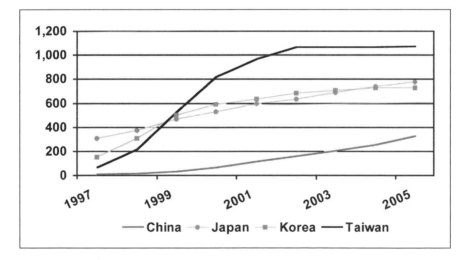

Exhibit 13.4   Mobile Phones (per 1,000 People) (*Source: Euromonitor*)

because many Taiwan companies invest directly into China via BVI or Hong Kong companies due to Taiwan's stringent regulations governing investing in China.

It is important to highlight the trade relationship between China and Taiwan, because the two economies have been integrating at a rapid rate. In 2000, trade between China and Taiwan totaled $32.4 billion, representing only 11.2 percent of Taiwan's foreign trade. At the end of 2004, trade between China and Taiwan totaled $62 billion, representing 18 percent of Taiwan's foreign trade. Export from Taiwan to China stood at 25.8 percent, and import from China to Taiwan represented 9.9 percent of Taiwan's total trade. As a result, Taiwan generated a total trade surplus of $28.3 billion vis-à-vis China in 2004.

While growth in Taiwan has slowed since, Hong Kong has rebounded. The average P/E (price/earnings ratio) ratio of the Taiwan Stock Exchange had sunk to a new historical low in 2004 at only 12.58. On the other hand, the average P/E ratio of Hong Kong Hang Seng Index had risen to 18.73 at the end of 2004. Many in Taiwan are concerned that if this trend continues, the hollowing out of Taiwan will not just be limited to its manufacturing base and operations hub, but its capital market as well.

The Culture and Behavior of Chinese Managers from Taiwan

About 80 percent of the population of Taiwan is Taiwanese, with most of the rest split between Hakka (from the south) and recent (since 1949) mainland immigrants. Regarding behavior in general and language in particular, the people on Taiwan are considered by other Chinese the most conservative. That is, neither Confucius's influence nor the Mandarin spoken was mitigated by Communist philosophies and rule. Consequently, their age, rank, and family play the most powerful roles among all Chinese. Companies tend to be managed directly from the top, and the decision-making style is autocratic. Managers are at the same time down-to-earth practical, but on occasion daring.

The entrepreneurial spirit runs deep. Indeed, a key role model representing these characteristics is Terry Gou, founder of Hon Hai Precision, a $28 billion dollar contract manufacturer of which he owns 30 percent. That makes him the richest man on the island and number 176 on *Forbes* most recent billionaire ranking at $3.2 billion. Terry Gou started his company in 1974 with 10 employees making plastic parts for televisions. Now the firm has production facilities in the United States, the United Kingdom, Ireland, the Czech Republic, and the mainland. In 1993 Hon Hai opened plants at Shenzhen and Kunshan. Foxconn currently has sales revenues of over $6 billion and is growing fast.

Of the Asian businesspeople in our studies of negotiation styles, those on Taiwan were most similar to Americans. Please note John's and Philip Cateora's descriptions from their *International Marketing*:[4]

Japan

> *Consistent with most descriptions of Japanese negotiation behavior, the results of this analysis suggest their style of interaction is among the least aggressive (or most polite). Threats, commands, and warnings appear to be deemphasized in favor of the more positive promises, recommendations, and commitments. Particularly indicative of their polite conversational style was their infrequent use of* no *and* you *and facial gazing, as well as more frequent silent periods.*

S. Korea

> *Perhaps one of the more interesting aspects of the analysis is the contrast of the Asian styles of negotiations. Non-Asians often generalize about the Orient; the findings demonstrate, however, that this is a mistake. Korean negotiators used considerably more*

punishments and commands than did the Japanese. Koreans used the word no *and interrupted more than three times as frequently as the Japanese. Moreover, no silent periods occurred between Korean negotiators.*

China (Northern)

The behaviors of the negotiators from Northern China (i.e., in and around Tianjin) were most remarkable in the emphasis on asking questions (34 percent). Indeed, 70 percent of the statements made by the Chinese negotiators were classified as information-exchange tactics. Other aspects of their behavior were quite similar to the Japanese, particularly the use of no *and* you *and silent periods.*

Taiwan

The behavior of the businesspeople in Taiwan was quite different from that in China and Japan but similar to that in Korea. The Chinese on Taiwan were exceptional in the time of facial gazing—on the average, almost 20 of 30 minutes. They asked fewer questions and provided more information (self-disclosures) than did any of the other Asian groups.

Compared with other Chinese, the businesspeople on Taiwan are about in the middle of the indirectness dimension, and generally provide honest information. They will hesitate to say "no," but not so much as their Mainland cousins. Corruption has faded dramatically as Taiwan has prospered. They also tend to be less formal, even less sophisticated. The senior decision maker at the table probably will not have much to say during negotiations.

The *Ménage à Trois* That Works

Some would call it simply a trade triangle. But, that geometrical metaphor misses the essential trait of the relationship among the

Unites States, China, and Taiwan. The fact is the three are in bed with one another—maybe not married—but clearly in bed. *Interdependence.*[5] Below are three representations of the relationship. Exhibit 13.5 gives you the numbers. Exhibit 13.6 provides Confucius's 1,000-word version—the key cog is certainly Taiwan in Mark Wuerker's 1985 political cartoon. And, finally there's the fascinating nuance of the Neil Bush, Winston Wang, Jiang Mianheng relationship so eloquently described in *BusinessWeek.*[6] Enjoy.

The executives at Grace Semiconductor Manufacturing Corp. know a thing or two about guanxi, the web of connections that fuel so much of business in China. The Shanghai-based company was cofounded by Jiang Mianheng, the son of former Chinese President Jiang Zemin. The other cofounder is Taiwan-born Winston Wong, whose father Y. C. Wang runs petrochemical

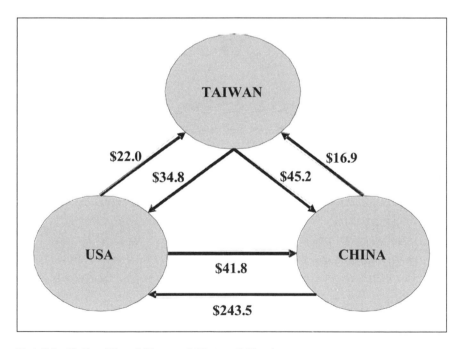

Exhibit 13.5   The *Ménage à Trois* of Trade (Billions $ of Merchandise) (*Source: Department of Commerce*)

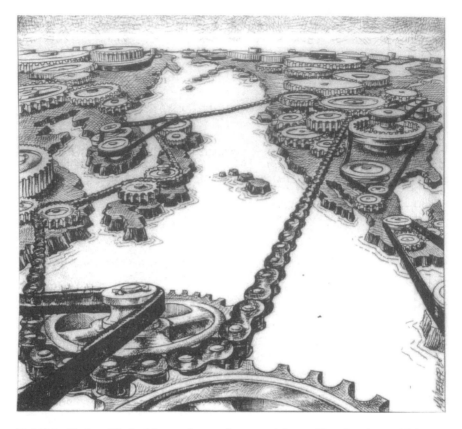

Exhibit 13.6   Global Interdependence with an Emphasis on Taiwan

maker Formosa Plastics and is probably the island's most power-ful businessman. That's not to say the two don't have pretty solid credentials: Wong founded Nanya Technology Corp. in Taiwan, while Jiang has a PhD in physics from Drexel University in Philadelphia and is vice-president of the Chinese Academy of Science. But as they set out to raise the billions of dollars needed to start a semiconductor company, their true-blue bloodlines didn't hurt.

So it should come as no surprise that Grace last year hired a certain Neil Bush. After all, he's the son of the former President

*and brother of President George W. Bush. Neil Bush's retainer
with Grace, which pays him $400,000 in stock annually over five
years, came to light during Bush's divorce proceedings in Texas.
Although the 48-year-old Bush admitted in a divorce deposition
that he has little knowledge of semiconductors, his family tree
offers plenty of Washington guanxi—not unlike Jiang and Wong.*

*So just what has Neil Bush done for Grace? Even the com-
pany seems a bit unclear on that point. According to a contract
that was filed with Bush's divorce papers, Grace hired him as a
consultant. Grace, however, says Bush is a director—and officials
decline to say anything more about his role. Nobody has accused
Grace or Bush of doing anything illegal, and Grace says Bush
didn't help the company obtain permits this year to import sensitive equipment from the U.S. used to etch silicon wafers. "Neil
played absolutely zero role in getting these licenses," says Daniel
Y. Wang, Grace's chief financial officer. Bush didn't return phone
calls to the Texas companies he runs, Ignite! Inc. in Austin, and
Crest Investments in Houston.*

*Still, there is little doubt that Grace could use a bit of help in
its dealings with the U.S. Grace is one of many Chinese and
Western companies that would benefit from a repeal of controls
on the sale of tech equipment that Western countries fear could
be used by the Chinese military. These restrictions, known as the
Wassenaar Arrangement after the Dutch town where the pact
was signed in 1996, require equipment vendors and their prospective Chinese customers to get government approval for sales
of advanced technologies.*

*For years, Wassenaar has been a headache for Chinese chip-
makers. While China has the expertise to produce low-end chips,
when it comes to making more advanced—and more profitable—
semiconductors that use ultrathin circuits, Grace and other Chinese companies have to rely on imported equipment. Wassenaar
is designed to keep gear from falling into the wrong hands by
ensuring that governments screen all potentially sensitive sales to
mainland companies. Some high-end technology "can be exported,
but with a lot of delay and a lot of paperwork," says Dorothy Lai,*

an analyst with market watcher Gartner Inc. in Hong Kong. For instance, semiconductor manufacturing equipment maker Applied Materials Inc. helped Grace get permits for its recent purchases of etching gear.

For its part, Grace is planning an expansion that may need a stamp of approval by U.S. authorities. The company hopes to build a second semiconductor plant in Shanghai capable of churning out chips from wafers 12 inches in diameter—which require the most advanced manufacturing gear available, and for which Grace's vendors would need a permit. To fund the expansion, Grace plans a $350 million private placement of shares, and is considering a public offering. So far, Grace has raised $1.3 billion from various investors, including $55 million from two international private equity funds. The company, which only began commercial production in September, expects to be making 10,000 wafers per month by yearend, and 27,000 by December, 2004. Grace is clearly an ambitious company—but one that knows a bit of guanxi can be as important to success as a roomful of engineers.

As all three representations so accurately depict, what affects one, affects the other two. At this writing the best example is the backing off by Senators Chuck Schumer and Lindsey Graham on trade sanctions against China for not raising the value of the yuan fast enough. We love Schumer's explanation: "We never wanted our bill to become law," Schumer said, adding that enough reforms have occurred in China so, "We don't have to fire the so-called nuclear weapon."[7] The fact is that if the United States were to slap such trade sanctions on China, China would sell U.S. Treasuries, driving the fragile U.S. economy to a major recession.

Yes, Taiwan's economy depends on the continued growth of both its partners. The best prescription for everyone's economic health is a political standdown, where threatening words and xenophobic political ploys are put aside. This is also the best prescription for peace across the Taiwan Strait.

Notes

1　Bruce Einhorn, Matt Kovac, Peter Engardio, Dexter Roberts, Frederick Balfour, and Cliff Edwards, "Why Taiwan Matters," *BusinessWeek*, May 16, 2005, pages 40–45.

2　Jason Dedrick and Ken Kraemer, *Asia's Computer Challenge* (New York: Oxford Univeristy Press, 1998).

3　Bruce Einhorn, et al.

4　Philip R. Cateora, and John L. Graham, *International Marketing* (14th edition, Burr Ridge, IL: McGraw-Hill 2007).

5　For perhaps the most comprehensive discussion of the interdependence see Richard C. Bush, *Untying the Knot, Making Peace in the Taiwan Strait* (Washington, DC: Brookings Institute, 2005).

6　Frederick Balfour, Bruce Einhorn, and Kate Murphy, "A Bush in the Hand Is Worth . . . a Lot," *BusinessWeek*, December 12, 2003, page 27.

7　"US Schumer, Graham Delay Sanctions Vote til Sept 29," *Market News International*, March 29, 2006.

SINGAPORE—ITS ROLE IN CHINA'S FUTURE

Singapore is often referred to as a "fine, fine place." That is, there are fines for almost everything, it seems, from spitting to chewing gum. The forms they hand you at the airport prominently mention the death penalty for drug trafficking. The government even subtracts its taxes directly from your bank account—a convenience many don't appreciate. It's a small island and most organized. An emphasis on ethical business practices at the very top of the government has yielded a dynamic business culture and affluent lifestyle for its citizens.

Almost 89 percent of the 4.6 million residents of Singapore speak Chinese as their first language. In fact, the island's residents are so Chinese that in 1965 Malaysia decided to divest itself of the regional *entrepôt*. This was a very interesting decision, indeed. Much of the economic success of the island country has resulted from its strong connections with relatives and companies in China. The authoritarian leaders of the former British colony have combined the Chinese work ethic and global *guanxi* with aggressive investments in the public education system to turn the small country into the financial and high-technology center of Southeast Asia. But, as direct trade with China continues to burgeon, how will Singapore's leaders and companies respond?

A Little History

Actually, Singapore only has a little history to tell. The story really starts in 1819 with the arrival of Sir Thomas Stamford Raffles, then a young British official of the East India Company. He was able to gain permission from the Malay rulers of the area to open a trading post on the island. It quickly became a regional center of trade, attracting merchants and ships from Asia, the Middle East, and Europe. The mixing of cultures caused the usual conflicts and the usual creativity. Most of these travelers were men, and when they settled, they often married local women. Even the Chinese population itself hailed from different parts of China, not just the south coast.

In 1867 the British made Singapore a crown colony. In 1869 the Suez Canal opened, thus making the shortest reach between Europe and China through the Strait of Malacca near Singapore rather than the Sunda Strait near Jakarta.

During the 1920s ties between the Straits-born Chinese on Singapore and the Chinese mainland rulers were strengthened by mutual consent and large investments. Furthermore, Mandarin became the dialect taught in Singapore's schools. During the 1930s and World War II Chinese nationalism was boosted by Japanese violence. After the war the British kept Singapore separate from the Malay Union, although both shared a common currency.

A group of mostly middle-class, British-educated Chinese led by Lee Kuan Yew formed the People's Action Party (PAP) in Singapore in 1954. PAP's stated purpose was ending British colonialism and joining the Malay Union. In 1956 the negotiations were begun in London, resulting in the granting of internal self-rule for Singaporeans in 1958. Shortly thereafter PAP was elected to power by a wide margin, and Lee Kuan Yew became prime minister. In 1963 Singapore left colonial control of the British and joined the newly created Malaysian state. The aforementioned Malaysian xenophobia (clearly expressed in a unanimous parliamentary vote) combined with some outside pressure from Indonesia to force a new and final separation of Singapore from Malaysia. Thus Singapore became an independent state on August 9, 1965. You can view a video presentation of this history that includes Lee Kuan Yew breaking into tears over the 1965 division at the city's historical museum. Indeed, the emotions of the man expressed so plainly and publicly explain part of his zeal to make the new nation succeed.

The Lee Kuan Yew government quickly focused on creating a "Singaporean identity" that infused Chinese (Mandarin), Malay, Indian, and English as official languages. English was designated as the official language for business. As a consequence, today 35 percent of Singaporeans speak Mandarin as their first language, 23 percent English, 14 percent Malay, 11 percent Hokkien, 6 percent Cantonese, 5 percent Teocheu, and 3 percent Tamil.

PAP has won every election since 1959 with overwhelming majorities, and Lee Kuan Yew remained prime minister until 1990. The government has been quite successful in stimulating the economy through incentives for export industries, improving labor laws, and providing tax relief. And the island nation to this day remains the region's most important transportation, educational, high-tech, and financial center.

Lee Kuan Yew

Because Lee Kuan Yew remains so central to the young Singapore, it is worthwhile to take a quick look at his personal and family background. We excerpt here from wikipedia.org:[1]

> *In his memoirs, Lee mentions that he was a fourth-generation Chinese Singaporean: his Hakka great-grandfather, Lee Bok Boon (born 1846), emigrated from the Dapu county of Guangdong province to the Straits Settlements in 1862.*
> *The eldest child of Lee Chin Koon and Chua Jim Neo, Lee Kuan Yew was born at 92 Kampong Java Road in Singapore, in a large and airy bungalow. As a child Lee was strongly influenced by*

British culture, due in part to his grandfather, Lee Hoon Leong, who had given his sons an English education. His grandfather gave him the name "Harry" in addition to his Chinese name (given by his father) Kuan Yew.

Lee and his wife Kwa Geok Choo were married on September 30, 1950. They have two sons and one daughter.

Several members of Lee's family hold prominent positions in Singaporean society, and his sons and daughter hold high government and government-linked posts.

His elder son Lee Hsien Loong, a former Brigadier-General, has been the Prime Minister since 2004, and Finance Minister of Singapore. He is also the Vice-Chairman of the Government of Singapore Investment Company (GIC) (Lee himself is the Chairman). Lee's younger son, Lee Hsien Yang, also a former Brigadier-General, is the President and Chief Executive Officer of SingTel, a pan-Asian telecommunications giant and Singapore's largest company by market capitalisation (listed on the Singapore Exchange, SGX). Sixty-two percent of SingTel is owned by Temasek Holdings, a prominent government holding company with controlling stakes in a variety of very large government-linked companies such as Singapore Airlines and DBS Bank. Temasek Holdings in turn is run by Executive Director and CEO Ho Ching, the wife of Lee's elder son, the Prime Minister. Lee's daughter, Lee Wei Ling, runs the National Neuroscience Institute, and remains unmarried. Lee's wife Kwa Geok Choo used to be a partner of the prominent legal firm Lee & Lee. His younger brothers, Dennis, Freddy, and Suan Yew were partners of the same firm. He also has a younger sister, Monica. However, Lee has consistently denied charges of nepotism, arguing that his family members' privileged positions are based on personal merit.

Lee was educated at Telok Kurau Primary School, Raffles Institution, and Raffles College. His university education was delayed by World War II and the 1942–1945 Japanese occupation of Singapore. During the occupation, he operated a successful black market business selling a tapioca-based glue called Stikfas. *Having taken Chinese and Japanese lessons since 1942, he was able to work as a transcriber of Allied wire reports for the Japanese, as well as being the English-language editor on the Japanese* Hodobu *(an information or propaganda department) from 1943 to 1944.*

After the war, he studied law at Fitzwilliam College, Cambridge in the United Kingdom, and briefly attended the London School of Economics. He returned to Singapore in 1949 to work as a lawyer in Laycock and Ong, the legal practice of John Laycock, a pioneer of multiracialism who, together with A. P. Rajah and C. C. Tan, had founded Singapore's first multiracial club open to Asians.

Over the years many have criticized Lee's and the government's heavy-handed control, particularly limiting individual rights—thus the "fine, fine place" comment. Many have described his regime as elitist and autocratic. He has often been accused of suppressing political opposition through both civil and criminal court actions. But he has also received international recognition for his good works and successes. His Corrupt Practices Investigation Bureau (CPIB) was given great power to investigate and arrest officials accused of corruption; and several ministers were charged and jailed as a part of the crackdown. Lee also believed that ministers should be paid well in order to maintain clean and honest government. In 1994 he proposed to link the salaries of ministers, judges, and top civil servants to the salaries of top professionals in the relevant sectors, arguing that this would help recruit and retain talented officials to serve the public sector. Indeed, one measure of his success in fighting corruption is the stellar rankings numbers listed for Singapore by Transparency International. But there is a downside to Lee's approach as displayed as part of the analysis included in *Foreign Policy's* annual ranking of the globalization of nations.[2] There the reader will see evidence of the good, the bad, and the uniqueness of Lee's approach. The good—Singapore is among the least corrupt of all nations and, at least in the 2005 rankings, the most global economy. The bad—it scores very low on the political freedom index. The unique—Singapore is all by itself among the other nations where freedom and corruption are generally negatively correlated.

Economic Trajectory

Singapore's economic growth rate has pretty much paralleled that of Hong Kong and the other Asian tigers. Now Singapore ranks behind only Japan and Hong Kong in per capita GDP—see Exhibit 14.1. Because the Singapore economy is smaller and more narrowly focused than the rest, it is more volatile, experiencing declines in 1985, 1998, and 2001. But, overall the growth rate remains impressive. See Exhibit 14.2.

The two metrics we use for information-communication infrastructure (personal computer and cell phone penetration levels) puts Singapore as one of the most technologically connected countries on the planet. (See Exhibits 14.3 and 14.4.) As mentioned above, *Foreign Policy* ranks Singapore as the most globalized economy (ahead of Ireland, Switzerland, the United States, the Netherlands, and Canada, in that order) based on four criteria: economic integration (Singapore ranks number 1), personal contact (number 3), technological connectivity (number 11), and political engagement (number 32). Its most outstanding characteristic is the first, where it scores highest on trade and FDI. As one might expect, it also scores quite high on the *guanxi*-related dimension, personal contact, which includes telephone usage, travel, and personal transfers. And, of course, these activities are supported by a very good information-communication infrastructure.

In the past Singapore's economic strength has been in the following areas:

- Electronics
- Chemicals
- Financial services
- Oil drilling equipment
- Petroleum refining

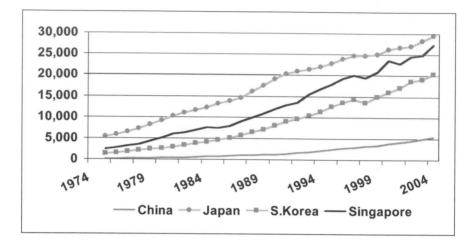

Exhibit 14.1   GDP per Capita PPP (Current International $)
(*Source: World Development Indicators*)

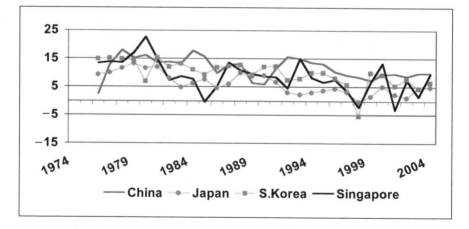

**Exhibit 14.2   GDP per Capita PPP—Percent Change
(Current International $)** (*Source: World Development Indicators*)

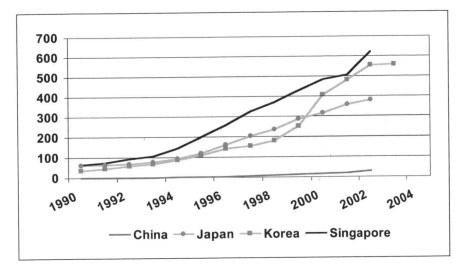

Exhibit 14.3   Personal Computers (per 1,000 People)
(*Source: World Development Indicators*)

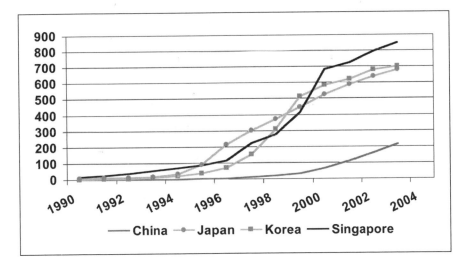

Exhibit 14.4   Mobile Phones (per 1,000 People)
(*Source: World Development Indicators*)

- Rubber processing and rubber products
- Processed food and beverages
- Ship repair
- Offshore platform construction
- Life sciences and health care
- Entrepôt trade

However, the government is now focusing on developing an "information economy."

For the twenty-first century it expects job growth and the best investment opportunities in related sectors:

- Arts and entertainment
- Financial services
- Chemicals
- Health-care services
- Information-communication technology
- Logistics and transport
- Region base for multinational corporations
- Research and development

Toward promotion of such commercial opportunities the government has entered into free-trade agreements with the widest variety of countries including:

- Australia
- New Zealand
- European Free Trade Association (Switzerland, Iceland, Liechtenstein, and Norway)
- United States
- Jordan

The government is also engaged in negotiations for similar agreements with:

- Bahrain
- Egypt

- Mexico
- Canada
- South Korea
- India
- Panama
- Chile
- ASEAN members
- China

Of course, Singapore's competitive advantage has always been based on its role as *entrepôt*, and it is continuing to develop the businesses in the area most closely related—transportation services. And, this "old" business remains its commercial strength vis-à-vis China. And, that brings us directly to Temasek Holdings, the company that owns and manages the Singapore government's direct investments. The word "Temasek" is an ancient Javanese name for Singapore. Temasek's diverse portfolio includes most of the business categories listed above and totals some $60–$70 billion. It owns 57 percent of Singapore International Airlines and 100 percent of PSA International. The latter is the number two firm globally in the ports business. PSA also operates the world's largest transshipment hub in Singapore where shippers have a choice of 200 shipping lines with connections to 600 ports in 123 countries.

The firm owns about $5 billion of Chinese assets across diverse industries. Temasek's top representative in China recently described their immediate plans for the PRC:

> *"Temasek is now placing great importance on Asia and invest-ment in China is an essential part of its business," Ms. Cheo Hock Kuan, Temasek's Senior Managing Director and Chief Representative for China told* Xinhua *[PRC People's Daily[3]] on Friday. Temasek has bolstered its presence in many Chinese indus-tries, including the banking and financial sector, energy and resources, transport and logistics, telecoms and media, pharmacy and health care.*
>
> *Ms. Cheo said Temasek is keen to invest in state-owned enter-prises (SOEs) or other large companies that serve as broad-based*

proxies for the economic transformation in China. "Temasek is also interested in investing in promising and fast growing businesses, particularly those that meet the growing consumer demands, or facilitate the increasing integration of China into the regional and global economy," said Ms. Cheo.

According to Cheo, a new cargo airline venture between Temasek, Singapore Airlines Cargo and China Great Wall Industry Corp plans to begin its operations in the first half of this year. Besides destinations within China, the new cargo airline will also serve destinations in the United States, Europe, North East Asia, and South West Asia. Cheo believes the new cargo airline will promote China's integration into the global economy.

Temasek's biggest investment in China is in the banking sector. Investment Managing Director Frank Tang told Xinhua *that Temasek reinforced cooperation with China's banks last year through its wholly owned Asia Financial Holdings (AFH). According to Tang, AFH has just completed a five percent stake purchase in the Bank of China (BOC) for 1.5 billion U.S. dollars, though Temasek originally hoped the stake could be 10 percent. But it will try to invest an additional 1 million dollars in BOC's initial public offering (IPO). Prior to this, AFH acquired a five percent stake in China Minsheng Banking Corp. LTD. in January last year and purchased a 5.1 percent stake in another big Chinese state commercial bank—China Construction Bank last August.*

Tang said China's banking reforms offer a good opportunity for Temasek to enter China. Temasek is confident for the future growth of financial industry in China as well as the whole of Asia, and believes it can create sustainable value for its shareholders.

PSA International already holds investments in 18 port projects in 11 countries—Singapore, Belgium, Brunei, India, Italy, Japan, the Netherlands, Portugual, South Korea, Thailand, and of course, China. In China it currently controls 36 berths in Hong Kong, Dalian, Fuzhou, and Guangzhou. And it has approval or is building an additional six berths, including a new facility at Tianjin.

So, Singapore will continue to simulate and participate in the growth of the greater China. It not only has the technological capabilities and the financial wherewithal, but it also has the cultural knowledge and *guanxi* to continue to make things happen in the global economy, particularly in support of China.

The Culture and Behavior of Chinese Managers in Singapore

The salient difference between the Chinese managers in Singapore and on the Chinese mainland is the historical influence of the British. The English language skills are of course most apparent. But underlying those are values for following rules and generally straightforward (not devious) business dealings. Relatedly, Singapore Chinese tend more toward individualism than most other Chinese. Things may move fast, even very fast, and decision making tends toward the autocratic. However, face, relationship building, and diligence will still be important considerations for your Chinese partners in Singapore. And, toward preserving relationships, the Singapore folks are known for eschewing the word no. But, despite their relatively reserved veneer, your negotiations in Singapore will still be tough.

Notes

1 Wikipedia.org, September 10, 2006.
2 "Measuring Globalization," *Foreign Policy*, May/June 2005, pp. 52–60.
3 "Singapore's Investment Arm Temasek Strengthens Presence in Dynamic Chinese Market," *People's Daily Online*, March 3, 2006.

CHAPTER 15

THE GREAT DIASPORA

W ho's running the planet these days? Yes, China's cheap labor is setting prices globally. And, of course, the United States military and economic power are unprecedented. Japan? The European Union? North Korea, Iran, Pakistan, and India are setting the nuclear weapons agenda. Fifteen of the nineteen terrorists who changed the world on September 11 were from Saudi Arabia.

But, the notion of "nation" is losing steam in the twenty-first century. Indeed, Joel Kotkin provided a completely different answer in his dated, but still excellent book, *Tribes*. He argued that tribes that span national boundaries have been leading the global economy for centuries, and, indeed, are still today. He describes in interesting detail the dominance of the Jews, the British, the Japanese, the Indians, and, of course, the Chinese. All these tribes have in common (1) a strong ethnic identity, with a sense of mutual dependence and emphasis on family structure; (2) a global network based on tribal trust that allows the group to function collectively; and (3) a passion for technology and a belief in education and scientific progress.[1] He also predicts the rising influence of new tribes—the Mormons and Armenians. While all the tribes make for very interesting reading, here we focus on the global Chinese diaspora.

As are all numbers about Chinese, the estimates of the population of overseas Chinese (excluding Singapore, Taiwan, and Hong Kong) are a bit iffy, but generally above 40 million. That's about the same population as California. Some 35 million live in the countries included in Exhibit 15.1, and about 30 million of those live in the Southeast Asian countries listed. Despite their relatively small percentages in all the countries of Southeast Asia, ethnic Chinese control an astonishingly great proportion of the economic activity there. This has frequently put them at odds with the native-dominated governments of those countries. Finally, note that most of the Chinese who have migrated from the mainland have come from just two southern coastal provinces: Fujian (Hokkien dialect) and Guangdong (Teochiu, Hakka, and Cantonese dialects).

The Waves of Migration

"In the north they make the rules, in the south we interpret them." Thus has been the mantra of the merchants along the south coast of China for thousands of years. The emperors have restricted trade, contact, and emigration. But the attractiveness of trade and the generally loose reins (or reigns depending how you think of them) of the north have motivated the Chinese to go overseas. Singapore historian Wang Gungwu describes four patterns of emigration in his book, *China and the Chinese Overseas*.[2]

- *The Trader Pattern:* Merchants and relatives of merchants that traveled and emigrated for commercial purposes.
- *The Coolie Pattern:* Peasant-class workers, landless laborers, and/or urban poor traveling supported by labor contracts. While many returned to China, many also stayed to build their own fortunes and futures. This pattern represents the largest group of overseas Chinese.

Location	Ethnic Chinese Population (thousands)	Percentage of Chinese of Total Population	Primary Linguistic Group(s)	Percentage of Market Capital Controlled by Chinese
Southeast Asia				
Indonesia	7310	3.6	Hokkien	73.0
Thailand	8323	13.6	Teochiu	81.0
Malaysia	6147	29.9	Hokkien, Hakka, Cantonese	69.0
Philippines	1522	2.0	Hokkien	50–60.0
Vietnam	1051	1.4	Cantonese	45.0
Myanmar	5000	10.0	Hokkien, Cantonese	—
Cambodia	300	2.7	Teochiu	70.0
Some Others				
Japan	234	0.2	—	—
India	168	0.0	—	—
United States	2723	1.0	Cantonese	—
Canada	920	3.1	Cantonese	—
Peru	540	2.2	—	—
Russia	1000	0.7	—	—
United Kingdom	250	0.4	—	—
France	225	0.4	—	—
Australia	320	2.0	—	—

Exhibit 15.1   Chinese Diaspora by the Numbers*

*Best estimates based on triangulation of sources: Lynn Pan (ed.), *The Encyclopedia of the Chinese Overseas* (Cambridge: Harvard University Press, 1999); George T. Haley, Chin Tiong Tan, and Usha C.V. Haley, *New Asian Emperors* (Oxford: Butterworth Heinemann, 1998); Murray Wiedenbaum and Samuel Hughes, *The Bamboo Network* (New York: Free Press, 1996); and Laurence J.C. Ma and Carolyn Cartier (eds.), *The Chinese Diaspora* (Boulder, CO: Rowman & Littlefield, 2003).

- *The Sojourner Pattern:* This much smaller group of Chinese left to advocate abroad the Chinese culture and way of life. People in this group have lobbied the foreign governments to allow for Chinese schools and such. Often they were sent by the home central governments to recapture control over the huge assets of overseas Chinese.
- *The Descent or Remigrant Pattern:* Increasingly overseas Chinese are losing their language and along with it their Chinese culture as successive generations live in other countries and adapt. Even so, the Chinese identity and work ethic persists and allows a special understanding and relationship with the mainland despite the latter's volatile politics.

The Southeast Asian Market

Given the numbers in Exhibit 15.1, the chance of running into a Chinese family-owned enterprise is quite large if your firm targets the fast-growing, half-billion person Southeast Asian market. All the Southeast Asian countries listed there are members of the increasingly dynamic multinational trade group, the Association of Southeast Asian Nations (ASEAN). The goals of the group are economic integration and cooperation through complementary industry programs; preferential trading, including reduced tariff and nontariff barriers; guaranteed member access to markets throughout the region; and harmonized investment incentives. Like all multinational market groups, ASEAN has experienced problems and false starts in attempting to unify the combined economies of its member nations. Most of the early economic growth came from trade outside the ASEAN group. Similarities in the kinds of products member nations had to export, in their natural resources, and other national assets hampered early attempts at intra-ASEAN trade. The steps countries took to expand and diversify their industrial base in order to foster intraregional trade when ASEAN was first created have resulted in the fastest-growing economies in the region and an increase in trade among members. See Exhibit 15.2.

Five major circumstances account for the vigorous economic growth of the ASEAN countries and their transformation from cheap-labor havens to industrialized nations: (1) the ASEAN governments' commitment to deregulation, liberalization, and privatization of their economies; (2) the decision to shift their economies from commodity-based to manufacturing-based; (3) the decision to specialize in manufacturing components in which they have a comparative advantage (this created more diversity in their industrial output and increased opportunities for trade); (4) Japan's emergence as a major provider of technology and capital necessary to upgrade manufacturing capability and develop new industries; and (5) the continued coordination, leadership, and financial control of the overseas Chinese network so long in place in the region.

Although there has never been an attempt to duplicate the supranational government of the European Union, each year the

Association	Member	Population (millions)	GDP ($ billions)	GDP per Capita	Imports of Goods and Service ($ billions)	Exports of Goods and Services ($ billions)
ASEAN Free Trade Area (AFTA)						
	Brunei	0.3	5.7	17,650	—	—
	Cambodia	12.3	3.9	317	2.3	2.3
	Indonesia	209.0	216.2	1,034	50.4	60.2
	Laos	5.4	2.5	465	—	—
	Malaysia	23.8	112.1	4,708	98.7	117.6
	Myanmar	48.3	—	—	—	—
	Philippines	78.3	91.1	1,165	37.6	34.0
	Singapore	4.6	112.0	27,118	—	—
	Thailand	61.2	174.6	2,853	72.7	94.6
	Vietnam	79.5	31.0	390	15.3	10.6

Exhibit 15.2 Southeast Asian Market Group (Constant PPP 1995 $)
(*Source: World Bank, 2006*)

group becomes more interrelated. ASEAN Vision 2020 is the most outward-looking commitment to regional goals ever accepted by the group. Among the targets that will lead to further integration is the commitment to implementing fully and as rapidly as possible the ASEAN free-trade area.

Just as was the case in the European Union, businesses are drafting plans for operation within a free-trade area. The ability to sell in an entire region without differing tariff and nontariff barriers is one of the important changes that will affect many parts of the marketing mix. Distribution can be centralized at the most cost-effective point rather than having distribution points dictated by tariff restrictions. Some standardization of branding will be necessary because large customers will buy at the regional level rather than bit by bit at the country level. Pricing can be more consistent, which will help reduce the smuggling and parallel importing that occur when there are major price differentials among countries because of different tariff schedules. In essence, marketing can become more regionally and centrally managed.

One result of the Asian financial crisis of 1997 to 1998 was the creation of ASEAN+3 (ASEAN plus China, Japan, and South Korea) to deal with trade and monetary issues facing Asia. Most countries of East Asia felt that they were both let down and put upon by the West, who they felt created much of the problem by pulling out in the midst of the crisis. Many thought the leading financial powers either declined to take part in the rescue operations, as the United States did in Thailand, or that they proposed unattainable solutions. The result was the creation of ASEAN+3, consisting of the foreign and finance ministers of each country, who meet annually after ASEAN meetings. Their first meeting was devoted to devising a system whereby the member countries share foreign exchange reserves to defend their currencies against future attack. Although still only tentative, there was also discussion among the members of ASEAN+3 of creating a common market and even a single currency or, perhaps, a new Asian entity encompassing both Northeast and Southeast Asia. Closer links between Southeast Asia and Northeast Asia are seen as a step toward strengthening Asia's role in the global economy and creating a global three-bloc configuration.

The Overseas Chinese Networks in ASEAN

Most Western analysts describe two primary ingredients of the networks of Chinese-controlled firms in Southeast Asia—social and financial. Of course, the Chinese folks actually involved in the networks don't see the distinction. Joel Kotkin describes this brocade of finance and *guanxi*:

> *Like the Jews of Poland and elsewhere in Europe, the Chinese in Southeast Asia dominated many critical commercial niches as traders, artisans, and skilled workers, often filling the "middleman" role between the dominant elite—made up of European merchants, plantation owners, and colonial officials—and the masses of native agriculturalists. Cut off from their native land, much like the Jews, they had little alternative but to engage in such activities as trading and money lending. As Rustam Sani, a senior fellow at the Malaysian Institute for Strategic and International Studies, explains: "They had no choice but to become active in business, in trade. Malays could retreat to the land because they owned the land. They could go back to the villages. But the Chinese had no choice except in business. . . . They became well entrenched."[3]*

The social ties (*guanxi*) of Chinese in Southeast Asia are of five sorts: *clans* based on family surname; *locality* based on origin in China; *dialect*; *guild* based on craft practiced; and *trust* based on experience or recommendation.[4] And, for any one executive, these individual relationships usually don't work in parallel, but rather in multiplicative, even exponential ways. Ram Charan reports one way in which social ties enhance competitiveness: "Networks are designed to empower managers to talk openly, candidly, and emotionally without fear, to enrich the quality of their decisions, to test each other's motives and build trust, and to encourage them to evaluate problems from the perspective of what is right for the customer and the company rather than from narrow functional or departmental interests."[5] Of course, the principal advantage of networks is the reduction of transaction costs among network members. That is, I don't have to shop around for the best price, I can trust my brother-in-law or former classmate to take care of me now and in the long run too.

The extent of the financial ties are best exemplified by two well-known examples—the Lippo Group centered in Indonesia and the Kuok Group of Malaysia. Most recently the Lippo Group was described in a press release by its new French/American joint venture partner, Esker Software:

> The Lippo Group *is a multibillion dollar asset base and revenue conglomerate with over ten thousand employees. Lippo was founded by its chairman, Dr. Mochtar Riady, over 30 years ago and has offices in China mainland, Hong Kong, and Macau; and Australia, Indonesia, Malaysia, Philippines and Singapore. Lippo Group has over 10 publicly-listed companies in different territories including Hong Kong, Indonesia, Philippines and Singapore. Lippo Group's main business covers five key areas:*
>
> * *Financial services—This comprises commercial banking, investment banking, life insurance, general insurance, securities broking and underwriting, asset management and mutual funds with focus on the Asia Pacific region.*
> * *Industrial activities—Lippo Group has invested in manufacturing industry e.g., electronic products, automotive parts, cement and household appliances such as refrigerators and air-conditioning units.*
> * *Infrastructure development—Lippo Group has invested and completed infrastructure projects in electric power generation and distribution, gas production, communication network, highways and water purification.*
> * *Strategic investments and services—These services include information technology, supermarket chains, department stores, entertainment business, schools and universities.*

- *Urban development and property investment—This includes fully integrated satellite cities, houses, condominiums, office towers, industrial estates, shopping malls, hotels, country clubs and golf courses. Lippo Group has a proven track record in transforming undeveloped plots into residential estates, commercial offices and shopping malls in Indonesia, China mainland and Malaysia.*

The Lippo Group has a team of qualified and experienced professionals who have a proven track record in the respective areas of business activities. Lippo Group believes in networking and sustaining long term relationship with its partners. Over the years, it has grown through joint ventures and strategic alliances with many of the world's leading manufacturing, construction and financial services companies. With its resources and capabilities, Lippo Group is set to move forward with its partners, and take advantage of the opportunities in the Asia Pacific economy.[6]

Of course, you may recall that the Lippo Group was embroiled in the controversy regarding offshore "Chinese money" contributed to the Clinton/Gore campaign coffers in 1996. Lippo means "energy" in Chinese, and the group is controlled by the Riady family through a series of private trusts. A native of Indonesia, Chairman Mochtar Riady studied banking in China and in the process developed a series of connections on the mainland. Most of Lippo's mainland investments have centered in Fujian province, the Riady family's former homeland. Family assets are estimated at well over $6 billion and involve cross-holdings with other large Chinese-owned conglomerates such as those owned by Hong Kong's Li Ka-shing.

The Kuok Group of Malaysia

The Kuok Group is led by Robert Kuok Hock Nien,[7] born in Johor Baru, Malaysia in 1923. He is currently listed as the wealthiest Malaysian by *Forbes* with personal holdings of more than

$5 billion. Although he has given more authority to the next gen-
eration, Kuok remains the patriarch in charge.

Kuok was born in 1923 in Johor Bahru, the son of a well-off
commodities trader. His ancestral town was in Fujian province,
China. At Raffles College in Singapore, he was a schoolmate of
Singapore's Lee Kuan Yew in the late 1940s. After graduation, he
worked at his father's company, and founded the Kuok Brothers
Sdn Bhd in 1949.

After founding the Kuok Brothers Sdn Bhd, Kuok immediately
began investing in the sugar refinery business. In 1957, Malaysia
gained its independence from the United Kingdom. Kuok seized
this opportunity to swiftly establish his business network throughout Malaysia, based on a vertical integration business model (raw
materials → processing → distribution). He also mastered the
intricacies of commodities trading in London in the 1950s. By the
1970s, he was known as the "Sugar King" as he controlled some
10 percent of the global sugar market. After proclaiming success
in the sugar refinery business, he quickly moved into other businesses and established the largest flour mill in Malaysia.

Since the 1960s, Kuok has relied heavily on his "gentlemanly"
way of doing business to become a mover and shaker in industry.
He was fast in recognizing opportunities at home and abroad, and
used his *guanxi* with government and industry to rapidly build
his empire. He also created strategic alliances with other commercial parties. He worked with local governments to form a
shipping company and later built hotels, office buildings, and convention centers. With partners, he founded banks. Aside from his
many enterprises in Malaysia, he operates in many other countries and regions including Singapore, Thailand, China, Indonesia, Fiji, the Philippines, and Australia. His business interests cut
across sugarcane plantations, sugar refinery, flour milling, animal
feed, oil, and mining to finance, hotels, properties, trading, and
freight. Kuok currently controls the Shangri-La Hotels and
Resorts Chain, Kerry Group, Perlis Plantations Bhd, and dozens
of other companies.

Similar to the Lippo and Kuok groups are several other Chinese-
owned and similarly diverse conglomerates in other ASEAN

countries. For example, in the Philippines Lucian Tan owns beer, tobacco, banking, and investment firms; and Henry Sy controls retailing, cement, and investment concerns. In Thailand the Lamsam family is involved in banking and real estate; and the Chearavanont family holds assets in agribusiness, real estate, and telecommunications. And, of course, in Indonesia the once mighty Salim group headed by the Lim family is a major factor in the economy there. The lists go on and on, and these represent only the largest firms.

Chinese Americans

As indicated in Exhibit 15.1, there are also about 4 million ethnic Chinese living in the United States and Canada. In the latter most have settled in British Columbia and Ontario; and in the former along the West Coast, particularly in California. In the United States almost 70 percent of Chinese Americans work in managerial, professional, and other white-collar positions; this corresponds to less than 60 percent for the entire U.S. population. The business success stories are many. Prominent among them are innovators in high-technology areas such as An Wang (founder of Wang Computers in the 1980s) or Jeffrey Yang (founder of Yahoo!Inc.). Chinese-American scientists have likewise contributed greatly—perhaps the best example has been Chang-Lin Tien, a Berkeley physicist who served as chancellor there from 1990 to 1997. If we focus on California for a moment, where more than 1 million Chinese-Americans reside, the future looks very good. Although Chinese Americans make up only 3 percent of the California population, they currently comprise 13 percent of the student body of the University of California system. And, at the oldest flagship campus, University of California Berkeley, 17 percent of the students identify themselves as Chinese American.

Strife in China and opportunity (the gold rushes and construction work) in North America brought the early waves of Chinese immigrants beginning in about 1850. A declining economy in the North America led to increased discrimination and targeted exclusion of Chinese immigrants in the 1880s (a head tax in Canada and a ban in the United States). Race-based restrictions on immigration were finally ended with the Immigration Act of 1965 in the United States. The act granted applicants from all nations equal status and equal quotas of 20,000 per year per country were established. That included a separate quota of 20,000 from Taiwan and 5,000 from Hong Kong, the latter in 1987. The population of immigrants from Taiwan grew more than tenfold to about 200,000 during the 1980s, and some 30,000 student visas were granted each year during this period ranking them third among all foreign students in the United States.

Don Lee, a Chinese-American reporter for the *Los Angeles Times*, filed an insightful report on the experiences of a fellow Chinese American trying to put his cultural skills to use in Shanghai.[8] It seems even Alex Xu has felt a bit shanghaied there. The story provides interesting reading and deep lessons about both the China market and Chinese-American participation in it. Enjoy:

Alex Xu has worked in the trenches at the old Broadway department stores, managed the complex finances of the Santa Anita racetrack and built thousands of homes in Southern California. But all that wasn't enough to prepare him for doing business in China.

Since coming here three years ago to start a chain of budget hotels, the 41-year-old Chinese American says, he has run into a maze of regulations and permits that, by comparison, makes California look like an easy place to do business. He says that he also has been pressured to pay bribes and that in one city, his employees were beaten by thugs. Sometimes Xu has fought back. But mostly, the math whiz turned entrepreneur has bided his time and sought out relatives and friends to help him get around obstacles.

He has opened nine GreenTree Inns in China and, along with a handful of other hotel companies, is racing to tap the nation's boom in business and leisure travel. "I'm far behind my original plan," said Xu, who splits his time between Shanghai and

Los Angeles, where he is president of American Pacific Homes Inc. and lives with his wife and two children.

Xu has flown back and forth so many times that he knows the pilots on China Eastern Airlines by name. Last year, he missed Christmas and his wife's and 11-year-old daughter's birthdays— he sent them a dozen roses each. "It's been a bumpy road," he said. Xu is among tens of thousands of overseas Chinese who have returned to their motherland for work and business opportunities. The Chinese call them "sea turtles"—a play on the characters hai gui, *which mean "returned from overseas studies." Many sea turtles from the United States come from California, home to more than 1.1 million ethnic Chinese. The Chinese diaspora, estimated at 35 million in Asia and elsewhere, gives China an advantage that other Asian economic powerhouses such as Japan and South Korea don't have.*

Overseas Chinese like Xu bring with them not only money— he and his backers have invested $20 million—but also sophisticated technology and management skills honed over many years. China desperately wants these to move beyond low-cost manufacturing and grow its high-tech and service industries, which many cities are trying to do. "Because Shanghai is developing, their experience will be precious," said Zhou Hong, division chief of Shanghai's Overseas Chinese Affairs office. He estimates that 15,000 Chinese from abroad have started businesses in the city. Chinese returnees have some obvious advantages over foreigners doing business in China. In addition to language, they tend to have greater familiarity with the culture and markets, as well as personal connections.

But success is far from assured, as Xu's experience illustrates. Xu lived away from China for a long time, more than most sea turtles, having moved to California in 1987 as a graduate student in mathematics at USC. But the native of Shandong province is no stranger to Shanghai. Xu's wife, Wang Wei, was born and grew up here, and the couple had traveled to Shanghai and other Chinese cities on numerous occasions. "When I vis-

ited China I always stayed in a five-star hotel," he said. "No one was offering business travelers an affordable option."

In late 2003, Xu drafted a business plan, enlisted an architectural firm in Orange County, hired four people in China and began to look for a site for his first GreenTree Inn. He found it in an empty vocational school in Jingan district in the middle of Shanghai a couple of blocks away from glitzy Nanjing Road. All he needed was government approval. As head of American Pacific Homes in Montclair, Xu is used to dealing with planning departments and community groups and waiting for permits. But he never expected that he would need approvals from 11 agencies to open a hotel in Shanghai. There was the police, the fire department, various business licensing bureaus and foreign enterprise offices.

In some cases, Xu had to clear one agency before he could move on to the next. Yet the tasks of the different bureaucracies weren't always specified. "Many times," he said, "they would kick the ball back to each other."

Xu had a dozen people on his payroll helping, including accountants and hotel managers. A college classmate of Xu's wife introduced him to a Shanghai government official who helped move the ball forward. Six months later, Xu had all but the final stamp of approval and was allowed to open his hotel for 30 days on a provisional basis. But the month passed and he heard nothing. The hotel was on tenterhooks; it couldn't check in any new guests. When the final go-ahead came three months later, Xu says, he was practically numb. He never had a grand opening because he didn't know when the hotel would clear the last hurdle. "People have the belief that because the Chinese government has an open-door policy, it must be very easy," he said during a recent three-week visit to China. "The learning curve to do business is a lot higher here."

Along the way, Xu also learned a few things about the Chinese approach. Three flag posts stand in front of his green, 140-room hotel; China's flag must be in the center. Every night, hotels must submit a record of all registered guests to the local police. And if you want plants and the street outside your door to be clean and well kept, it helps to have a friend on the neighborhood committee. The next eight hotels came together faster, including two more in Shanghai, but not always without trouble. Xu was reluctant to discuss specifics, but he said that in one city, a restaurant tenant in Xu's newly acquired property refused to move out.

On a recent weekend, the tenant hired thugs who jumped behind the hotel counter and attacked some of Xu's managers. GreenTree called 110, China's 911, but the police, he said, looked the other way. Xu wasn't at the site at the time, but his managers hired guards to keep the restaurant closed and hold the gang at bay. "They realized we were deadly serious and agreed to move out in three days," Xu said.

In Southern California, Xu lives a quiet, comfortable life, albeit a busy one. In addition to his home-building business—the main projects are in Ventura County—he invests in properties such as office and medical buildings in the San Gabriel Valley. Xu admits he is a workaholic, answering e-mails at 3 in the morning to his employees in China who are at work. "The kids and I just got used to it," his wife said, adding that "it all happened gradually." In 2002, Xu flew to China twice for business. He made four trips the next year, then eight in 2004 and 10 in 2005. When he's not working, Wei said, Xu likes to play board games at home with his children, Ashley and 6-year-old Brian.

Xu didn't have an easy childhood, growing up poor in a farming village near Weihai, a port city southeast of Beijing. His father was a doctor of Chinese medicine, but during the Cultural Revolution he picked up a farm hoe, planting wheat and corn in the summer and potatoes and radishes in the fall. Xu's mother went to work with the local government. Between them, they earned about $12 a month, which they used to buy salt, oil and clothes. Xu recalls that he and his younger brother and sister tasted meat only three times a year. Xu flourished in school, graduating from the Beijing Institute of Technology at age 20. While working as a research analyst at a government agency *specializing in aerospace, he studied English at night. He won a scholarship to USC.*

He had earned master's degrees in applied mathematics and engineering and was studying for a doctorate when he met Brian Fleming, an American executive. Xu was tutoring Fleming's daughter in math, and one evening, he confided in him: Business was his passion, not academics. A month later in 1990, Fleming, then chief financial officer of Broadway Stores Inc., offered Xu a job in the company's financial systems department. A year later Broadway was in bankruptcy reorganization; it would eventually see its name replaced by Macy's. Fleming left three years later for Santa Anita Realty Enterprises Inc. and took Xu with him as the company's finance director. "Alex is a genius in math. He has an incredible ability to focus," said Fleming, 62, now chief financial officer at BCBG Max Azria Group Inc., a Los Angeles-area fashion company.

Xu hopes to build hundreds of GreenTree Inns throughout China. He has 10 under development and plans to open 50 this year, most in southern China. At less than $30 a night on average, GreenTree Inns cost a fraction of the price of many five-star hotels that are favored by executives. Xu believes that most corporate travelers won't mind giving up a swimming pool, a big health center and luxury restaurants. What they want, he says, are a good location, comfortable bed, clean facility and Internet access, which is free in every room at GreenTree. Chinese travelers also want a tasty breakfast buffet. For a little more than $2, Xu offers a mix of Western and Chinese dishes, including eight to 10 vegetables, much of it prepared from the freezer to reduce waste.

Until now, the occupancy rate of GreenTree Inns open at least six months has been running at 90% or higher, Xu said. That compares with a national average of 60% to 70% for all hotels, said Zhang Minghou, a spokesman for the China Hotel Assn. By the association's count, China has about 200,000 lodging places, including 10,000 that are star-rated by the government. Zhang estimates that the hotel market for business travel is growing at least 10% a year. "This is an emerging market with a large potential," he said. Zhang recently visited a GreenTree Inn in Shenzhen, though he didn't stay overnight. He says he went away generally impressed with the location and cleanliness of the facility.

But he adds that it's too early to tell whether Xu and Green-Tree will succeed. A pair of state-owned hotel operators and international chain Super 8 Motels are aggressively targeting budget-conscious business travelers, and many others are trying to enter the market.

Xu says he doesn't worry about competitors as much as he does his management and the chain's ability to grow while maintaining high standards and principles. For the most part, Xu says, he lets the staff run the hotel and work with local officials and vendors as needed. But he draws the line at bribery. One utility company, Xu says, insisted that GreenTree pad the rates. When the hotel said no, the utility representative told Xu, "Sorry, you won't have gas." The hotel switched to higher-cost diesel fuel.

"I probably will never get used to the way it's done here," Xu said. "But I don't want to. We have to be different and not be afraid."

Managerial Behaviors of Overseas Chinese

All the largest firms are enmeshed in business operations on the mainland as well as Southeast Asia. Chinese Americans manage most of the trade between the United States and China. Most experts agree also that the Chinese executives running all these operations tend toward a hands-on approach, transfers of knowledge and people across diverse businesses, reference to qualitative information and holistic views gleaned from personal contacts, and action-driven decision making.

Additionally, these overseas Chinese managers are at least bicultural and therefore are capable of thinking and conversing as "natives" in their native countries. But they can also turn on the entrepreneurial spirit and skillful bargaining of their south coast Chinese ancestors quite quickly. They will continue to be tough customers and even tougher competitors, particularly on their home turf.

The commercial values and behaviors of overseas Chinese will be best indicated by their fluency in Chinese dialects, the recency of their immigration, and the location of their university experience. So as you get to know the Chinese folks across the negotiation table, whether they be in Bangkok or Boston, it makes sense to take an interest in their personal history. And, it may also be just plain interesting!

Notes

1 Joel Kotkin, *Tribes: How Race, Religion, and Identity Determine Success in the New Global Economy* (New York: Random House, 1992), from the back cover.
2 Gungwu Wang, *China and the Overseas Chinese* (Singapore: Times Academic Press, 1991).
3 The quote is based on an interview with Hal Plotkin reported in Joel Kotkin's *Tribes*.
4 Tiong Chen Chin, Usha C.V. Haley, and George T. Haley, *New Asian Emperors*.
5 Ram Charan, "How Networks Reshape Organizations— for Results," *Harvard Business Review*, Reprint No. 91530, 1991, p. 49.
6 Press release, Esker Software, October 20, 2005.
7 Much of the biographical information about Robert Kuok is taken directly from the Chinese Overseas Data Bank based in Singapore. See www.huayinet.org.
8 Don Lee, "Returning Chinese Find a Tough Market," *Los Angeles Times*, March 5, 2006, pp. C1 and C5.

PART IV

NEGOTIATING AND ENFORCING INTELLECTUAL PROPERTY RIGHTS (IPRs)

FEARS ABOUT INTELLECTUAL PROPERTY RIGHTS: PIRATES INTO POLICEMEN?[1]

A quick quiz to start—in what country do intellectual property pirates steal the most money from American firms? You'll find the interesting answer later in the chapter. Hint: It's not China!

During the last decade American politicians and the media have focused on three reasons to vilify China—the violation of human rights by the Chinese government, the proliferation of nuclear arms by China, and the almost universal disregard of intellectual property rights (IPRs) by individuals and organizations in China. For American executives the last issue (in the form of fears about piracy, counterfeiting, and technology theft) has been the primary reason for their second thoughts about doing business in China.

Before discussing the debate swirling around China and IPRs, it is important first to understand the fundamental justification for the ownership of ideas. IPRs are fictional rights created to encourage innovations and creativity by protecting the labor of

authors and inventors while at the same time promoting dissemination of ideas and information and competition. Through the
years, the pendulum has swung between favoring *dissemination
and competition* and emphasizing *protection and exclusion*. In fact,
during the last century, the United States has gone through different periods in which IPRs were paramount (favoring exclusion
and protection) and where antitrust was dominant (favoring dissemination and competition). The twenty-first century has begun
with the balance tipped steeply toward IPRs—the World Trade
Organization (WTO) attempting to enforce strong protections
and exclusions through the TRIPS Agreement (1994 Agreement
on Trade-Related Aspects of Intellectual Property Protection)
sections of the GATT (General Agreement on Trade and Tarrifs).

WACKY PACKAGING GIVES KNOCKOFFS AWAY

BEIJING—The entertaining part of buying Chinese knockoff
DVDs and CDs is the packaging.

For instance, stores overflow with compilation albums that
infringe on the intellectual property rights of several U.S. companies at once.

One hot seller, America's Greatest Country Hits, includes
songs by non-country artists Richard Marx and Gregory Hines.
Christmas albums frequently throw in the *Titanic* love theme "My
Heart Will Go On" so there's an excuse to use cover art of
Leonardo DiCaprio's chin burrowing Kate Winslet's nape. . . .

A pirated DVD of the TriStar film *The Wonder Boys* includes
English subtitles that refer to Michael Douglas's professor, Grady
Tripp, as the "auspicious emperor of leather." One DVD box of
The Fugitive features images of star Harrison Ford from his film
Six Days, Seven Nights but a description of *A River Runs Through It*,
a film Ford wasn't in.

However, "attempting" is the key word in the previous sentence. On November 9, 2001, the day before China was officially admitted into the WTO, Microsoft Windows XP was launched with an official price tag of about $180. Meanwhile, on the streets of Shanghai, pirated copies of XP had been selling for about $2 a "copy" for weeks. Bill Gates shouldn't have taken it too personally—estimates are that 95 percent of all software in use in China is pirated. Indeed, Mr. Gates was overjoyed on a recent visit to Shanghai when the mayor there promised to clamp down— by ordering his own staff to stop buying pirated copies! And it's not just software. Procter & Gamble complains that 40 percent of its shampoos marketed in China are knockoffs. Honda estimates that 60 percent of Honda motorcycles sold in China are

There are several theories on why the packaging is so strange. One possible reason for rampant misspellings—Whitey Husto, Madamma—is that counterfeiters use computer scanners to transfer the images and words from legitimate material onto their screens to manipulate it. Scanners are notorious for incorrect letter recognition.

As for the twisted lyrics, the most sensible explanation may come from a Beijing shop owner who would only give his surname, Li: "Sometimes the legitimate entertainment company creates a Chinese version of the product with a translation of the lyrics in Chinese. . . . The bootleggers may try to translate the Chinese back into English, which is difficult because each Chinese character is a concept."

Excerpted from Steve Friess' "Product Piracy Poses Biggest Threat to China's Economic Status," *USA Today*, June 28, 2001, p. B6.

not Hondas. Estimates of lost revenues from such piracy range widely—the highest one we've run across is $16 billion annually. Perhaps the anecdotes reported in the box are humorous, but $16 billion is not a funny number in this context.

While it is certainly true that there are massive amounts of pirated software, CDs, and brand names in China, one need only look back in history to understand why. Most readers would be surprised to find that the United States was once a pirate vis-à-vis Europe and Britain. As the United States developed economically, socially, and technologically, the problem of piracy vis-à-vis the other countries eventually disappeared. As demonstrated later in this chapter, other developed or developing countries such as the United States, Japan, and Taiwan also traveled the same road of development in terms of IPRs.

As China develops economically and socially, the problem of IPR violations will become less severe. As per capita income rises, more and more people will be able to afford to pay reasonable prices for books, music CDs, DVDs, and the like. As Chinese companies begin to develop new technologies, they will need IP protections in order to be profitable and grow. Ultimately, the rate of economic progress will largely determine whether most of China's companies or citizens will abide by the IPR rules mandated by the WTO, although more fundamental considerations such as legal consciousness, political culture, and cultural values cannot be ignored.

Under pressure from the United States in the 1990s, the Chinese government passed legislation for regulating IPRs and for enforcing IPR violations in China. In fact, violations of the IPR laws can lead to criminal prosecution and imprisonment. Most importantly, with China's membership in the WTO, it has agreed to abide by TRIPS.

TRIPS requires China to take positive steps to protect the property rights in the country. China has to adopt and implement national legislation which sets specific standards and actively enforce them, whether it is ready for TRIPS or not.

TRIPS

TRIPS is a part of the multilateral trade agreements that were made binding on members in the Final Act of the Uruguay Round. Adhering to the TRIPS agreement is obligatory for all countries that join the WTO, now including China, and is part of the WTO's common institutional framework.

The agreement covers all intellectual property rights, patents, trademarks, copyrights, and trade secrets, including relatively new ones such as semiconductor chip rights. It incorporates the Berne Convention for copyright norms and adds additional copyright protection for computer software, databases, and sound recordings. TRIPS adopts a patent law minimum well above the previous standards of the 1883 Paris Convention, extending both subject matter covered and term of protection. Patent rights are extended to virtually all subject matter (with the exception of plants and animals other than microorganisms), including pharmaceutical products, chemicals, pesticides, and plant varieties, and are to be granted for 20 years.

Semiconductor chips and the layout designs of integrated circuits are protected under a *sui generis* (special or more specific) system. Countries are required to provide adequate and effective enforcement mechanisms both internally and at the border. Countries must also provide for both civil and criminal penalties for infractions. The agreement makes the WTO's dispute settlement mechanism available to address conflicts arising under TRIPS and significantly provides for the possibility of cross-sectoral retaliation against countries that fail to abide by WTO's dispute settlement body's rulings.

TRIPS proponents helped to devise an enforcement mechanism linking intellectual property protection to trade leverage in order to compel developing countries to respond. Now violations in intellectual property can lead to sanctions on goods. The WTO is empowered to monitor compliance to ensure that defendants carry out their obligations within a reasonable time period. If the defendants fail to comply, the WTO will authorize the complainant to impose retaliatory trade sanctions if requested to do so. This gives the WTO power to enforce the TRIPS agreement.

This far-reaching agreement has important implications for innovation, economic development, the future location of industry, and the global division of labor. Indeed, it has been argued that the dramatic expansion of the scope of intellectual property rights embodied in the TRIPS agreement reduces the options available to developing nations by effectively blocking the route that developed countries followed before them. It raises the price of information and technology by extending the monopoly privileges of rights holders, and requires countries such as China to play a much greater role in defending them. It is interesting to note that industrialized countries such as the United States and Japan built much of their economic prowess by appropriating others' intellectual property. With the TRIPS agreement, this option seems to be foreclosed for later developing countries.

It is even more interesting to note that *without private sector activism, there would be no TRIPS* today. In Professor Susan K. Sell's outstanding work, one gets to understand and see how and why TRIPS was a stunning triumph for the U.S. commercial interests and their lobbyists who worked tirelessly to influence and advocate the TRIPS Agreement. In fact, a handful of American firms, together with like-minded companies in Europe and Japan, negotiated and devised a consensual blueprint for the TRIPS agreement which was pushed by the U.S. government and ultimately adopted by GATT. This "trilateral group" was able to effectively advocate and institutionalize an IPR regime based on protection and exclusion rather than on competition and diffusion.

It is under this IPR environment that China enters WTO and becomes a card-carrying member of the international community. For better or worse, TRIPS is here to stay. But to understand how China will develop under the TRIPS regime, it is important to look back in history.

A Historical Perspective

The history of the transformation of intellectual property pirates into policemen has been quite consistent around the world and over the years.

The United States

It was not until sometime in the nineteenth century that the United States became a net exporter of technology. Before that it offered lax protection for foreigners' IPRs and built much of its industrial prowess on European technology in general and British technology in particular. Indeed, the story goes that Benjamin Franklin regularly reprinted the works of British authors in his newspaper ignoring their copyrights in the process. In the early days of steam engine technology, Britain forbade the export of engines, parts, and skilled personnel. The United States imported all three regardless. It is obvious that the decision was made in the United States that at that stage of economic development, the best policy for the United States was lax enforcement of foreign IPRs.

This preference for weak protection of IPRs changed in the latter half of the nineteenth century as American firms began to achieve technological breakthroughs. American firms, such as the Edison Company, pressed for strong IPR protection in the negotiations over the Paris Convention. Over a hundred years later, this strategy would again be used by the Intellectual Property Committee to push its agenda which led to the TRIPS agreement, as IPR owners from developed countries (Europe, Japan, and the United States) realize the monopolistic potential of IPRs.

Japan

After World War II Japan was viewed a country that imitated American technology and products. Indeed, Japanese companies were regarded as great imitators of American products but laggards in innovations. The Japanese were also famous for reverse engineering. The Japanese attitude about IPRs probably was not that different from that of the United States about a century and a half earlier—it needed to learn from the West and catch up. Needless to say, the Japanese enforcement of foreign IPRs was lax.

However, by the 1980s, as Japan became a veritable economic power, Japanese companies became seriously interested in developing and protecting their IPRs. Japanese companies have become leaders in applying for and obtaining new patents with the U.S. Patents and Trademarks Office. The pirates have become the policemen as Japanese companies seek strong protections for their IPRs as members of the trilateral group pushing through the TRIPS agreement during the Uruguay round of GATT.

Taiwan

The case of Taiwan can perhaps be best used to illustrate the point that economic, technological, social, and political changes can dramatically affect a country's view and compliance with IPRs imposed by outside forces such as the TRIPS agreement.

In the 1980s, Taiwan was regarded as the counterfeit capital of the world. Violation of various forms of IPRs ranging from copyrights to trademarks to patents was rampant. Counterfeiting of computer hardware and software, electronic goods, video and audiocassettes, watches, and textiles was commonplace despite the tremendous pressure put on by the United States. In order to comply with U.S. demands, various laws were passed with great fanfare, complemented by severe penalties, mass educational campaigns, and increased news coverage.

If Taiwan government's actions pleased American interests, it certainly did not please many within its border. The most prestigious economic newspaper in Taiwan, *Jingji Ribao* (Economics Daily), argued that the the government should not rush out to legislate laws that benefit others and harm its own. Some went so far as to denounce Taiwan lawyers who had represented American intellectual property holders as "traitors." U.S. threats and demands were regarded by many as American excesses and ignored by many. This anger helps to explain why the IPRs agreements and concessions wrung so painfully from Taiwan had such little real impact on corporate or individual behavior.

That American pressure had caused an unprecedented revision of intellectual property law in Taiwan is undeniable. But, it was not foreign pressure that yielded the current compliance. In the 1990s, Taiwan became "Silicon Valley East." Its economic ascent and its increasing importance in the personal computer supply chain as well as leading-edge technologies in wafer foundries reflected Taiwan's new capabilities to generate its own world-class technology if it was to compete with other advanced economies. Additionally, various domestic groups including engineers behind Taiwan's burgeoning software business, publishers, and many in the indigenous film and entertainment industries were confronted with mainland China piracy (among others). These *new* victims of infringement began to support stronger IPR protections both at home and abroad.

This point is borne out by one author's personal experience in the representation of a number of Taiwan's high-tech companies. As recently as five years ago, most of these companies were defendants in patent infringement lawsuits. In the last few years, as some of these companies have accumulated substantial portfolios of patents and other IPRs, they too begain to seek redress for violation by both U.S. and foreign companies in not only the U.S. courts, but foreign courts as well. The pirates have become owners of IPRs. Or as William Alford so elegantly puts it, "As Pirates Become Proprietors . . ." Indeed, we are now witness to the first mainland firm to sue an American company over patent (for flash-drive design) infringement—it will be fascinating to watch Netac (based in Shenzen) take on PNY Technologies of New Jersey in Texas in the coming months.

In addition, for many years, the Taiwan judiciary lacked integrity, competence, and independence. In recent years, the court system has improved markedly. It is now seen as an effective means of remedying infringement and is a viable venue for the resolution of IPR problems. Moreover, the concept of "rule of law" has become more and more accepted by businesses and individuals alike. Taiwan now ranks as one of the most vigorous countries in the enforcement of IPR violations in Asia.

As can be seen from the experience of United States, Japan, and Taiwan, external pressure and externally imposed IPR legislation can only go so far. It is only when a country has reached a certain stage in its economic, technological, social, and political development that its government, companies, and citizens have the capability, maturity, and incentive to pay for and to observe certain intellectual property rights.

The Case of China

From time to time, the mass media including leading newspapers such as the *New York Times* and *Wall Street Journal* report stories about intellectual property piracy in China. These stories usually go as follows: "For the longest time, the Chinese pirates have been getting a free ride on the creative genius of Western authors and inventors. As a result, they have brought about the greatest trade deficit in the United States, culminating in a $202 billion trade deficit in 2005. Every year, the United States loses more than $4 billion because of intellectual property piracy in China. Tired of this enormous trade deficit and the millions of pirated copies of Microsoft Windows and Office and counterfeit Mickey Mouse T-shirts, the United States is mounting a noble crusade not only to protect the United States' intellectual property interests but also to teach China about the needed ethical values, technological development, and fair play in global economic integration."

These stories contain some truths as to the extent of the Chinese piracy problem and its adverse impact on the U.S. economy. However, they omit some of the most important aspects of the on-going U.S.-China intellectual property conflict. First, this noble crusade did not begin in the 1990s; it has been ongoing since the turn of the twentieth century. So far, it has not produced very effective results, apart from putting lots of IP laws on Chinese statute books and occasional anticounterfeiting raids. For example, P&G reports that some 1,000 raids on counterfeit sellers of their products have yielded only 10 convictions in the last three years. Second, it has failed to point out that China and the West have significant political, social, economic, and cultural differences that militate against intellectual property law reforms in China. Third, the crusade has so far failed to convince the Chinese and their leaders of the benefits of intellectual property rights to China, even if China has become part of the WTO and must abide by TRIPS.

Although prominent legal scholars such as William Alford, author of the wonderful *To Steal a Book Is an Elegant Offense*, have repeatedly tried to make the case that China cannot be coerced into complying with the Western formulated IPRs regime, these stories continue to confuse American scholars, policymakers, the mass media, and the general public and prevent them from understanding the roots of the Chinese piracy problem.

The History of China and Intellectual Property Laws

China did not attempt to introduce substantial intellectual property protection until the early twentieth century. To protect the IPRs of its nationals, the United States, which had only acceded to the Paris Convention for the Protection of Industrial Property in 1883, used its military and economic might to force China to sign a commercial treaty in 1903. The Chinese revolution occurred in 1911, and China introduced a substantive copyright law in 1910, patent law in 1912, and trademark law in 1923.

Despite these laws, the piracy problem was exacerbated by increasing industrialization. The failure of this first conversion attempt by the United States can be attributed to three reasons.

First, the United States failed to consider the relevance of its intellectual property model to China and premised the new regime on a registration system. Because of uniquely Chinese problems such as geographical isolation, high levels of corruption, and strong regional protectionism, the registration system for the intellectual property turned out to be ineffective and the enforcement nearly impossible.

Second, the United States was unable to convince the Chinese government why intellectual property laws would benefit China. To many officials, law reforms were merely unfortunate short-term expedient answers for complying with overbearing Western demands. Third, the United States did not rally the support of Chinese holders of IPRs behind the new intellectual property regime. The United States also failed to train Chinese officials with responsibilities in the field and to educate the Chinese populace about the importance and reasons behind IPRs. Instead, the United States presumed that political pressure would suffice to induce adoption and widespread adhesion to the IPR laws.

In 1977, when Deng Xiaoping assumed power, he called for "four modernizations" aimed at enabling China to reach world-class strength in agriculture, industry, science and technology, and military matters by the end of the century. It was under such a pretext that in 1979 the United States and China concluded a trade agreement in which each side recognized the importance of effective protection of patents, trademarks, and copyrights and to take measures under its laws and regulations to protect the works of citizens of other nations.

However, within China, the debate about the efficacy of IPRs for China's economic development remained. Those in favor of a strong IPR protection regime argued that it provided meaningful material incentives for innovation and creativity, that it facilitated faster technology transfer by foreigners, and that it aided China's technology development and also would protect China's scientific advances abroad. Those opposing argued that a strong IPR protection regime was intrinsically antithetical to socialism, might lead to the total domination of the Western "literary-industrial complex" as to retard the development of indigenous science and so leave China dependent on the outside world economically, scientifically, and militarily, and would risk draining China's limited foreign exchange reserves to pay royalties.

By the mid-1980s, however, American businesses became impatient with the lack of progress in intellectual property protection in China. They urged the U.S. Trade Representative (USTR) to put pressure on China. China was thus 'persuaded' to pass a new copyright law and enact new implemention regulations in 1990, signing a Memorandum of Understanding on Intellectual Property in 1992 ("1992 MOU"), signing the Agreement Regarding IPRs ("1995 agreement"), and concluding another accord ("1996 accord") which merely reaffirmed China's commitment to protect IPRs under the 1995 Agreement.

Since the 1996 accord and with an eye toward joining the WTO, the Chinese government has made substantial efforts to improve intellectual property protection with tough enforcement measures including jailing or putting to death serious infringers. However, intellectual property piracy is still rampant in China today. This has led some keen commentators to suggest that the American intellectual property policy toward China has been ineffective.

Obstacles to Chinese Adoption of Western IPRs

There are four kinds of obstacles that hinder Chinese adoption of western IPR regimes. They are cultural, political, nationalistic, and legal in nature.

Confucianism and Traditional Chinese Cultural Values

As you read Chapters 2 and 5, you must have realized that Confucianism had been China's dominant political, social, and cultural philosophy until the beginning of the twentieth century. To the Chinese, the past was the embodiment of cultural and social values. Chinese children were taught to memorize verbatim the classics and histories, and their success in the imperial examinations depended to a large degree on their abilities to recite the Confucian Four Books and the Five Classics. It was small wonder that when the Chinese grew up, they were by training compilers, as compared to composers.

Unlike Westerners today, the Chinese in the imperial past did not consider copying or imitation a moral offense. On the contrary, since IPRs allow only a few to monopolize these needed materials, IPRs actually contradicted traditional Chinese moral standards. It is interesting to note that to a very large extent, this compiling tradition was similar to that held by Westerners before the emergence of the contemporary notion of authorship in the eighteenth century. In fact, it is reported that even William Shakespeare engaged regularly in activity that we would call plagiarism but he and his fellow Elizabethan playwrights saw as acceptable, if not even complimentary. Like the Chinese, writers regarded imitation as the sincerest form of flattery and a necessary component of the creative process.

Finally, creativity was considered a collective benefit to the community and posterity. Creating or compiling literary works was for the sake of sheer scholarship, not profit. In the pecking order of traditional Chinese society based on Confucianism, merchants were considered the lowest among the scholar-official (si), farmer (nong), artisan (gong), and merchant (shang) classes.

Socialist Centrally Planned Economic System

From 1949 to the early 1980s, China's Communist government implemented the socialist economic system whereby property belongs to the state and the people rather than private owners. Numerous mass campaigns and endless class struggles that took place during the Mao era demonized ownership of private property, whether real or intellectual. Specifically, during the Cultural Revolution, the government heavily criticized scientists, lawyers, writers, artists, and intellectuals and condemned them to harsh labor, banished them to farms, or punished them with prison terms. Even worse, during the Cultural Revolution many Chinese developed contempt for authorship and any kind of creative efforts. Thoughtful intellectuals and professionals became the bane of the Communist Party. An oft-cited comment by one comrade during the Cultural Revolution stated, "[i]s it necessary for a steel worker to put his name on a steel ingot that he produces in the course of his duty? If not, why should a member of the intelligentsia enjoy the privilege of putting his name on what he produces?" Even more telling, all the scientific textbooks failed to attribute the discoveries and inventions of great scientists or inventors such as Newton or Edison. They simply labeled scientific laws in ways that did not mention the names of the great scientists or inventors. Finally, from 1966 to 1971, all theater was banned except for the eight model revolutionary "operas."

This socialist view of the function of creative works has had a similar impact on the Chinese as the Confucian view. It represents a continuation of the centuries old notion that intellectual property is public property to be shared and enjoyed by all. Intellectual property is not private property that should benefit and enrich the authors and inventors.

The Middle Kingdom, Xenophobia, and Nationalism

It is difficult to imagine that in 1793, Emperor Qianlong of China sent King George III of England a letter stating, "We possess all things. I set no value on objects strange or ingenious, and have no use for your country's manufactures."

This kind of ethnocentricism brought China two centuries of humiliation as the military prowess and the scientific progress of the West had proven Qianlong wrong. While the great majority of the ruling scholar-official class regarded foreign affairs and Western enterprises as beneath them, the xenophobic and nationalistic sentiments among the populace as a result of humiliation made reforms difficult. As outlined in Chapter 2, the Opium War, Taiping Rebellion, Sino-Japanese War, and many other wars and defeats brought unequal treaties that not only shattered China's confidence, but created unbearable hardship. By the turn of the twentieth century, foreign industries and investments had dominated almost all modern industries and enterprises in China, disrupted the previously self-sufficient agrarian economy, destroyed the native handcraft industries, and shattered traditional family relationships.

The 1911 Revolution did not bring much relief to China's suffering. Social instability, wars, and intensified foreign imperialism continued to bombard China, although the new intelligensia began to advocate acceptance of Western philosophy and institutions. In 1949 the Chinese Communist Party established the People's Republic of China. Despite the change in government, China continued to toil under the burden of history and the humiliation it received at the hand of Western imperialism during the nineteenth and twentieth centuries. The many attacks by Western powers that caused China to adopt a self-strengthening world view persisted and actually was used by Mao very effectively. Many Chinese believed it was right to freely reproduce or to tolerate the unauthorized reproduction of foreign works that would help strengthen the country. Many, in fact, believed that copying was necessary for China to catch up with Western developed countries. To date, the Chinese sometimes refer to pirated computer programs as "patriotic software," believing that it speeds the nation's modernization at little or no cost, after China had been "pillaged" by the West for two centuries.

Laws with Chinese Characteristics

As discussed in Chapter 5, China had a legal tradition distinct from that of the West. Not only did the Chinese view law as only a supplemental means for maintaining social control, but they also regarded law as an arbitrary, cumbersome, and much less preferred way of governance. The Confucian concept of "li" was the way to govern. Under this tradition, the Chinese lived by the concept of "li" (rituals), rather than the concept of "fa" (law). Chinese who were guided by "li" understood their roles, responsibilities, and obligations to others and to society. They were also more accommodating to other people and were more eager to avoid confrontation and conflict in order to preserve harmony. As a result, explicit laws and regulations were not necessary and litigations were to be avoided almost at any cost.

Even though Mao sought to overturn many aspects of the Confucian tradition, formal laws were still denounced as inherently bureaucratic, hampered by legislative formalities and fed on professional interests, slow to come, rigid in procedure, prone to ramifying into technical details and yet unable to cover all the circumstances of the ever changing social relationships. Instead, he instituted socialist laws that operate within the boundaries of policy directives, under the guidance of policy principles and supplemented by various policy tools (such as a Party or government circular or notice). Thus, throughout the Cultural Revolution and even today, laws are still considered as a concrete formulation of the Party's policy. They are intended to be flexible and can be formulated on an interim or trial use basis.

Thus, Chinese laws in general are broadly drafted, leaving the detailed rules to be provided by the relevant administrations under the State Council. It is often the detailed administrative implementation of rules that provides the concrete information about the definition, limits, and practical implication of legal rights established in the laws. To determine the applicability and effectiveness of a provision, one must examine all the laws and supplemental documents, including administrative rules and judicial interpretations, in all the relevant and related areas. In most cases, the more specific and updated provisions prevail.

Thus, Chinese laws have indeed unique and distinctive characteristics influenced in part by the Confucian notion of governance and in part by Mao's Communist ideals. Contrary to the American system of separation of executive, legislative, and judicial power, the Chinese laws are much influenced by the policies of the Party. Couple that with the relative immaturity of the judiciary, and it should not be surprising that China's "Laws with Chinese Charateristics" that have baffled us for so long will continue to do so in the future. Thus, this plus the other factors discussed in this section question whether China would be able to effectively adopt and enforce the intellectual property laws mandated by TRIPS, in spite of the Chinese government's efforts to try to stamp out intellectual property violation.

Morality, Legitimacy, and IPRs

We have attempted to outline some of the historical, cultural, economic, and political reasons why intellectual property laws imposed on China by the West may encounter difficulties. However, it is even *more* important to understand why people in general, not just people in China, do not obey intellectual property laws.

Violation of Intellectual Property Laws Is Not Unique to China

The success of Napster (downloading software) and vast evidence indicating that CDs, computer software, tapes, and other copyrighted materials are often used illegally in the United States are but two good examples. A body of research supports this claim. For example, investigators have reported that a substantial proportion of both business executives and other members of businesses report the illegal copying of computer software. Similarly, it has been estimated that over one-half of college students in the United States use illegal software. These studies support estimates that between 50 and 90 percent of all computer software used is unauthorized. Finally, a study of other thefts of intellectual property such as taping a record album or a movie reveals that such actions are widely regarded as acceptable practices.

You will find in Exhibit 16.1 a listing of the estimated piracy rates for computer software around the world. The highest per-

Highest Piracy Rates		Lowest Piracy Rates	
Vietnam	92%	United States	22%
Ukraine	91%	New Zealand	23%
China	90%	Austria	25%
Zimbabwe	90%	Sweden	26%
Indonesia	87%	United Kingdom	27%
Russia	87%	Denmark	27%
Nigeria	84%	Switzerland	28%
Tunisia	84%	Japan	28%
Algeria	83%	Finland	29%
Kenya	83%	Germany	29%
Paraguay	83%	Belgium	29%
Pakistan	82%	Netherlands	30%
Bolivia	80%	Norway	31%
El Salvador	80%	Australia	32%
Nicaragua	80%	Israel	33%
Thailand	79%	UAE	43%
Venezuela	79%	Canada	36%
Guatemala	78%	South Africa	37%
Dominican Republic	77%	Ireland	38%
Lebanon	75%	Portugal	40%

**Exhibit 16.1   Piracy Rates, Top and Bottom 20
(Computer Software)** (*Source: Business Software Alliance,
www.bsa.org/globalstudy*)

centage is in Vietnam, followed closely by Ukraine and China. The
lowest rates are in the United States. So where is piracy the biggest
problem for American companies? It's actually in the United States.
The loss totals estimated for American firms in the United States
were $6.6 billion in 2004. China did come in second at $3.6 billion, followed by France ($2.9 billion), Germany ($2.3 billion, and
the United Kingdom ($2.0 billion). Perhaps the Brits are making
up for their own losses to us during the nineteenth century!

Why Do People Disobey Intellectual Property Laws?

It has been suggested that the traditional approach to safeguarding intellectual property—punitive laws meant to deter illegal use—have not succeeded and will not succeed. Research shows that in general threats of punishment do not deter people from law breaking. In intellectual property, the fear of punishment is so remote that deterrence is almost completely ineffective. In fact, Professor Tom Tyler suggests that it is unfortunate that authorities in the area of intellectual property use this strategy widely. He argues that whether it involves warnings on videocassettes or threats to sue university copy stores, the predominant strategy is to create a legal entitlement and then seek to enforce that entitlement with a threat. The result is widespread noncompliance with the law.

The Importance of Morality and Legitimacy

To induce public compliance, it is necessary to have a situation in which citizens voluntarily obey the law. Therefore, the effectiveness of intellectual property law is heavily dependent on gaining voluntary cooperation with the law, not on threats of punishment. It has been suggested that gaining voluntary cooperation with the law involves creating a culture that promotes compliance. Research suggests two factors that are important to gaining voluntary compliance: morality (Confucius is smiling!) and legitimacy. Morality is concerned with an individual's personal feelings about what is right or wrong. Legitimacy involves one's feeling that one ought to obey the law. Both of these factor promote voluntary compliance.

Individual morality, it is argued, is the primary factor shaping law-related behavior, followed by a sense of legitimacy as to the law and processes. Widespread research supports the proposition that judgments about fairness influence behavior. Most people simply do what they think is right or fair. In the case of intellectual property law, the finding by Professor Tyler is that there is a lack of public feeling that breaking intellectual property laws is wrong; therefore, there is little reason for people to follow IP laws. Thus it is crucial to understand public feelings about what is fair, whether it is in the United States or China. More research is needed to determine peoples' feelings about the morality of violating IP law and harmonizing the law to consumers' notions of right and wrong.

The second factor that induces compliance with law is the feeling of obligation to obey the law—legitimacy. When people feel that the law is legitimate, they feel that they "ought to obey" all laws, not just those that are consistent with their own moral principles. Thus, in order to induce widespread acceptance of IP laws, the goal ought to be enhancing the overall legitimacy of the law-making and law-enforcement systems. If people believe the laws are passed by authorities working in their interest and *following fair procedures*—not just in the interest of the special interest groups who stand to gain by the law at the expense of others—they will afford the law more legitimacy and tend to follow laws more closely. In essence, the key to effective laws is the creation of an underlying public culture whose values support the voluntary compliance with legal rules that are perceived to be fair.

Is TRIPS Moral and/or Legitimate?

The failure of Western IPR owners to understand the importance of these studies, in addition to China's differences from the West regarding legal traditions, history, and stages of economic development, is noteworthy. First and most fundamentally, the process by which TRIPS was adopted by the WTO was unfair in the eyes of many. TRIPS was a "stunning triumph for commercial interests and lobbyists" of the powerful trilateral group comprising a handful of the world's most powerful corporations. How can people in China view the IP laws as legitimate if they believe the laws were enacted and implemented following unfair procedures and only benefitting the rich and the powerful?

Is China's Crisis of Morality and Legitimacy a Result of American Hypocrisy?

In fact, there is a crisis of legitimacy with regard to IP laws. The vast majority of the Chinese population does not see these laws as enforcing important interests. As a result, there is no public acceptance of the need for such laws, and people do not see activities that infringe them as morally wrong. For example, while one author was visiting China in August 2002, a leading IPR authority in China, Professor Liu Chuntain of the Renmin University of Beijing, was engaged in a popular China Central TV talk show "Shi Hua Shi Shuo" concerning IPRs in China. Although Professor Liu strenuously advocated the merits of strong IPRs for China's development, it was quite clear that the majority of the audience thought otherwise. To the masses, it is also a matter of economics and legitimacy. For them, China has a legitimate interest in having unlimited access to foreign technology during its development process, and pirating can ensure that they can get these works at reasonable prices. This view is supported by some Western commentators. In fact, the current American IP policy is said to involve considerable hypocrisy, as the United States resisted giving adequate protection to foreign authors for many years, during which time America emerged from its period as a developing country.

American Aggressive Unilateralism

One reason IPRs has become such a dominant feature of American foreign policy is political expediency. Since 1985, under pressure from powerful industries and needing justification for the economic success of East Asian nations, the United States moved toward adopting a new trade policy commonly known as "aggressive unilateralism." The Reagan and Bush administrations embraced laissez-faire economics and opposed industrial policy. At the time, the latter was increasingly being credited for the success of the East Asian economies. The American government's aggressive unilateralism was based on the fundamental notion that the East Asian economic success should instead be explained in terms of the countries in East Asia having engaged in unfair trade practices. Thereby attention was deflected from the antithetical idea that government intervention may have played a constructive role in the success of these economies.

But in contrast to the political motives we have identified, American complaints about China have been framed in the language of fairness—that the theft of American IP by Chinese pirates is unfair. This approach casts doubt on the morality of our approach to IPRs given America's own history in terms of IP (that we are now advocating a stance we previously rejected) and that we are not honest about our motives (that our political motives are now dressed up in the language of fairness).

American-Induced Human Rights Abuses in China

To make matters worse, our aggressive IP policy also seeks to impose criminal sanctions on violators of IPRs in China, thus making us a potential accomplice to grave human rights violations there. It would seem outrageous that China, rated by Amnesty International as having one of the worst human rights records of any country in the world, should be persuaded by the West to use a criminal system that is characterized by political interference and that lacks basic procedural safeguards. The West purports to be concerned about human rights violations in China and often condemns China. Yet it has no problem fostering policies that may run counter to human rights when its own political interests are at stake. In fact, it has been reported that the Chinese government, in its eager attempts to please the West, has employed some of the most unsavory characters and procedures to enforce intellectual property law violations. As of 1998, it has been reported that at least 14 defendants have been sentenced to death for producing counterfeit goods. Thus, although the introduction of criminal sanctions for the infringement of IPR violations might meet the immediate concerns of American corporations, it has serious moral problems.

Since the heavy-handed strategies and tactics employed by the West have so far failed (and will likely to continue to fail) to convince the Chinese to internalize and implement our IPRs regime, we believe it is time for us to reexamine the existing paradigm and look for a new approach to developing countries. Yes, TRIPS is here to stay until the manifest unfairness against developing nations causes backlashes which might lead to massive demonstrations and renegotiations. The riots in Seattle and other cities around the world protesting globalization are signs that ordinary people are not content to let giant corporations dictate the agenda. Despite the political influence of the large multinational pharmaceutical giants, the constant uproar over AIDS drugs should also be instructive that profit maximization that we in the West have grown so accustomed to accepting may not be the "only truth."

The Evolving American View toward IPRs— the Pendulum Is Swinging Back

This current trend does not apply to only developing countries. More Americans are getting more and more unhappy about the monopoly power that entrenched commercial interests have been exerting via the use of IPRs. The music industry, despite its victory over Napster through the legal efforts of the Recording Industry Association of America (RIAA), will not be able to stop other forms of sharing. In fact, it is ironic that after the March 15, 2001, injunction directing Napster to block users from sharing copyrighted songs, the sales of albums continued to slide. More ominously, leading intellectual property scholars such as Stanford Law School professor and technology pundit Lawrence Lessig are now on the record as opposing the increasing abusive use of intellectual property laws. "Copyright and patent law, ostensibly designed to protect innovation, now have become tools large companies can use to maintain their dominance and control," Lessig said in his keynote address at the LinuxWorld Conference and Expo.

What to Do?

Some Suggestions on How to Encourage Compliance in the Long Run

The fact that most Chinese people and perhaps their leaders do not yet quite appreciate the importance of IPRs is not the same as the fact that it is unimportant for China. In fact, there are voices within China that are calling for China to quickly adopt the Western intellectual property framework so that it can stimulate its developments in science and technology. It could be argued that it is vital for China to develop a viable intellectual property regime, for without it, emerging Chinese companies cannot protect their intellectual properties and are likely to suffer more than American companies.

The question, then, is not whether China needs intellectual property laws. Rather, it is a question of how to persuade and help China quickly adopt an IPR regime that the Chinese would embrace and enforce vigorously. Then and only then will we start to see piracy in China begin to decline to the benefit of both American and Chinese companies whose goals are to innovate and compete fairly under free market conditions.

Peter Yu makes several suggestions by which America can help China to change from a pirate to partner. Among his recommendations are:

1. Abandon the coercive American IPR policy.
2. Foster a better understanding of China by the American people by joint conferences, research, awareness programs, and so forth.
3. Convince the Chinese leaders why IP protection will benefit China.
4. Promote a local China IP industry.
5. Promote individual rights and the rule of law in China.
6. Educate the Chinese officials about IPRs.
7. Educate the Chinese populace about IPRs.

8. Be patient with the Chinese during the transitional period.
9. Assist China to reform its IP laws.
10. Develop a new and harmonized international IP regime.

Although Peter Yu's suggestions are comprehensive, far reaching, and perhaps too idealistic, they are not too be taken lightly. In fact, if the United States really wants Chinese people and organizations to obey IP laws, the United States has to be fair and realistic. The aggressive unilateralism and hypocrisy which underpin the current U.S. imposed IPR regime and TRIPS need to be reexamined seriously. As psychological studies clearly tell us, the Chinese people and government must believe that the IPR regime imposed by the West is both moral and legitimate—and integrity and fairness play big parts—in order for them to accept it.

A very important part of the fairness issue is that China must be allowed to develop economically. The United States will have to respect China's sovereignty and its desire for economic, technological, and cultural development. It must avoid exaggerated demands for the recognition of IP as a form of inalienable right more important than China's progress. If the United States is perceived as using IPRs to try to retard the economic growth and progress of China, no amount of threats, coercion, and trade sanctions will be able to deter Chinese piracy.

How to Make TRIPS Work in the Near Term

Despite some leading scholars and commentators' urging that the West abandon the coercive policy of TRIPS or develop a new and harmonized international IPR regime, it is unlikely that the hard won gains by the developed nations at the behest of the giant multinational corporations will be so easily given up. Therefore, it is only realistic to expect that developing countries such as China learn to navigate within the confines of the existing TRIPS agreement.

Pro-Competitive Strategy within the Context of TRIPS

Professor Jerome H. Reichman has proposed a pro-competitive strategy for implementing the TRIPS agreement despite its pro-developed country bias. He suggests that a worldwide implementation of TRIPS, however, is not guaranteed because compliance by any individual state depends on its own national policies. He argues that there are many potential gains in complying with the TRIPS agreement, especially in light of the growing tendency of developed nations to adopt anti-competitive, highly protectionist industrial policies in reaction to the prospect of rapid economic growth among developing countries. The strategy includes:

1. Accommodating established intellectual property regimes to national development goals.
2. Using competition law to curb the abuse of market power.
3. Fashioning an IP regime to stimulate local innovation.
4. Resisting the drive for stronger international IPRs.
5. Strengthening national infrastructures for the acquisition and dissemination of scientific and technical knowledge.

Conclusion

History teaches that as the United States, Japan, and Taiwan developed economically, politically, and socially, problems with IP piracy gradually disappeared. The last 15 years teach us that China has a distinct cultural, social, technological, and political background that could not be so easily overcome by American coercive IPR policy. Psychological studies teach that people everywhere, not just in China, will abide by IP laws that are morally defensible and procedurally legitimate. Reality teaches that the actions the United States government takes will have important implications as to whether or how fast China becomes a true partner or a reluctant participant (euphemism for pirate) in the new IPR world order under TRIPS.

It is therefore most important for us to introduce a competitive mechanism whereby China can participate meaningfully. By virtue of joining the WTO, China enjoys both the benefits and obligations of a more competitive business environment. Industries ranging from automobiles to telecommunications to computers are braced for the onslaught of competition as import taxes and restrictions are reduced.

In order for the United States to effectively promote its IPR agenda, it is important for us to adopt a well-thought-out and cooperative approach to this issue. A bilateral approach to engaging and inducing the Chinese leaders at different levels and consumers to buy into the concept of the importance of intellectual property must be used. The continued use of the old "tried and true" but ineffective methods of coercion, threats, and negative criticism will not help in speeding the adoption of IPRs in China. Finally, as previously demonstrated, it took the United States, Japan, and Taiwan as developing nations years to begin earnestly adopting IPRs as part of their social and commercial fabrics. We must have realistic expectations that China in due time, when its economic circumstance, social outlook, legal institution, and technological prowess have all advanced to a higher levels, will become an avid advocate and enforcer of legitimate IPRs.

In this chapter we have discussed the IPR problem at the level of policy making. This provides the crucial context for the next chapter wherein we provide specific advice for managers on how to (1) effectively negotiate IPR issues with Chinese clients and (2) how to address violations including comments on both prevention and remediation.

Notes

1   The following books and articles were essential in developing this chapter: William Alford, *To Steal a Book Is an Elegant Offense* (Stanford, CA: Stanford University Press, 1995); M. Blakeney, *Trade-Related Aspects of Intellectual Property Rights: A Concise Guide to TRIPS Agreement* (London: Sweet & Maxwell, 1996); Robert Burrell, "A Case Study of Cultural Imperialism: The Imposition of Copyright on

China," in Lionel Bently and Spyros M. Maniatis, *Perspectives on Intellectual Property Series*, v. 4 (London: Queen Mary and Westfield College, Universtiy of London, 1998); Confucius, *Confucian Analects* (New York: Square $ Series, 1951); Jason Dedrich and Ken Kraemer, *Asia's Computer Challenge* (New York: Oxford University Press, 1998); John King Fairbank and Merle Goldman, *China: A New History* (Cambridge, MA: Belknap Press, 2006); Peter Feng, *Intellectual Property in China* (Hong Kong: Sweet & Maxwell Asia, 1997); Ernst Philip Goldschmidt, *Medieval Texts and Their First Appearance in Print* (London: Oxford University Press, 1940); Immanuel Chung-yueh Hseu, *The Rise of Modern China* (New York: Oxford University Press, 2000); David J. Jeremy, *Transatlantic Industrial Revolution: The Diffusion of Textile Technologies between Britian and America, 1790–1830* (London: University of London, 1978); J. H. Reichman, "From Free Riders to Fair Followers: Global Competition under the TRIPS Agreement" (New York: N.Y.U.J. *International Law of Politics*, 11, 1997); Susan K. Sell, *Private Power, Public Law: The Globalization of Intellectual Property Rights* (Cambridge, UK: Cambridge University Press, 2003); Christopher May and Susan K. Sell, *Intellectual Property Rights: A Critical History* (Boulder, CO: Lynne Rienners Publishers, 2006); Susan K. Sell, *Power and Ideas: North-South Politics of Intellectual Property and Antitrust* (Cambridge, UK: Cambridge University Press, 2003); E. Alan Lind and Tom R. Tyler, *The Social Psychology of Procedural Justice* (New York: Plenum, 1988); Tom R. Tyler (ed.), *Social Justice in a Diverse Society* (Boulder, CO: Westview Press, 1997); Elisabeth Uphoff, *Intellectual Property and US Relations with Indonesia, Malaysia, Signapore, and Thailand* (Ithica, NY: SEAP Cornell University monograph, 1991); Peter K. Yu, *Intellectual Property and Information Wealth* (New York: Praeger, 2006); Peter K. Yu, *The Second Coming of Intellectual Property Rights in China* (New York: Cardozo School of Law, Yeshiva University, 11, 2002).

NEGOTIATING AND ENFORCING INTELLECTUAL PROPERTY RIGHTS

Bill Gates's negotiation strategy with Chinese software pirates demonstrates both guile and patience. He accidentally revealed his strategy in 1998 in an interview at the University of Washington:[1]

> *Although about 3 million computers get sold every year in China, people don't pay for the software. Someday they will, though. And as long as they're going to steal it, we want them to steal ours. They'll get sort of addicted, and then we'll somehow figure out how to collect something in the next decade.*

Well, it didn't take a decade for this marketing-product trial approach to work. On April 18, 2006, one day ahead of Chinese President Hu Jintao's arrival in Redmond, Washington, for dinner at Gates's home on his way to a meeting with George W. Bush, Mr. Gates inked a deal with Lenova for $1.2 billion of software for the Chinese firm's computers. Brilliant!

To stay competitive in global markets, most agree that manufacturing in China is a must. Everyone also points out the balance that must be struck between the opportunities and the hard-to-measure risks. Moreover, many opportunities and threats coexist, making it even more difficult to evaluate the true risks of doing business in China. As noted in Chapter 16, one of the major concerns for foreign investors, especially for those who run core intellectual property companies, is how to protect, negotiate, and enforce intellectual property rights (IPR) in the rough and tumble Middle Kingdom. In this chapter, we discuss issues focusing on the interests of foreign investors or traders like you. First, we very briefly cover the nation's intellectual property laws and its enforcement system. Second, we discuss the practical aspects of protection of and enforcement of intellectual property rights.

China's Current IPR Protection System

Prior to the 1980s, the Western intellectual property guidelines were not recognized in China. China's current intellectual property system was developed as a result of the nation's economic reform since the 1980s. Through its massive economic and legal reform over the past two decades, China has increasingly recognized the value of a strong IPR regime. Particularly since the mid-1990s, the Chinese government has reshaped its IPR legislation, making its market safer for foreign investment.

The current system includes laws and regulations on patent, trademark, copyright, trade secrets, and unfair competition. In the past two decades, China has strengthened its enforcement institutions: judicial organs, administrative agencies, and other functional departments. Recall that the Chinese government largely operates under a centralized executive—the State Council. The administrative agencies and local governments serve as arms of the central executive. Currently, in order to enforce IP law, administrative agencies are often taking more significant positions than judiciary agencies. The administrative responsibilities for IPR enforcement are spread across three agencies.

China is a newcomer to establishing judicial protection of IPR. During the last decade or so, the Chinese government significantly enhanced its judicial enforcement against IPR violations. In June 1993, an Intellectual Property Rights Tribunal was established in the Beijing Intermediate People's Court as the first court with jurisdiction exclusively over IP cases. The court of appeal for this tribunal is the Beijing High People's Court. Subsequently, other IP courts have been established in some other provinces, major cities, and Special Economic Zones.

Certain nonjudicial functional departments can be also considered as part of the IPR movement. For example, the General Administration of Customs (GAC) is a functional department participating in the international cooperation on IPR enforcement to safeguard fair and legitimate trade against activities of counterfeiting, pirating, and smuggling.

As part of its efforts to rejoin the global economic community, China has made progress toward harmonizing its IPR protection system with international norms. The 1979 U.S.-China Agreement on Trade Relations marked the beginning of China's legislative efforts to enter onto the international stage. On June 3, 1980, China became a member of the World Intellectual Property Organization (WIPO). China is now a member of the Paris Convention for the Protection of Industrial Property (PCPIP) and the Patent Cooperation Treaty (PCT).

As a member of the PCT, the Chinese State Intellectual Property Office (SIPO) has begun to serve as a Receiving Office, International Searching Authority (ISA), and International Preliminary Examining Authority (IPEA). Since the language for a patent application is prescribed by the Receiving Office of the PCT, Chinese has become one of the PCT working languages. Upon joining the WTO, China made further efforts to bring its IP laws in line with the international system. China has recently revised its IP laws to comply with the standards of the World Intellectual Property Organization (WIPO) and the regulations of the WTO.

Sources of China's IP Laws and Enforcement System

Three kinds of intellectual property are considered here separately: patents, trademarks, and copyrights.

Patents

Upon founding of the PRC, the Chinese government adopted the Provisional Regulations on the Protection of Invention Rights and Patent Rights in 1950. The regulations were later replaced by the Regulations for Rewarding Inventions in 1963. China's first Patent Law, based on the 1963 regulations, was made official in 1984, and it has been revised in 1992 and in 2000. The current Implementing Rules of the Patent Law of the PRC was adopted in 2001.

The current Patent Law and its Implementing Rules allow a party to appeal to a special committee for reconsideration of the Patent Office's opinion in rejecting a patent application and, further, may appeal a Patent Office's decision to the Beijing's Number One Intermediate People's Court. It also provides that a patent holder may seek injunctive actions via court order to halt patent violations pending proceedings of patent prosecution or litigation. The new law also makes the foreign application procedures conform to the procedures under the WIPO. For example, the new Implementing Rules of the Copyright Law added a lengthy chapter named "International Patent Applications" to conform to PCT provisions.

Under the PRC Patent Law, there are two government agencies with the authority to enforce patent rights: administrative agencies and judicial organs of the People's Courts. The main administrative agency is the SIPO. The Chinese Patent Office (CPO) under the SIPO is in charge of receiving and examining patent applications, granting patent rights, examining and determining requests for reexamination and invalidation, and other administrative functions given by the SIPO under the Patent Law. Patent applicants may institute legal proceedings in the People's Court if they are not satisfied with the decision made by SIPO and its Reexamination Board, and parties in a patent dispute may also seek judicial remedies over patent dispute.

Jurisdiction of the courts depends on the type of patent disputes involved. For patent disputes over the validity of a patent or its compulsory license, the Beijing Intermediate People's Court is the court of first instance, and the Beijing High People's Court is the court of appeal. For patent disputes over infringement, proprietorship and assignment contract of patent rights, and fees to use an invention for a pending patent application, the provincial intermediate people's court where the disputes first arose is the court of first instance, and the provincial high people's court where the disputes arose is the court of appeal. For patent disputes over patent license contracts, the local people's court where the transaction occurs is the court of first instance, and the relevant intermediate court is the court of appeal.

Foreign Entities to Apply to Patents

Under China's Patent Law, any foreign individual or enterprise that has no regular domicile or place of business in China shall entrust a patent agency, as designated by the SIPO, to act as his, her, or its agent in handling patent-related matters. If an independent foreign enterprise or other entity has established business in China, it is has been qualified as an independent legal entity in China, and thus can, according to the same procedures applicable to Chinese legal entities, directly authorize a Chinese patent agency to handle the matter. By the end of 2002, there were 60 foreign-related patent agencies designated by the SIPO.

A foreign entity may also seek patent protection in China by filing a PCT patent application designating China. As mentioned earlier, the language for a patent application is prescribed by the receiving office of the PCT (i.e., SIPO in China). When a foreign entity files a PCT patent application, both English and Chinese are acceptable for the application in the international phase, but after entering into the national phase, a Chinese translation of the application must be provided to SIPO if the original PCT application was filed in a language other than Chinese.

Note that, pursuant to China's Patent Law, the Chinese patent application process adopts the first-to-file rule, that is, where two or more applicants file patent applications for an identical invention or creation, the patent right shall be granted to the applicant whose application is filed first. The duration (counted from the date of filing) of a Chinese patent is 20 years for invention and 10 years for utility models and designs.

As mentioned earlier, the SIPO is in charge of receiving and examining patent applications. But if a patent applicant is not satisfied with the decision made by the SIPO and its Reexamination Board, she or he may instigate legal proceedings in the People's Court.

Foreign Entities to Protect Patent Rights in Disputes

For a foreign patentee or interested party seeking protection against patent infringement, there are three legal remedies available: administrative proceedings, civil proceedings, or criminal proceedings. The patent administrative authorities are SIPO and local patent administrative offices. For judicial proceedings over patent infringement, whether civil or criminal, the court presiding over the locale where the infringing goods are made has the jurisdiction. If place of manufacturing is not clear, a suit may be brought before the court where the goods are sold or used.

In an administrative proceeding, a party may request that the relevant patent administrative authority intervene. The patent administrative authority may conduct necessary investigations, mediation, or make decisions on matters to stop infringing activities or enforce compensatory or punitive measures.

A party may, if not satisfied with a decision of the patent administrative authority, directly instigate judicial proceedings in the

People's Court. In a judicial proceeding, a court may make judgments to stop infringing acts, confiscate illegal properties, or apply compensatory or punitive measures. Where facing serious patent infringement or counterfeiting claims, a party may bring lawsuits to court to prosecute the infringing party. For judicial proceedings, the cases regarding patent matters mostly start in the Intermediate People's Court. A party has the right to one appeal to a higher court, usually the Higher People's Court. Thus, the decision made in the court of appeal is considered final.

Trademarks

The Chinese government adopted the Provisional Regulations on the Protection of Invention Rights and Patent Rights in 1950. The regulations were later replaced by the Regulations for Administration of Trademarks in 1963. China's first Trademark Law, based on the 1963 regulations, was formalized in 1982, and it has been revised twice since, in 1993 and 2001. The Implementing Rules of Trademark Law were revised in 2002.

One of the major reasons for the recent revision is to have the law conform with the WTO requirements and to make the foreign application procedures fall under the guidelines of the WIPO. For example, under the newly revised Implementing Rules of the Trademark Law, the breadth of the requirement that foreigners and foreign enterprises must appoint state-designated trademark agencies has been reduced by defining "foreigners and foreign enterprises" as those that have no regular domicile or place of business in China. The revised Trademark Law introduces provisions giving holders of registered trademarks and interested parties the right to seek preliminary injunctions against infringers.

Trademark protection also has two-tier enforcement in China: administrative and judicial enforcement. The Trademark Office (TMO) under the State Administration for Industry of China (SAIC) is in charge of the registration and administration of trademarks and the implementation of international treaties and agreements regarding foreign-related trademark matters. The People's Courts where the trademark infringement takes place has the jurisdictional power to hear cases.

Foreign Entities to Register Trademarks

Seeking trademark registration is very important since the Chinese trademark registration adheres to a strict first-to-file rule rather than the first-to-use rule that is followed in the U.S. system. In other words, foreign trademark holders should register patents in China as early as possible.

Under China's Trademark Law, any foreign individual or enterprise without regular domicile or business in China who intends to apply for the registration of a trademark or for matters concerning a trademark in China shall entrust a trademark agency designated by the SAIC to act as its agent. Furthermore, the foreign individual or enterprise shall file an application in accordance with any agreement concluded between the PRC and the country to which the applicant belongs, or according to the international treaty to which both countries are parties, or on the basis of the principle of reciprocity.

Foreign Entities to Protect
Trademark Rights in Disputes

A foreign trademark holder who enters the Chinese market needs to engage capable business experts and legal professionals to develop trademark protection strategies and prepare for legal battle when trademark related disputes arise. For trademark infringement cases, an infringed party may seek remedies through three proceedings: administrative, civil, and criminal. Therefore, upon discovering trademark infringement, a trademark holder may either report the infringement to the local AIC or go directly to the people's courts.

In administrative proceedings, the local (county level and above) Administration for Industry and Commerce (AIC) is authorized to receive the complaints, and the SAIC is its highest administrative authority. The local AIC may conduct necessary investigations, decide to mediate, order halting the infringing activities, seize or destroy infringing goods and instrumentalities, and enforce compensatory or punitive measures. Since the local AIC has experienced professionals to oversee market conditions and handle trademark matters, it is often preferred for a trademark holder first go to the AIC where the case will be investigated.

Litigation in courts, either as civil or criminal proceedings, is another option for enforcing trademark rights. Litigation has inherent advantages in certain circumstances, for example, giving the trademark holder more assurance of the enforcement measures, higher remedial awards, and broader market publicity and consumer awareness. Thus, judicial enforcement may be a preferred option over administrative enforcement for high-profile litigation.

However, alternative dispute resolution methods, compared to litigation, can be a less costly, faster, and more flexible way to resolve trademark disputes. Like other commercial matters, trademark disputes are especially suited for arbitration, which is often economically less expensive and procedurally more flexible. This is especially true in cases where trade secrets protection is an issue.

Copyright

The Chinese government adopted a Decision Concerning the Improvement and Development of Publishing at the first PRC National Publication Conference in 1950. Beginning in 1979, the government set forth a series of administrative regulations on copyright protection. The first PRC Copyright Law was formalized in 1990 and revised in 2001. The current Implementing Rules of the Copyright Law were adopted in 2002.

Similar to the newly revised Patent Law and Trademark Law, the current Copyright Law has introduced many changes to bring it in line with the Berne Convention for the Protection of Literary and Artistic Works (BCPLAW) and the TRIPS. The revisions also made equitable remedies available to victims of copyright infringement so that an aggrieved party may seek a preliminary injunction to preserve assets and evidence.

In China, copyright protection, like patent and trademark protection, has two-tier enforcement: administrative and judicial. As the government administrative agency, the National Copyright Administration (NCA) handles most copyright matters, including the administration of foreign-related copyright matters and approval of establishment of foreign-related copyright agencies. Furthermore, the NCA supervises all local copyright administration departments.

Foreign Entities to Seek Copyright Protection

The Chinese Copyright Law adopts the rule of automatic protection, and, since China joined the Berne Convention, the principle of national treatment applies to foreigners. An infringed party must bring the suit within two years from the date the piracy has been uncovered. Considering the time frame and the insubstantial costs, a foreign copyright owner may want to register the copyright in China to facilitate future enforcement action.

Since copyright enforcement measures are time-limited, foreign copyright owners intending to enter the Chinese market should first seek legal protection in China. To benefit from legal protection, works of foreigners must be either first published in China or published outside China where the author's country and China are both members of any international copyright agreement. For long-term copyright protection, the copyright owner should ensure that his or her work falls within the scope of copyrightable subject matters and meets specific requirements relating to ownership, duration, and other limitations.

For foreign copyright owners, licensing agreements with competent Chinese entities may offer a long-lasting solution to copyright protection in China, which may enhance the foreign investors' competitive market position and thus create more profits through copyright-protected production and distribution in domestic and global markets. The licensing agreements with Chinese partners also give the local licensees more incentive to seek copyright enforcement against infringement.

Like patent or trademark rights, copyrights in China can be enforced through three channels: administrative, civil, and criminal proceedings. The NCA and its local copyright offices may apply administrative measures to impose fines or penalties, or to confiscate property obtained through piracy.

Through a judicial proceeding or a preliminary injunction, property preservation is available to a copyright owner if he or she has evidence to establish that another party is committing an act of infringement. Upon finding copyright infringement, foreign copyright owners may bring suits in courts for civil remedies or for criminal prosecutions.

PRC Anti-Unfair Competition Law

The Paris Convention states that member countries shall fill in the gaps in IPR protection left by patent, trademark, and copyright laws and provide effective protection against acts of unfair competition. To bring its legislation in line with the Paris Convention, China has adopted a series of legislative measures including the PRC Anti-Unfair Competition Law which was instituted in 1993. Regulations against unfair competition are also described in other laws such as the PRC Product Quality Law and the PRC Advertising Law.

The Anti-Unfair Competition Law and related regulations provide a framework for the protection of nonregistrable IPRs. The laws address certain trading practices, which include passing off registered trademarks, trade names, and trade addresses or packaging, counterfeiting, disclosure of trade secrets, bribery and kickbacks, monopolies, antidumping, and other anticompetitive activities and matters related to consumer protection.

Foreign business entities whose rights are infringed upon may bring their case to the SAIC for investigation. The SAIC and its local administrations are authorized to order that infringing activities stop; they can also confiscate or destoy illegal income or properties, and impose administrative fines. The SAIC and its local departments, if necessary, may refer the case to court, and the infringed party may also choose to file directly a lawsuit in court with jurisdiction for civil proceeding or criminal prosecution.

Protection and Enforcement of IPR in Practice

In theory and on paper IPR protection seems straightforward in China. The rules and enforcement agencies and authorities are all in place. However, the enormity of the problem and a fundamental cultural distaste for "ownership of ideas" (particularly by foreigners) combine to overwhelm the system. The system places emphasis on public enforcement against IPR infringement mainly through administrative agencies (rather than civil or criminal approaches). And, the major administrative power over counterfeiting is not centralized but divided among different agencies. Thus, the door to corruption and bribery is propped wide open.

Recent legislative reform in China has introduced numerous revisions in the IP laws. The new changes provide preliminary injunction relief to infringed patent holders or trademark owners. For foreign-related IP issues, the new laws relaxed prior requirements that the foreign entities must entrust state-designated patent or trademark agencies by narrowing the definition of "foreigner and foreign enterprises" as only those having no regular domicile or place of business in China. But these are minor advances. Major improvements will result only with the passage of time and the increasing development of intellectual property by Chinese firms themselves.

The remedies for American companies operating in China are several: (1) prevention; (2) codeveloping intellectual property with Chinese partners; (3) negotiation or alternative dispute resolution; (4) complaints to the Chinese authorities; and (5) complaints to the U.S. government or the WTO.

Prevention

The best means of prevention is to engage local legal representation and diligently register intellectual property with the appropriate local agencies as described above.

Codeveloping Intellectual Property with Chinese Partners

One of the originators of "open innovation" is Philips Research in the Netherlands. Thirty years ago this company pioneered the concept of partnering to develop new ideas and partnering to market new ideas. Open innovation for Philips also means it buys ideas from research and development partners and then sells ideas to marketing partners, rather than developing and marketing all its own ideas. One current project well exemplifies its innovative approach to developing and protecting intellectual property in China:

> *The PHENIX Initiative is a commercial, industrial, and R&D cooperative launched by a consortium of Chinese and European partners, led by France Telecom. It received the support of the EU-China Working Group on Digital Olympics, of the MOST (Chinese Ministry of Science and Technology), the BOCOG (Beijing Organizing Committee for the Games of the XXIX Olympiad), and was cofinanced by the European Union. Philips Research (Europe and East Asia in Shanghai) participated in the project, which was aimed at studying the commercial potential in China for mobile interactive services, analyzing digital video broadcasting–handheld (DVB-H) positioning in China, and developing innovative concepts in the area of mobile services, particularly targeting the upcoming Olympic games.[2]*

Many American firms have established design and R&D centers in China already. However, American government high-tech export restrictions and competitive angst prevent associations for American firms in China such as the PHENIX Initiative. And such collaborative efforts can be effective in developing R&D and promoting protection, and, in turn, IP protection systems in China.

Negotiation and Alternative Dispute Resolution

Foreign investors involved in disputes relating to IPR as well as international trade contracts or joint ventures in China are sometimes willing to settle their disputes in a flexible, informal, less expensive, and less confrontational manner. As mentioned in Chapter 6, ways of alternative dispute resolution that are often adopted in China include arbitration and mediation.

Arbitration is traditionally perceived in the international community as an effective method to resolve commercial disputes.

Recall that China has adopted a bifurcated arbitration system involving both domestic and international systems, which provide separate tribunals and procedures. The international arbitration tribunal in China is the China International Economic and Trade Arbitration Commission (CIETAC). The CIETAC is headquartered in Beijing and has branch offices in Shanghai and Shenzhen. It is the official arbitration agency in China, handling international commercial disputes.

The New York Convention on the Recognition and Enforcement of Foreign Arbitral Awards (New York Convention) is a very important international treaty affecting the international commercial arbitration process. For enforcement of arbitral awards regarding international commercial transactions, the New York Convention provides guidelines for the mutual recognition and reciprocal enforcement of arbitral awards made by its members. Most of the major trading countries, including China, have ratified the Convention. Thus international arbitral awards made in China can be enforced in the United States and vice versa.

Arbitration is a private dispute resolution process, and based on the PRC Arbitration Law, arbitration agencies are not part of state administrative agencies and do not depend on courts. Arbitration is, however, subject to state supervision. The state can intervene through courts at the prearbitration stage, during the arbitration process, and after arbitration. Disputing parties may also apply to courts on issues such as validity and enforcement of arbitral awards. Thus arbitration proceedings are interrelated with litigation.

There are certain benefits and advantages to arbitration as opposed to litigation, especially in dealing with international investments and trades. First, handling foreign-related commercial disputes often requires application of special laws and rules and requires special knowledge in the field. The choice of law and tribunal in arbitration, as opposed to litigation in a court, may provide the disputing parties' opportunities to appoint appropriate arbitrators with requisite knowledge and seek decision under a particular law of arbitration.

Second, cost-effectiveness may be a factor to consider in using arbitration rather than litigation. An unchallenged arbitration process is usually faster than the judicial process. But be aware that speedy relief may be unlikely for disputes involving technology or intellectual property. Moreover, confidentiality is another benefit of arbitration, especially where trade secrets or confidential financial information is involved.

The PRC Arbitration Law was formalized only in 1994, and the practice of the CIETAC is relatively immature, especially compared with those in developed countries. As a consequence, lack of expertise in judging foreign-related cases is often problematic. Also, the practical connection of arbitration with the courts and influence by a superior authority may override benefits of fairness and cost-effectiveness associated with the arbitration process. Furthermore, local protectionism may sometimes render arbitration ineffective, and even a successful arbitral award in favor of foreign parties may be limited because of lack of knowledge by the courts about the New York Convention.

Mediation, an informal, nonadversarial process to resolve disputes through voluntary agreement, is a traditional way and today is still extensively adopted in China to solve civil disputes. As mentioned in Chapter 6, there are four types of mediation practices in China: civil mediation, arbitrational mediation, administrative mediation, and judicial mediation. The basic rules on mediation in China are the People's Mediation Commission Organic Rules.

Beijing Conciliation Center is one of the major organizations in China governing civil mediation, conciliation, and other alternative dispute resolutions. The center may handle foreign-related disputes relating to trade, investment, technology transfer, finance, insurance, and other business transactions.

Foreign parties may also use mediation as a "filtering process" before proceedings to arbitration or litigation, or as a "joint process" to facilitate settlements during proceedings of arbitration or litigation. The arbitration rules concerning disputes that involve foreign parties usually permit an arbitration tribunal to mediate a case, in the hope that the mediation will in fact render arbitration unnecessary. The PRC civil procedure law permits pretrial and in-court mediation to facilitate settlement. Compulsive mediation, however, is prohibited.

As a dispute resolution alternative, mediation, as opposed to arbitration or litigation, is advantageous because it is generally quick, flexible, cost-effective, and less destructive than other approaches. It may enable the disputing parties to keep a friendly relationship. As we discuss in Chapter 3, Chinese managers emphasize long-term reputation [*manzi*] in business transactions and are far more willing to deal with business partners that are highly recommended by trusted business contacts and colleagues. If everything goes smoothly, they tend to keep long-lasting, friendly relationships with their partners for later mutual benefit. Therefore, the benefits to resolving disputes via mediation are obvious if it is permitted under the circumstances.

However, compared to litigation, mediation has far fewer legally binding constraints to both disputing parties. Mediation agreements reached through voluntary consent are usually not enforceable or regulated by courts. Thus, for certain cases involving serious IPR violations or complicated technology matters, mediation may be considered as a "facilitating" mechanism coupled with arbitration or litigation. Moreover, to ensure a successful mediation process in resolving foreign-related disputes, appointment of competent mediators with requisite professional skills and legal knowledge is crucial.

Chinese Authorities

Given infringements and/or violations of IP laws, complaints should be filed with the appropriate Chinese authorities as outlined in the first section of this chapter.

The American Government and the WTO

Finally, American firms can file complaints with the U.S. government although the help provided is limited by law. The Commerce Department[3] reports:

> *Many companies, particularly SMEs that discover their products are being infringed in China, contact the Department of Commerce for assistance. Because intellectual property rights are private rights, the Department can provide only limited direct assistance. In many cases, the United States government can provide companies with information in navigating China's legal system, including lists of local investigative firms and attorneys and share our experience and expertise in China. However, the Department of Commerce cannot provide American companies with legal advice or advocate on a company's behalf without the company first taking legal action.*
>
> *When a company encounters blatant infringement of its IPR, the right holder should hire local counsel and pursue a preliminary investigation on one's own or through a contracted professional firm, keeping in mind that U.S. companies should ensure compliance with Chinese law, which restricts private investigation to certain forms of "market research" investigations. Once the initial investigation is complete, the company should determine if further action and possible costs related with such actions are worth pursuing. Right holders will have the option to initiate actions or seek redress through either the judicial or administrative system. Foreign rights holders have had considerably less success in encouraging criminal prosecution of IPR violations, particularly when copyright infringements are involved.*
>
> *Once a company decides to pursue a remedy, the Department of Commerce, through our Washington DC or China-based offices will monitor the case, if requested to do so by the company. The U.S. Government cannot intervene in the case, however we can inquire about its status or contact government officials about concerns related to the effective administration of legal remedies available to IP holders. The Department of Commerce is most*

likely to become involved in a case where evidence indicates China is not complying with its enforcement under the WTO TRIPS Agreement. As with other types of commercial disputes, the Department's efforts in assisting with IPR disputes are aimed at achieving a fair and timely resolution in accordance with international commitments, Chinese laws and in advancing adequate legal and judicial protection for all parties.

We strongly emphasize that the information provided above by no means constitutes legal advice and should not be substituted advice of counsel. Its intended purpose is to provide an overview of China's IPR environment, available enforcement mechanisms, and Chinese government offices sharing jurisdiction over IPR protection and enforcement. We recommend that U.S. companies seeking to do business in China or are facing IPR infringement issues, retain qualified U.S. and/or Chinese legal counsel and pursue their rights through China's IPR enforcement regime.

We fully agree with the Commerce Department's last caveat. Please don't take this information as legal advice. Your own counsel should be consulted about your specific circumstances, particularly in China.

As we state throughout the book, you must have the long term in mind when addressing the Chinese market and business system. Decisions regarding intellectual property should be made with confidence that the Chinese regime of IPR will continue to tighten toward world standards, and the speed at which this takes place will be directly related to China's own IP productivity. So once again your patience will be required.

Notes

1   Charles Piller, "How Piracy Opens Doors for Windows," *Los Angeles Times*, April 9, 2006, pp. C1–C10.
2   Philips Research *Password*, issue 26, February 2006, p. 14.
3   "Protecting Your Intellectual Property Rights in China," www.mac.doc.gov.

PART V

CONCLUSIONS

CHAPTER 18

SPECULATION ABOUT THE FUTURE OF CHINESE AND AMERICAN COMMERCIAL RELATIONS

Remember what we said at the end of Chapter 1 about the luck associated with the number 8. Indeed, if you've made it all the way through our book, you are bound to prosper in your commercial dealings in China. We aren't saying it will be easy. But we've tried to provide a guide suggesting where your best efforts will best pay off. Maybe a little luck will help too!

China has always been hugely important to the United States. In fact, the reason this country exists is China. Recall the Boston Tea Party. Our complaint then was the British tax, and more important their prohibition of our Yankee traders dealing directly with the merchants in Canton. Back in 1776 trade with China influenced politics in the most profound way.

Now, circa 2007 politics are influencing trade with China in a bad way. It's so easy for politicians on both sides of the isle (and both sides of the Pacific) to use xenophobia for their selfish political purposes. Republicans tell us that the Chinese will try to kill us. Democrats tell us that the Chinese are trying to steal our jobs. John has been quite consistent in his criticism of such political pandering over the years. We've included two OPEDs from the *Orange County Register* that make the point that still needs to be made, the first from May 11, 2001, and the second from June 12, 2005.

China Options

It's going to be a hot summer. In addition to a lack of air conditioning, one of the sorer sources of heat will be U.S./China frictions. In June, once again Congress will vote on Permanently Normalized Trade Relations (PNTR) with China. The spy plane fiasco and recent rhetoric regarding Taiwan will make things much more difficult this time around.

Moreover, the year 2000 trade figures will be prominent in the discussions. For the last 20 years Japan has been the trade deficit dominator. However, in 2000, for the first time in history it was China. Last year our merchandise trade deficit with China was $84 billion compared to only $81 billion with Japan. Job losses in America will be blamed on China. During all the years we faced the Soviet missiles, at least we were never able to blame our unemployment on the Russkies. Japan was clearly culpable—right? And now we have China to blame for both job losses and military tensions. Watch out, Beijing.

Also decided this summer will be the location of the 2008 Olympic Games. Congress is currently revving up to pass a resolution recommending that the IOC not give the Games to Beijing— a kind of punishment for human rights violations and aggressiveness toward Taiwan. This is not a thoughtful resolution. Instead, Congress should be urging the IOC to put the burden of the games on China. There are two gains to this gambit.

First, China is provided a big carrot (incentive) for better behavior. President Bush has been quite expert in applying the "big stick" so far. Moreover, 2008 is a special year for many Chinese making this carrot particularly attractive. The number eight is the luckiest single digit, closely associated with "making money" and property. The number is no minor matter.

And, China will make money—NBC has already agreed to pay the IOC $1.2 billion for the 2008 Summer Games broadcast rights. McDonalds, Motorola, and General Motors will be spending big, too.

Of course, the prestige and pride will be plentiful, as well. Indeed, if China is smart about the whole thing, they'll invite Taiwan to participate in hosting the Games. The rowing events might be held at Sun-Moon Lake in the center of the island, for example. Or, perhaps baseball would be appropriate for Taipei. All this is consistent with the ping-pong diplomacy that worked so well in the 1970s.

The second gain is even greater. Foisting the Games on China for 2008 puts the Chinese leadership under a microscope for the next seven years. The whole world will be watching China. Those in power will have huge financial incentives to invite the world press to Beijing and to see China in the best light. If the Chinese government misbehaves, it won't be just Chinese dissidents and American politicians complaining.

There are three axioms of international relations. (1) Trade causes peace; (2) politicians cause wars; and (3) wars cause deaths, on both sides. The trade involved in China's entry into the World Trade Organization, PNTR, and the 2008 Olympic Games can be good for all concerned. Free enterprise has taken root in China and the seeds of democracy are there if one bothers to look. Trade is a kind of fertilizer for both.

Finally, as our leaders in Washington (and theirs in Taipei and Beijing) consider their options over the summer, included must be the potential casualties on all sides if shooting starts across the Straits of Taiwan.

I hope I didn't hear Mr. Bush, in a casual conversation with a reporter, volunteer my 17-year-old son for duty in that action.

> *In 2008 I would much rather be reading about our sons and daughters winning Olympic Gold Medals instead of Medals of Honor, particularly the posthumous kind.*[1]

Fortunately for all of us, coolness prevailed on Capitol Hill, and all three gifts—WTO, PNTR, and the 2008 Games—were granted to China. But the attractiveness of making China "the big enemy" remained great in Washington well into 2005.

Who's Menacing Whom?

> *Be a pattern to others, and then all will go well: for as a whole city is affected by the corrupt passions of great men, so it is likewise reformed by their moderation.*
>
> —CICERO, CIRCA 50 B.C.

Apparently Secretary of Defense Rumsfeld and President Bush missed the old Roman's missive on leadership. Their dream of "world" democracy can never be accomplished by the gun. Indeed, consider how well their rhetoric is working with China. Last week in Singapore Rumsfeld publicly pondered, "Since no nation threatens China, one must wonder: Why this growing investment [in arms]?" The Chinese responded in their usual way, their answer was a question. A Foreign Ministry official queried, "Do you truly believe that China is under no threat whatsoever from any part of the world?"

It is abundantly manifest that no one is interested in attacking China, not North Korea or Japan, or even the United States. In fact, the reason China has a 2-million-man army is to control its own historically unruly population. But, before Middle East terrorism took center stage on September 11, 2001, China actually was the big threat America prepared for in the military exercises and budget meetings of the time. And, by the way, the United States does menace China, that is, if you count flying spy planes and sailing aircraft carrier task forces along their coast.

Imagine Chinese military aircraft over Catalina or their submarines near the port of Los Angeles. Wouldn't that be "menacing" to us? So, it just isn't clear who's menacing whom.

The reality is that today's trade-based economic interdependence precludes anyone from attacking anyone. Despite the cacophony of saber rattling in Washington, Beijing, and Taipei, nobody can afford a war across the narrow straits separating the mainland from Taiwan. And democracy is coming to China fast anyway, via the pacific practices of commerce, WTO, Wal-Mart, the 2008 Olympics in Beijing, the 2010 World's Fair in Shanghai, and such.

So why Rumsfeld's rough rhetoric? Simply, it sells well at home. Xenophobia has been so used by politicians to consolidate political strength at home since even before Cicero's time. The problem is that harsh words yield harsh words. Brandishing weapons leads to brandishing weapons, and worse, using them.

Since Mr. Bush took office in 2001 the budget busting build of military expenditures has been menacing both at home and abroad. In 2000 we spent $301 billion on defense, in 2003 more than $417 billion (this ignoring the costs of the fighting in Iraq and Afghanistan). And how has the "bring 'em on" Bush foreign policy affected our so-called enemies? Over the same time period North Korea grew its spending from $1.4 billion to $1.8 billion, Iran $12 billion to $18 billion, and China $22 billion to $32 billion. The CIA says the last number is more like $67 billion. But, given the bad information the CIA gave us about weapons in Iraq, I prefer the Swedish estimates as above (SIPRI Yearbook 2004). Of course, China is now capable of delivering perhaps a couple of dozen nuclear missiles (of their 400+) to the west coast of the United States. Both North Korea and Iran have recently tested ballistic missiles and aspire to the prestige of nuclear weaponry.

Iraq? The war we started there is turning into a slow disaster. It's been 27 months since we invaded and we continue to spend money at the rate of $7 billion per month. Of course, tragically, on average 66 Americans have been killed and more than

500 have been wounded each month as well. And the carnage continues with civilian casualties spinning out of control and 85 American lives lost just last month (May). There's no good news in the numbers.

Nor is there a good solution to the conundrum of our own creation in Iraq. The costs of staying are clear. The costs of leaving are less so. Perhaps a Nixonian declaration of "peace with honor" would work for President Bush?

But I do have some advice for the President on the broader topics of national security and foreign relations. Recognize that even the bad guys around the world imitate you, so please set a different type of example for them. Your bluster, bullying, threats a la "Evil Axis," and premature conflagrations are ruining our military and our country, and killing thousands around the world. Relaxing trade restrictions, as you did recently by permitting Iran to move toward WTO membership, is one effective way to promote global peace and democracy. Another would be unilateral cuts in military spending and nuclear weapons. The Russians and we each have enough nuclear arms (more than 10,000 each) to end all life on the planet, let alone China. Perhaps other countries won't bother growing their expensive nuclear arsenals if the leader of the most powerful country the earth has ever known has the courage to lead by wise "moderation . . ."[2]

China and the Unites States need each other. Everyone knows this. And with growing globalization we certainly cannot ignore each other. Many feel that the world economy is undergoing a new revolution as a China-led Asia returns to its historical role as the center of world affairs.[3] One factor that complicates diplomacy between the two countries is something most corporate executives can identify with. American politicians tend to have a background in law while Chinese officials are almost all trained in engineering.[4] So at top levels there's an extra professional cultural divide—Chinese *engineers* versus American *attorneys*. Engineers by training strive for "better," and lawyers prepare for the "worst." Unfortunately, the one trait they seem to share is the shameful use of xenophobia as a tool to consolidate their power.

So, *at the political level* we need to make policies based not on a fear of China, but on the recognition that trade ultimately keeps China on a path toward peace and global prosperity. China must be seen as an opportunity rather than a threat. Such a positive perspective of the Middle Kingdom is good for the 1.4 billion Chinese on the planet, and the rest of us as well.

And, of course, we have the pandas. Smarter than our giving China the 2008 Games is China giving Taiwan TuanTuan and YuanYuan. That is, the PRC government has officially offered a pair of pandas to the Taipei zoo, and the government on Taiwan is considering the gift as we write. But really, how can anyone resist pandas? Despite the wariness of the politicians in Taipei— they called them "Trojan pandas"—70 percent of the people polled preferred to welcome the cute bears to Taiwan. Brilliant! Let's keep China on this peaceful path.

But much more important than what pandas, presidents, and prime ministers do is what you do. Both a Finnish sales manager and an English author would agree. John tells the story of a delayed flight in Xian:

> *I had been in China a couple of weeks. I was tired. The fog had delayed my flight from Xian to Shanghai by four hours. I was standing in a long line at the counter to check in again. I started chatting with the older chap in line ahead of me. Juhani Kari introduced himself as a Finnish sales manager at ABB. He asked me what I did for a living. I responded, "I teach international business." He replied, "There is no such thing as international business. There's only interpersonal business." A wise man, indeed!*

And English poet, journalist, and anthropologist Rudyard Kipling said more than a century ago: "Oh, East is East, and West is West, and never the twain shall meet." Since then most have imbued his words with an undeserved pessimism. Some even wrongly say he was wrong.[5] The problem is that not many have bothered to read his entire poem, *The Ballad of East and West*:

> *Oh, East is East, and West is West, and never the twain shall meet,*
> *Till Earth and Sky stand presently at God's great Judgment*
>   *Seat;*
> *But there is neither East nor West, border, nor breed, nor birth,*
> *When two strong men stand face to face, though they come from*
>   *the ends of the earth!*

The poem can stand some editing for these more modern times. It should include the other directions—North is North and South is South. And the last line properly should read, "When two strong *people* stand face to face." But Kipling's positive sentiment remains. Differences between countries and cultures, no matter how difficult, can be worked out when people talk to each other face to face. Kipling rightly places the responsibility for international cooperation not on companies or governments, but instead directly on the shoulders of individual managers, present and future, like you. So, please work hard!

Notes

1   John L. Graham, "China Options," *Orange County Register*, May 11, 2001, page D3.
2   John L. Graham, "Who's Menacing Whom?" *Orange County Register*, June 12, 2005, page D3.
3   Martin Wolf, "The World Begins to Feel the Dragon's Breath on Its Back," *Financial Times*, December 14, 2005, p. 15.
4   Robert Lawrence Kuhn, "A Problem of Perception," *BusinessWeek*, April 24, 2006, pp. 33–34.
5   Michael Elliot, "Killing Off Kipling," *Newsweek*, December 29, 1977, pp. 52–55

INDEX

ABOUT THE AUTHORS

N. Mark Lam is an attorney and business advisor specializing in East-West negotiations, and is the CEO of the world's largest Internet radio network, Live.365.com. His area of expertise is in forming global alliances and resolving business and legal conflicts for global high-tech companies, including Philips Electronics and Hon Hai Precision Industry Co., Ltd.

John L. Graham is a Profesor of International Business at the Paul Merage School of Business, University of California, Irvine, and a world recognized scholar in the area of international business negotiations and international marketing. During the last 25 years, he has provided advice and training to executive groups at Fortune 500 companies and other institutions, including Toyota, Intel, Ford, AT&T, and the U.S. State Department.